CRITICAL TRUSTS LAW:
READING ROGER COTTERRELL

Critical Trusts Law:
Reading Roger Cotterrell

Nick Piška

Hayley Gibson

COUNTERPRESS
COVENTRY

First published 2024
Counterpress, Coventry
http://counterpress.org.uk

ISBN: 978-1-910761-23-6 (Paperback)
ISBN: 978-1-910761-24-3 (ePDF)

Typeset in 10.5 on 12pt Sabon

Global print and distribution by Ingram

Contents

Preface

Nick Piška and Hayley Gibson

In May 2016 a group of trust lawyers and activists met at The Shard, London, to discuss the relationship of pension trusts and global corporate capitalism. During a break, standing at the large glass windows looking down at the City of London, Nick Piška and Adam Gearey reflected on the paucity of critical trusts scholarship given the role of trusts in the global financial crisis and rising wealth inequality. The conversation naturally turned to the work of Roger Cotterrell on trusts, one of the few theoretical-doctrinal interventions to have linked trusts to questions of power and inequality, and the seed of an idea for a symposium revisiting themes Roger's work on trusts was sown.

At Kent Law School we have been setting Roger Cotterrell's articles on trusts as 'core reading' on our Equity & Trusts module for many years. Introducing trusts to undergraduate students might appear daunting enough, but introducing the trust idea, trust doctrine, and a critique of the trust form simultaneously has been challenging and exhilarating in (almost) equal measure. Each year we find different nuances and different points to emphasize in Cotterrell's works as the legal, social, economic and theoretical milieu has shifted—and each year our students bring different questions and ideas to the seminars and assessments.

In 2017, 30 years since the publication of his first article in a trilogy of articles on trusts law—'Power, Property and the Law of Trusts: A Partial Agenda for Critical Legal Studies'[1]—we hosted a symposium

---

1. Roger Cotterrell, 'Power, Property and the Law of Trusts: A Partial Agenda for Critical Legal Scholarship,' *Journal of Law and Society* 14 (1987); Roger Cotterrell, 'Some Sociological Aspects of the Controversy Around the Legal Validity of Private Purpose Trusts,' in *Equity and Contemporary Legal Developments* ed. Stephen Goldstein (1992); Roger Cotterrell, 'Trusting in Law: Legal and Moral Concepts of

on Roger Cotterrell's work on trusts in Canterbury.[2] This was an opportunity to bring together academics and activists whose work reflected a 'critical ethos' to consider trusts through the lenses of ideology, power, and wealth inequality, while drawing on theoretical insights from sociology and critical theory.[3]

This edited collection brings together a number of the papers presented at that symposium. Themes explored in the chapters include ideology and the (in)visibility of power; the abuse of trusts; the gendering of trusts; and the implications of trusts regimes for questions of tax, finance and banking. Some, in a nod to Cotterrell's 'partial agenda' for critical trusts scholarship, set out new agendas for trusts scholarship. Many turn to developments in trusts practice since the publication of Cotterrell's articles (for example developments in asset protection trusts) not only to mark the 30 year retrospective of the symposium, but to attest to the continued prescience of Cotterrell's initial, 'partial,' agenda.

A long time has passed since the symposium, and this collection has been delayed by various factors—pandemic, personal and institutional. We'd like to thank the authors for their contributions, and their patience and support in getting the collection over the line.

The symposium and ensuing collection couldn't have happened without support from various groups and individuals. Thanks to the SLSA and the Kent Law School's Social Critiques of Law (SoCriL) research group—led by Donatella Alessandrini and Emilie Cloatre—for financial support for the symposium. We'd like to thank Raúl Madden for research assistance in editing some of the chapters. Illan rua Wall and Gil Leung at Counterpress have given us amazing support and encouragement throughout. And finally special thanks to Roger Cotterrell who provided an Afterword for this collection.

Nick Piška and Hayley Gibson
April 2024

Trust,' *Current Law Problems* 46 (1993).
2. We held the symposium at Friends Meeting House and Pilgrims Hospice in Canterbury, which gave a relaxed, 'town hall' activism atmosphere to proceedings compared to the stuffiness of University lecture theatres and seminar rooms.
3. Many contributors are members of the Equity & Trusts Research Network, hosted by Kent Law School, which works in collaboration with the Trusts & Estates Collaborative Research Network of the Law & Society Association. For more information on these research networks please visit https://research.kent.ac.uk/equity-and-trusts/.

1

An Introduction to Critical Trusts Law

Nick Piška*

This edited collection provides a snapshot of an emerging body of critical scholarship on trusts. Critical trusts law is best understood as an ethos towards trusts law, scholarship and practice rather than a coherent or singular 'critical theory.' It is an ethos that questions legal dogma, scholarship that criticises law in the name of dogmas, and practices of exclusion and inequality. Each of the chapters in this collection is oriented, in one way or another, towards social justice rather than individual property or power.

The chapters were first presented at a symposium in 2017 on the 30th anniversary of the publication of the first of Roger Cotterrell's three publications on the law of trusts.[1] Although there have been many criticisms of the law of trusts over the centuries, Cotterrell's 1987 article—'Power, Property and the Law of Trusts: A Partial Agenda for Critical Legal Scholarship'[2]—outlined for the first time a critical, socio-legal approach to the law of trusts, further developed in subsequent articles in 1992[3] and 1993.[4] This trilogy of articles provided, and still provides, a rich set of conceptual tools for the critical analysis

---

* Kent Law School, UK. I'd like to thank Hayley Gibson for discussions about critical trusts law, and Iain Frame, Rosemary Hunter and Illan rua Wall for comments on earlier drafts of this introduction.
1. Power, Property and the Law of Trusts Revisited: Roger Cotterrell's Contribution to Critical Trusts Scholarship, University of Kent, 25-26 October 2017.
2. Roger Cotterrell, 'Power, Property and the Law of Trusts: A Partial Agenda for Critical Legal Scholarship,' *Journal of Law and Society* 14 (1987).
3. Roger Cotterrell, 'Some Sociological Aspects of the Controversy around the Legal Validity of Private Purpose Trusts,' in *Equity and Contemporary Legal Developments* ed. Stephen Goldstein (1992).
4. Roger Cotterrell, 'Trusting in Law: Legal and Moral Concepts of Trust,' *Current Law Problems* 46 (1993).

of trust law and practice which doesn't start from unchanging legal dogma but from a sociological explanation of legal doctrine and legal change. Thirty years on the need for critical trusts scholarship couldn't have been more pressing. The Global Financial Crisis of 2007 exposed the use of trusts on financial markets and led to a greater interest in wealth inequality and how wealth is structured. The work of economists such as Thomas Piketty laid bare the massive wealth inequality between the top 1% and the rest of society.[5] His *Capital in the Twenty-First Century*, first published in 2013, demonstrated that wealth grows at a greater rate than economic growth, which brought home to critical legal scholars the role that legal tools enabling the retention of wealth across generations, such as trusts, have in perpetuating wealth inequality.[6] The Panama Papers were leaked in 2016, exposing the use of offshore legal entities such as trusts by wealthy clients for illegal or unethical purposes, and—shortly after the symposium in 2017—the Paradise Papers were leaked.[7]

It was against this background that we invited contributions to the symposium to respond to the themes and theoretical challenges of Cotterrell's work, in particular questions of power, ideology and inequality. The chapters in the collection include topics concerning settlor-power and structural power; 'limited duty trusts' and asset protection trusts; charitable trusts and pensions trusts; the interface of trusts, taxation and fiscal policy; the interplay of privacy and transparency, the hidden and the visible; and the gendering of trusts. The focus is predominantly on express trusts, in recognition that it is the adaptation of trusts law to the particular ends of settlors by those drafting trusts that most directly raises questions of power, ideology and inequality.[8] This introduction to critical trusts law situates Cotterrell's work on trusts in light of the changing jurisprudential, economic and political landscape,[9] before providing an overview of current trends in critical trusts scholarship and of the chapters in this collection.

---

5. Facundo Alvaredo, Anthony B. Atkinson, Thomas Piketty and Emmanuel Saez, 'The Top 1 Percent in International and Historical Perspective,' *Journal of Economic Perspectives* 27 (2013).

6. Thomas Piketty, *Capital in the Twenty-First Century*, trans. Arthur Goldhammer (London: Harvard University Press, 2017).

7. See Frederik Obermaier and Bastian Obermayer, *The Panama Papers: Breaking the Story of How the Rich and Powerful Hide Their Money* (London: Oneworld Publications, 2017).

8. It should not be thought that trusts imposed by law do not give rise to similar considerations. While this is most stark in the context of trusts of the family home, a critique of trusts arising for breach of fiduciary obligation in commercial contexts, for example, is also deserving of critique.

9. Also see Roger Cotterrell's 'Afterword' in this collection.

Critical Trusts Law in Retrospect

Cotterrell's 1987 Critique: Ideology and Sociological Analysis

'Critical legal theory' is a broad category encompassing a 'considerable diversity' of (often conflicting) theoretical frameworks and methodologies, often associated with the critique of the liberal understanding of law.[10] In the US, Critical Legal Studies (US CLS) developed as a successor movement to legal realism and has largely disappeared as a distinctive movement, instead assimilated into critical race and gender approaches to law, and now often represented in Law and Society and Law and Humanities journals and conferences.[11] In Britain, a distinct branch of critical legal theory developed through the Critical Legal Conference (CLC).[12] This was, and continues to be, an overtly political and theoretically oriented movement, although it does not have a monopoly on critical approaches to law—like US CLS, critical approaches have developed outside of the original 'conference.'[13]

One commonality between US CLS and the CLC was the desire to challenge the assumptions of 'orthodox jurisprudence.' In the 1980s, this was liberal jurisprudence which saw law as neutral and objective.[14] One approach to critical legal theory that was prevalent at the time, drawing on Marx and the Frankfurt School, was ideology critique.[15] As Alan Hunt observed: 'There is one important and very visible difference between liberal and critical theory: critical theory employs the concept

10. Peter Fitzpatrick and Alan Hunt, 'Critical Legal Studies: Introduction,' *Journal of Law and Society* 14 (1987), 1.
11. See Margaret Davies, *Asking the Law Question*, 3rd ed. (Sydney: Lawbook Co, 2008), 183–212.
12. Fitzpatrick and Hunt, 'Critical Legal Studies,' 1–3.
13. See Costas Douzinas, 'A Short History of the British Critical Legal Conference or, the Responsibility of the Critic,' *Law and Critique* 25 (2014).
14. See Corinne Blalock, 'Neoliberalism and the Crisis of Legal Theory,' *Law and Contemporary Problems* 17 (2014).
15. For an overview of Marxism in legal theory, see Robert Fine, 'Marxism and the Social Theory of Law' in *An Introduction to Law and Social Theory*, ed. Reza Banakar and Max Travers (Oxford: Hart Publishing, 2002). This wasn't the only approach—postmodern and feminist approaches were also flourishing: see, for example, Costas Douzinas and Ronnie Warrington, 'On the Deconstruction of Jurisprudence: Fin(n)is Philosophiae,' *Journal of Law and Society* 14 (1987) and Anne Bottomley, Susie Gibson and Belinda Meteyard, 'Dworkin; Which Dworkin? Taking Feminism Seriously,' *Journal of Law and Society* 14 (1987). Also see Costas Douzinas and Ronnie Warrington with Shaun McVeigh (eds.), *Postmodern Jurisprudence: The Law of the Text in the Text of the Law* (Routledge, 1993); and Costas Douzinas, Peter Goodrich and Yifat Hachamovitch, eds., *Politics, Postmodernity and Critical Legal Studies: The Legality of the Contingent* (Routledge, 1994).

of "ideology".'[16] Law masked ideas and beliefs, and its unequal effects, not simply as 'false consciousness', but possibly constituting or legitimizing those effects. Critical approaches sought to unmask or otherwise expose law's founding beliefs and its practical effects, and to this end was overtly concerned with oppression and class, gender and race.

Cotterrell's 1987 article was published the year following the first Critical Legal Conference, held at the University of Kent.[17] Many of the papers at that conference were published in a special issue of the *Journal of Law and* Society.[18] Three tensions run through that collection, reflecting some nascent tensions within the CLC. The first was the attempt to distinguish the British CLC from US CLS. Peter Fitzpatrick and Alan Hunt, in their introduction to the special issue, recognised some overlap in rejecting 'the dominant tradition of Anglo-American legal scholarship, the expository orthodoxy or, more crudely, the "black-letter law" tradition,'[19] a shared rejection of the limits of socio-legal approaches, and a shared concern with the politics of law. Cotterrell however noted 'crucial inadequacies' with US CLS which made it an inappropriate starting point for developing critical legal studies. First was its focus on analysis of legal doctrine at the expense of social, economic and political context. Secondly, Cotterrell noted the theoretical inadequacy of US CLS. This is a point he had made with more force in an earlier article:

> Much is often left unsaid in CLS literature about the exact theoretical foundations of the enterprise, or quite generalised allusions are made to large and often undifferentiated bodies of theory ('Marx', 'Lukacs', 'Habermas', 'Foucault', 'The Frankfurt School').[20]

It seemed that there was 'a rejection of any need for a theory of critique' in US CLS, whereas the CLC consistently sought a theory of critique—or at least asking what is critical about critical legal studies.[21] Thirdly, US CLS was inadequate due to its lack of interdisciplinarity; it was largely

---

16. Alan Hunt, 'The Critique of Law: What is "Critical" about Critical Legal Theory?' *Journal of Law and Society* 14 (1984).
17. The CLC was founded in 1984, held a one-day workshop at Birkbeck Law School in 1985, and held its first full conference at the University of Kent in 1986.
18. The special issue was also published as an edited collection in the same year: Peter Fitzpatrick and Alan Hunt, eds., *Critical Legal Studies* (Oxford: Basil Blackwell, 1987).
19. Fitzpatrick and Hunt, 'Critical Legal Studies: Introduction,' 1.
20. Roger Cotterrell, 'Critique and Law: The Problematic Legacy of the Frankfurt School,' *Tidskrift för Rättssociologi* 3 (1986), 102.
21. See Hunt, 'The Critique of Law.' Also see Julia Chryssostalis and Patricia Tuitt (eds.), 'Instances of Critique,' *Law and Critique* 16 (2005).

a law school phenomenon; US CLS needed to 'escape from the "intellectual ghetto" of the law school.'[22]

While there were important differences between US CLS and British CLC[23]—theoretically, methodologically and politically—with hindsight the attempts to draw a sharp distinction between them hid the commonalities and sacrificed the potential for further collaboration.

A second tension within that collection was between critical legal studies and socio-legal or sociological approaches. Fitzpatrick and Hunt's introduction noted socio-legal approaches as an attempt to escape orthodox jurisprudence, but stated they had limitations (without further explanation).[24] Cotterrell's work was firmly within a broad sociological approach, but he was keen to blur the boundaries between critical and socio-legal approaches; indeed, for Cotterrell, 'critique of law is in its fundamentals a sociological analysis of law.'[25] While Cotterrell sought to distinguish his analysis from 'law and society' approaches which rested on empiricism, positivism and pragmatism,[26] he also recognised the importance of empirical work.[27]

A third tension was between Marxist critiques of law, drawing on the Frankfurt School, and postmodern critiques of law, drawing on Foucault and Derrida (amongst others). As Fitzpatrick and Hunt prophetically asked: 'It remains to be seen if the critical legal studies movement can accommodate the gulf between these two traditions.'[28] While Cotterrell clearly identified more with the former, his conception of critique was more methodological than the radical critique associated with some CLC scholarship. A radical critique would require a 'moral vision,' and while he noted that the Frankfurt School of Critical Theory might contribute towards developing a moral vision, as things stood the strands were 'inadequate and because of their inadequacy the *sociological* critique of doctrine and institutions appears,' he wrote, to have 'an overriding priority in current work.'[29]

So what was critique for Cotterrell? Cotterrell had considered this in more detail in an article published a year earlier, where he had distinguished 'critique' and 'critical theory.'

---

22. Cotterrell, 'Power, Property and the Law of Trusts,' 78.
23. See Costas Douzinas, 'Oubliez Critique,' *Law and Critique* 16 (2005) and Cotterrell's Afterword in this collection.
24. Fitzpatrick and Hunt, 'Critical Legal Studies: Introduction,' 1.
25. Cotterrell, 'Power, Property and the Law of Trusts,' 79 (emphasis in original).
26. Cotterrell, 'Power, Property and the Law of Trusts,' 79.
27. See Cotterrell, 'Critique and Law.'
28. Fitzpatrick and Hunt, 'Critical Legal Studies: Introduction,' 2.
29. Cotterrell, 'Power, Property and the Law of Trusts,' 80–81.

Essentially, critique is the method by which knowledge proclaimed as
'true' is revealed as partial and critical theory is a theory of method.
Understood in this way critical theory is a very special kind of social
theory or perhaps not social theory at all. Its task is to expound
and justify the methods and rationale of critique. Since critique is a
permanent task—in my view a necessary responsibility of all serious
scholars—critical theory is concerned with what may be relatively time-
less matters, including moral and philosophical issues which concern the
responsibilities of the individual to his/her society, and the moral worth
of a social order judged against the possibilities of realising the autonomy
and authenticity of individuals within it.[30]

It is *critique* that he developed further in the 1987 article, which he
explained as follows:

Above all it is explicitly to refuse to accept legal doctrine on its own
terms; that is, to refuse to accept it in the terms in which it justifies
itself (as the unfolding of legal logic; as the self-evident embodiment of
rationality; as the purely technical instrument of policies originating from
'non-legal' (political) sources). Critique of law asks of legal doctrine in
a radical questioning: why does this doctrine exist? What is it for? Why
has it taken its particular form and content?[31]

It may surprise doctrinal scholars that the starting point of Cotterrell's
critique was doctrine. For Cotterrell law is both instrumental and
ideological. Critical analysis aimed at the demystification of law: how
does law structure and guarantee, on the one hand, yet legitimate and
hide, on the other, the exercise of power?

The critical logic of legal doctrine is a logic in terms of social and political
causes and effects of doctrinal developments. The form and content of
legal doctrine is to be explained in terms of the empirical conditions in
which law as doctrine and legal institutions exist in society. ... Legal doctrine thus reflects and contributes to wider currents of ideology. Critical
legal scholarship needs to show how and with what consequences it
does this.[32]

This is what Cotterrell meant by a critique of law being a sociological
analysis. This is not a deterministic or reductive theory of law though;
it is simply recognition that law, as a social phenomenon, 'is to be

---

30. Cotterrell, 'Critique and Law,' 107–108.
31. Cotterrell, 'Power, Property and the Law of Trusts,' 78.
32. Cotterrell, 'Power, Property and the Law of Trusts,' 79.

understood as obtaining all its specific characteristics from its place within a broader social environment.'[33] The sociological analysis Cotterrell adopted was rooted in doctrine and a contextual approach, using critical theory as a method; it was not an empirical sociology.

Cotterrell's critique of the trust form starts with what are often considered the orthodox doctrinal components of the trust—the beneficiary principle and fiduciary obligations—in light of a line of questioning that does not start within the logic of doctrine but externally. Cotterrell argued that trusts extend and intensify the ideological function of *property*, which hides or silences inequalities through a methodological separation of persons and things. Trusts further separate persons and things through the notion of the fund and the figures of trustee and beneficiary. Consequently, the trust both concentrates property-power (through the formation of large funds) and hides property-power (through the splitting of visible legal and invisible beneficial ownership). This critical framework explains the ideological significance of the beneficiary principle and the rule against non-charitable purpose trusts (a trust must be for persons, not purposes, because the ideology of property requires that property is owned by a person; it cannot abide ownerless property); fiduciary obligations (the ideology of property presents owners as not owing obligations to the world but rather being owed special obligations); and charitable purpose trusts (the requirement that they are for the public benefit construes the public as a collective owner).

Methodologically, the argument progresses by way of a series of bifurcations: law (doctrine) is both instrumental (facilitative of the exercise of power) and ideological (silencing or hiding the exercise of power); property gives rise to property-power and property-security; property is concerned with persons and things; trusts are an extension of persons (from individuals to collectivities) and things (from tangible things to abstract value as a fund); trusts extend and mystify the property-power (of beneficiaries, and we could add settlors and trustees) and property-security.

The Intellectual Context of Cotterrell's 'Partial Agenda'

Cotterrell's contextual and ideological critique of trusts did not arrive in an intellectual vacuum. Lawrence Friedman, as part of the University of Wisconsin Law School's 'law in action' approach, had already published

---

33. Cotterrell, 'Power, Property and the Law of Trusts,' 79.

'The Dynastic Trust' in 1964.[34] In 1979 Michael Chesterman's *Charities, Trusts and Social Welfare* was published in the 'Law in Context' series.[35] While the focus of this ground-breaking textbook was the law of charity, it inevitably included a great deal on the law of trusts, including historical and fiscal contextualisation to explain the doctrinal developments and policy considerations. This set the scene (and provided much of the material for the chapters on charitable trusts) for his subsequent collaboration with Graham Moffat in the same series, *Trusts Law: Text and Materials*, first published in 1988, a major contribution to the contextual approach to trusts law. Michael Chesterman's 1984 paper 'Family Settlements on Trust: Landowners and the Rising Bourgeoisie' made a further important contribution to the contextual approach to trusts law. This paper explained the emergence of certain trust orthodoxies in the eighteenth and nineteenth centuries, such as the rule in *Saunders v Vautier* concerning premature termination of beneficial interests and the decision in *Brandon v Robinson* concerning the assignment of beneficial interests and protective trusts. Each of these developments enabled the emergence of the idea of the trust as a fund: 'a mixed collection of all forms of property ... which together constitute a floating fund of investments.'[36] Chesterman explains these developments as law's 'responsiveness to economic and ideological forces,'[37] most notably the 'growth in commercial and industrial capital within a society still dominated politically by landed interests.'[38] His point is that the old law of trusts was concerned with preserving specific property for dynastic reasons, but that with a shift to mercantile and industrial capitalism and the emerging bourgeoisie, property needed to be more mobile and this contributed to the development of what are now taken to be trust law orthodoxies.

> In the last resort, the family trust and law relating to it, with all their powerful moral and ideological overtones, combine to protect accumulated private wealth. What this paper has attempted to show is the extent

---

34. Lawrence M. Friedman, 'The Dynastic Trust,' *Yale Law Journal* 73 (1964). Also see Lawrence M. Friedman, 'The Law of the Living, the Law of the Dead: Property, Succession, and Society,' *Wisconsin Law Review* (1966).

35. Michael Chesterman, *Charities, Trusts and Social Welfare* (London: Weidenfeld and Nicolson, 1979).

36. Michael Chesterman, 'Family Settlements on Trust: Landowners and the Rising Bourgeoisie,' in *Law, Economy and Society, 1750-1914: Essays in the History of English Law*, ed. G.R. Rubin and David Sugarman (Oxford: Professional Books Ltd, 1984), 124.

37. Chesterman, 'Family Settlements on Trust,' 157.

38. Chesterman, 'Family Settlements on Trust,' 164.

to which, and the processes by which, they may undergo major adaptation, when the composition of the class of private wealth-holders most dominant in society is altered in accordance with society's own political and economic development.[39]

Like Chesterman before him, in his 1987 article Cotterrell highlighted the importance of the emergence of the fund and how the trust was a mechanism for extending the idea of the fund beyond common law's blockages.

In 1987 another important contribution to critical trusts law was published, Gregory Alexander's 'The Transformation of Trusts as a Legal Category, 1800-1914.'[40] Like Chesterman, Alexander looked to contextualise the emergence of the category of the trust. Unlike Chesterman, Alexander's focus was on how the trust became a category distinct from contract, gift and conveyance through the development of its detailed rules and distinctions, but like Chesterman his interest was in 'the contingent and ideological character of legal categories.'[41] This article explicitly drew on the CLS work of Duncan Kennedy, describing the emergent orthodoxy in the law of trusts in the 'Classical' period in US jurisprudence of 1870 to 1920. One of the main themes of the article was 'that throughout the development of what we now think of as the modern law of trusts courts were anxious to prevent equitable doctrines applicable to trusts from undermining analogous common-law doctrines, which even by the late eighteenth century were beginning to reflected an individualistic social outlook.'[42] Alexander explained how categorization isn't simply a pragmatic, value-neutral exercise but ideological: 'precisely because their function is to organize our accumulated legal norms, categorical schemes do have normative power.'[43]

> Sketching the outline of their ideology, the Classics held the following preferences: adjudication by rules rather than discretionary standards, the judicial role restricted to facilitating private intentions rather than public regulation, individual self-determination maximized rather than collective paternalism.[44]

---

39. Chesterman, 'Family Settlements on Trust,' 167.
40. Gregory S. Alexander, 'The Transformation of Trusts as a Legal Category, 1800-1914,' *Law & History Review* 5 (1987).
41 Alexander, 'The Transformation of Trusts,' 303.
42. Alexander, 'The Transformation of Trusts,' 304.
43. Alexander, 'The Transformation of Trusts,' 314.
44. Alexander, 'The Transformation of Trusts,' 315.

Like Chesterman, Alexander was interested in ideology and the construction of trusts orthodoxy. Unlike Chesterman, who put the development of trusts law in economic and political context, Alexander very much focused on detailed consideration of the case law, highlighting one of the differences between US CLS's internal approach and the external approaches of the nascent CLC.

In 1988 Moffat and Chesterman's *Trusts Law* was published in the Law in Context series.[45] This book sought to 'present the law of trusts in a wholly new way,' namely to present the social and legal context in which trusts appear, which in turn required an understanding of the functions that trusts perform and attention to social and legal history, because 'the origins of many of the laws that presently govern trusts established to preserve family wealth or promote charitable activity are only explicable in terms of old modes of preserving family wealth or acting charitably.'[46] A key problem for the book was that with an emphasis on the different contexts in which trusts operate—private family wealth, commercial trusts, pension trusts, charitable trusts, various trusts imposed by law—it might be that there is no trust law after all, hence the plural in the book's title. Nevertheless, the authors maintained that the trust concept or idea had a 'unifying influence.' In *Trusts Law* this tension between fragmentation and a unifying notion of the trust idea was resolved by simply recognising that it is a productive tension that exists within the subject itself, an understanding of which is necessary to understanding legal change: 'the competing influences on legal development of the claims of pure conceptual clarity as against pressures for pragmatic resolution of practical problems. An adequate understanding of trusts law requires that both these influences be taken into account by the student.'[47]

Two alternative approaches to the problem of fragmentation to that taken in *Trusts Law* could be taken, both of which are relevant to Cotterrell's subsequent work on trusts. One would recognise that increasing fragmentation leads not to a single law of trusts but rather to specialisms of trust law; distinct disciplines of law relating to small family trusts, large discretionary trusts (in terms of beneficiaries and value), asset protection trusts, unit trusts, pension trusts, charitable

---

45. Graham Moffat and Michael Chesterman with John Dewar, *Trusts Law: Text and Materials*, 1st ed. (London: Weidenfeld and Nicolson, 1988). The 1987 article is extracted at length in the first edition of *Trusts Law*, and has remained in every edition since.
46. Moffat and Chesterman, *Trusts Law*, xv.
47. Moffat and Chesterman, *Trusts Law*, xvi.

trusts and so on.[48] Indeed, this may well be the direction of travel, in which case the question turns to how much 'trust law'—both from case law but also statute and regulation—is mandatory, ie applicable to 'all' trusts, and how much is optional, and whether there is a single 'irreducible core' of trusts law.[49]

A more radical approach would jettison 'the trust' as a legal category, and instead analyse areas of law underpinned by a social understanding of trusting. Indeed, in a 1992 article Moffat suggested exactly this:

> In what sense can we still talk of a subject called the law of trusts which is coherent, whether in concept or subject-matter, and which should be studied? ... Exploring and analysing the relationship between trust as a social phenomenon and as a legal form may provide fresh insights for our understanding of the law of trust.[50]

Cotterrell's subsequent articles would explore the transformations in trusts and the relation of trust as a social phenomenon and the legal forms of the trust.

Supplementing Form with Transformation: Three Typologies of Trust

Cotterrell published two further articles on trusts, in 1992—'Some Sociological Aspects of the Controversy around the Legal Validity of Private Purpose Trusts'—and 1993—'Trusting in Law: Legal and Moral Concepts of Trust.' While the focus of the 1987 article was a critique of the orthodox trust form, Cotterrell's 1992 and 1993 articles supplemented a critique of form with a critique of transformation.[51] These articles continue his sociological approach starting with conceptual issues that doctrinal (ie legal) analysis can't resolve, but did so without the direct references to critique or critical legal studies that are present in the 1987 article.

---

48. See Graham Moffat, 'Pension Funds: A Fragmentation of Trust Law?' *Modern Law Review* 56 (1993).
49. See David Hayton, 'The Irreducible Core Content of Trusteeship,' in *Trends in Contemporary Trust Law*, ed. A.J. Oakley (Oxford: Clarendon Press, 1996); John H. Langbein, 'Mandatory Rules in the Law of Trusts,' *Northwestern University Law Review* 98 (2004); John H. Langbein, 'Burn the Rembrandt? Trust Law's Limits on the Settlor's Power to Direct Investments,' *Boston University Law Review* 90 (2010).
50. See Graham Moffat, 'Trusts Law: A Song without End?' *Modern Law Review* 55 (1992), 137. Also see Graham Moffat, 'Pension Funds: A Fragmentation of Trust Law?' *Modern Law Review* 56 (1993), 488–492.
51. Cotterrell, 'Some Sociological Aspects,' 302-303; Cotterrell, 'Trusting in Law,' 75–76.

The 1992 article again focused on a trust orthodoxy: the beneficiary principle and the rule against private purpose trusts. To that end he was continuing his exploration of the relationship between trusts and property conceptions. The doctrinal dilemma Cotterrell looked at was the origins and effects of this orthodoxy: when and why did a rule emerge that trusts must be for persons or charitable purposes and not for private purposes? This conceptual issue is at heart an 'ideological dispute' about what constitutes a 'true trust.'[52] Cotterrell's critique is of the very idea of orthodoxy, as conceptions of the trust change with the changing social, economic and ideological contexts. To this end Cotterrell contrasts two conceptions of the trust: a moralistic conception and a property-receptacle conception that became dominant in the nineteenth century:

> In general … the moralistic conception puts primary emphasis on the sanctity of the trust creator's lawful intention, while the property-receptacle conception emphasises the importance of all property being subject to definite beneficial entitlements.[53]

Cotterrell argued that far from being essential trust orthodoxy, the beneficiary principle did not emerge until purpose trusts became a threat to the conception of the trust as a 'property-receptacle.' Drawing on Gregory Alexander's 1987 article with particular reference to the tension between rights of free alienation as opposed to restraints on alienation in the law of trusts, Cotterrell argued that purpose trusts were conceived as taking property away from family members:

> The trust creator's freedom of alienation, expressed in the setting up of a trust for abstract purposes unrelated to the specific interests of family members who survive him, cannot usually be justified as serving any socially useful family purposes.[54]

If unfettered, free alienability was the goal, then purposes should be upheld, and if they promoted concrete use-value they may also be tolerated, but otherwise they were at odds with the rationality of modern law:

> The precedents so established survived into a society ordered by a different world view, in which trusts were part of a structure of property law adapting to the developing demands of commerce and a modern

---

52. Cotterrell, 'Some Sociological Aspects,' 314.
53. Cotterrell, 'Some Sociological Aspects,' 313.
54. Cotterrell, 'Some Sociological Aspects,' 319.

economy. Cases which may originally have merely illustrated the general outlook that equity should fulfil, insofar as practicable, the last wishes of a testator expressed as a moral obligation, later seemed sentimental, anomalous and archaic decisions at odds with the rationality of modern trust law; a rationality centred on the economic utility of trust arrangements as convenient and efficient devices by which property holdings could be planned and regulated for the benefit of specific persons or categories of persons.[55]

As to the future of the beneficiary principle, for Cotterrell this would depend in part on the continuing hold of the property-receptacle conception of the trust:

> To the extent that the property-receptacle conception of the trust continues to dominate trust law …, it seems reasonable to expect that firm assertions of the beneficiary principle will continue.[56]

The old purpose trusts were limited in nature and therefore acceptable, but the 'scope, variety and ambition' of new purposes trusts were quite different.[57] This highlights the political stakes of this doctrinal dilemma and Cotterrell's intervention: the doctrinal orthodoxy emerged in a particular economic and political context, but in the 1980s the economic and political context was changing, and brought the doctrinal dilemma of the beneficiary principle to the fore and challenged the property-receptable conception underpinning the beneficiary principle. This sets the scene for the 1993 article.

While the 1987 and 1992 articles had a focus on property, and the beneficiary principle played a key role in both, the 1993 article turned to the relationship between moral or social trust and the law of trusts and fiduciary obligations. Here Cotterrell drew on social theories concerning social trust (most notably Luhmann's systems theory) as a means of shedding light on the transformation of trusts. This analysis again entailed putting trusts in their 'wider theoretical context,'[58] but this article put more emphasis on patterns of change than the previous articles. Despite the shift in emphasis, the article also returned to questions of power, notably the power and dependence involved in trusting relationships. Cotterrell moved from—or supplemented—property-power to looking at the networks of relationships involved

55. Cotterrell, 'Some Sociological Aspects,' 327–328.
56. Cotterrell, 'Some Sociological Aspects,' 332.
57. Cotterrell, 'Some Sociological Aspects,' 333.
58. Cotterrell, 'Trusting in Law,' 76.

in trusts (trustee-beneficiary; settlor-trustee; and settlor-beneficiary).[59]

For Cotterrell, the personal trust involved in trusting puts the person trusting at risk because of the inverse power relation. Law can be a means of reversing relations of power. In doing so it shifts trust from personal and interpersonal relations to trust in law and systems:

> To the extent that law controls trustees, the risk of relying on them is reduced and the moral relationship of trust is displaced from the trustee and attached to law itself. Thus, law's significance is to reduce the risk of interpersonal trust. Instead of having to put one's moral trust purely in the trustee, one can have confidence in law which guarantees the trustee's proper behaviour.[60]

Cotterrell identified a major issue in modern trusts: the reversal or regulation of the power imbalance achieved by 'orthodox' trust law, underpinned by the beneficial principle and fiduciary obligations, may no longer be adequate due to the size of modern trusts and expertise of those involved in the trust (entailing trustees having more power and discretion in the administration of the fund and beneficiaries having fewer opportunities to hold trustees to account).[61] Developing the 1992 typology of trusts, Cotterrell added 'capital management' to moralistic and property-receptacle. He went on to suggest a conceptual movement (if not an exact historical transition) from moralistic conception to property-receptacle, but that the latter has two stages: initially it was concerned with equitable proprietary rights fitting the common law model, but with a shift to capital management it became a disembodied capital fund.[62] And it is in these latter trusts that size and expertise became a real problem.

The Changing Contexts of Trusts Law and Practice

The legal, political and economic context in which Cotterrell's articles were published, and developments in trusts law and practice since, are important to understanding critical trusts law then and now. In England, the rise of 'neoliberalism' (which in this context can be taken to mean deregulation and financialisation) had a number of consequences. The 1980s saw the deregulation of the City of London, with the so-called

---

59. Cotterrell, 'Trusting in Law,' 77–78.
60. Cotterrell, 'Trusting in Law,' 79.
61. Cotterrell, 'Trusting in Law,' 79.
62. Cotterrell, 'Trusting in Law,' 90.

'Big Bang' on 27 October 1986. However default trust law concerning investment remained as it had been since the Trustee Investment Act 1961, which limited the power of trustees to invest in shares, and the power to delegate the administration of trust to 'experts' was also limited.[63] HM Treasury consequently consulted on the need to change investment and delegation laws relating to trusts, as trust law was falling behind.[64] This led to a reference to the Law Commission to consider the powers and duties of trustees, which in turn led to the Trustee Act 2000.[65] That Act considerably widened trustees' powers of investment and delegation. Although for many it merely codified what well-drafted trust instruments were already allowing, it brought about a complete reversal in 'default law': while previously trust law was cautious and limited, subject to settlors extending trustees' powers in the trust instrument, now default trust law provides very wide powers to trustees, subject to settlors restricting those powers in the trust instrument. These changes were in fact an extension of changes already introduced in the context of pension trusts (an example of Cotterrell's 'capital management trusts') under the Pensions Act 1995, and reflected policies first elaborated by the law and economics movement, most notably Langbein and Posner who, building on the work of the economist Harry Markowitz, had long made the case for developing trust law in accordance with the economic logic of portfolio theory.[66] The capital management model of the trust now represents the new trust orthodoxy as expressed by the Trustee Act 2000: wide investment powers subject to a duty to consider the 'standard investment criteria,' which is modelled on modern portfolio theory, a duty to obtain and consider 'proper advice' (meaning specialist financial advice), coupled with a general power of delegation and a special delegation regime for asset managers, with an expectation that trustees are professional governors of wealth.[67]

---

63. See L.M. Clements, 'Bringing Trusts into the Twenty-First Century,' *Web Journal of Current Legal Issues* 2 (2004), accessed 15 April 2024, https://www.bailii.org/uk/other/journals/WebJCLI/2004/issue2/clements2.html.
64. HM Treasury, 'Investment Powers of Trustees: A Consultation Document,' May 1996.
65. Law Commission, *Trustees' Powers and Duties* (Law Com No 260, 1999).
66. See John H. Langbein and Richard A. Posner, 'The Revolution in Trust Investment Law,' *American Bar Association Journal* 62 (1976), 'Market Funds and Trust-Investment Law,' *American Bar Foundation Research Journal* (1976) and 'Market Funds and Trust-Investment Law: II,' *American Bar Foundation Research Journal* (1977).
67. See Joshua Getzler, 'Legislative Incursions into Modern Trusts Doctrine in England: The Trustee Act 2000 and the Contracts (Rights of Third Parties) Act 1999,'

In order for the Trustee Bill to maintain support in the House of Lords, the Lord Chancellor undertook to refer certain questions to the Law Commission, in particular concerning trustee exemption clauses.[68] There was a concern that widening the powers of trustees might expose funds to too much risk, particularly in light of the recent decision in *Armitage v Nurse*[69] confirming the validity of clauses excluding liability for gross negligence. The Trustee Act itself confirmed the possibility of excluding liability for breach of the duty of care and skill. The Law Commission's consultation paper provisionally proposed prohibiting clauses excluding liability for gross negligence but, following a consultation response from the Financial Markets Law Committee (concerning the risk to London as a global centre for bond-trading if exclusion clauses were to be regulated) and further discussion with the Society of Trust and Estate Practitioners (STEP), the final report dropped this proposal in favour of an unenforceable rule of practice whereby trust drafters should draw settlors' attention to any clause excluding or limiting trustee liability.[70] The concerns of the financial markets were thereby addressed, and the centrality of settlor intention confirmed in the work of the Law Commission. These transformations in trust law, led by free-market economic thinking, may well have contributed to the impending financial crisis.[71]

Offshore, things were changing too. For example, Cayman Islands STAR trusts were introduced in 1997, kick-starting (or maybe turbo-charging) a race-to-the-bottom amongst jurisdictions, including many US states. The changes were fast and dramatic: perpetuity periods were extended or abolished; non-charitable purpose trusts and asset protection trusts with suitable firewall legislation protecting against creditors flourished; confidentiality laws reduced disclosure obligations; and the rise of what Lionel Smith has dubbed 'massively discretionary trusts':

> trust structures in which the trustees' dispositive discretions do not merely qualify the beneficial interests, but effectively displace them, one might even say overwhelm them.[72]

Global Jurist Topics 2 (2002).

68.   Law Commission, *Trustee Exemption Clauses* (Consultation Paper No 171, 2002), paras 1.1–1.12.

69.   [1998] Ch 241.

70.   See Law Commission, *Trustee Exemption Clauses* (Law Com No 301, 2006).

71.   See Joshua Getzler, 'Fiduciary Investment in the Shadow of Financial Crisis: Was Lord Eldon Right?' *Journal of Equity* 3 (2009).

72.   Lionel Smith, 'Massively Discretionary Trusts,' *Current Legal Problems* (2017),

These trusts include a wide range of powers, most importantly widely drawn powers of appointment and powers to remove or add beneficiaries to the class of objects. A 'letter of wishes' is central to the functioning of these trusts.[73] The letter of wishes is a non-binding statement of wishes to be taken into account when exercising powers. It might request that trustees consult and take account of settlor's wishes in exercise of powers; it might request to treat some beneficiary or beneficiaries as principal or primary beneficiary; it might request that trustees exercise powers in a particular manner, eg a long-term distribution strategy. The letter of wishes exists in a sort of no-man's land between a trust document expressing what trustees are to do and not to do and something more ephemeral with no obligations, making it difficult for beneficiaries to pin-down but also making it difficult to know exactly how a trustee will exercise a power, meaning that trust property is in extended-limbo (beyond the usual discretionary trust).

A new orthodoxy emerged that has become the hegemonic trusts discourse: the primacy of settlor-autonomy, conceding almost unlimited flexibility in the structuring of trusts; in particular, the extension and proliferation of powers given to trustees, third parties and settlors; the watering down of obligations and duties trustees are subject to; and the triumph of the contractualisation thesis which in turns raises questions over the 'ownership' of the fund. While the new orthodoxy might suggest a challenge to Cotterrell's argument, in particular the property-receptacle argument, this is something Cotterrell had already noticed in referring to capital management. And despite everything, the trust remains a property-receptacle insofar as it shields assets from creditors.

In light of these developments, Cotterrell's work, and the 1993 article in particular, was prophetic; indeed, we have to point out to our students that Cotterrell wrote this article *before* the Trustee Act 2000. The increasing (necessity of) expertise and technical competence in trust practice, leading to a desire for more power and more discretion on behalf of trustees and their delegees, has been coupled with a reduction in legal accountability despite the rising risk of error and increasing moral distance between trustees and beneficiaries.

27–28.

73. See Stephen Moverley Smith and Andrew Holden, 'Letters of Wishes and the Ongoing Role of the Settlor,' *Trusts & Trustees* 20 (2014).

Interregnum

Despite all the radical transformations in trust law and practice, the period from 1995 to around 2008 saw relatively little published critical trusts law scholarship. Neither volume of *The Critical Lawyers' Handbook* included a chapter on trusts.[74] That isn't to say there wasn't any critical scholarship on trusts, but the scholarship focused on one particularly important context: ownership of the family home following relationship breakdown. Feminist scholarship in this context was extremely important, particularly in reconsidering the meanings and significance of financial contribution and intention in light of women's immaterial labour.[75]

Why was there such little critique of the trust beyond specific domains such the family home? One explanation might be that it was—and remains—a context which was both more readily understood by students and also more directly material to the lives of those engaged in the debates, unlike many of the developments of trusts on the financial markets and in far-away jurisdictions used by high-net-worth-individuals. The focus on that context might have meant other developments in trusts law and practice went uncommented on.

Another explanation might be that Marxist approaches to political economy largely disappeared from the CLC in the 1990s, with 'postmodernist' approaches in the ascendancy.[76] To the extent that questions of political economy were raised, these were not at the level of private law but rather theory, public law or international economic law. Private law, and trusts in particular, did not receive a great deal of attention. However, that only explains the absence of critical trusts scholarship in the context of the CLC; it doesn't explain why outside of that particular movement a critical scholarship did not emerge. Outside of the CLC, trusts scholarship tended to be in the hands of orthodox jurisprudence, focusing on niche doctrinal issues rather than larger questions of theory or sociological jurisprudence.

---

74. Although as ever the non-inclusion of a chapter in a collection can be down to a multitude of reasons. There is no chapter on trusts in the more recent collection, Emilios Christodoulidis, Ruth Dukes and Marco Goldoni, eds., *Research Handbook on Critical Legal Theory* (Edward Elgar Publishing, 2019): one was intended to be included but the author wasn't able to complete it.

75. For example, Rosemary Auchmuty, 'Unfair Shares for Women: The Rhetoric of Equality and the Reality of Inequality,' in *Feminist Perspectives on Land Law*, Anne Bottomley and Hilary Lim eds. (London: Routledge-Cavendish, 2007). Also see Susan Scott-Hunt and Hilary Lim, eds., *Feminist Perspectives on Equity and Trusts* (London: Cavendish Publishing, 2001).

76. See Douzinas, 'A Short History of the British Critical Legal Conference,' 189–195.

Redux

The Global Financial Crisis 2007-2008 put political economy and wealth inequality—and with them Marx—back on the agenda at the CLC and for trusts scholars with a critical ethos, even if not affiliating themselves with the CLC. The work of Anthony Atkinson, Thomas Piketty, Joseph Stiglitz and Gabriel Zucman, amongst many others, provided detailed analysis of the problem of wealth inequality. That this was linked to how assets are held and distributed over time made it impossible not to look again at the role of law—and in particular trusts—in structuring wealth. In this context a number of new contributions to critical trusts scholarship emerged, although mostly still outside the CLC movement.

Doctrinal Critique, or Reactionary Doctrinalism

One form of 'critical' response to the changes in trusts law and practice is a doctrinal critique, what I call 'reactionary doctrinalism.' Here the doctrinal scholar holds up the 'true trust,' rooted in trust orthodoxy, to the trust aberrations that have been appearing mainly in offshore jurisdictions that basically give the settlor what they want.[77] Lionel Smith's excellent articles are shining examples of this approach:

> A trust has a certain logic to it, and there are aspects of this logic that are not susceptible to freedom of choice. ... I believe as much as anyone in freedom of choice. But I believe the rules of private law reflect important truths about interpersonal justice.[78]

Those truths are basically a reassertion of the beneficiary principle: you need beneficiaries to hold trustees to account; without beneficiaries to hold trustees to account there is unfiltered power in the hands of the trustees, which is basically ownership. As Smith states:

> It is a deformation of the trust to create a structure in which there is no real beneficiary; and it is a deformation of the trust to create a device in which beneficiaries have no significant rights.[79]

---

77. And not just scholars, practitioners too. See e.g. Tony Molloy QC, 'High-Net-Worth Trusts in the Twenty-First Century: Confiscatory Taxes and Duties?' in *Trusts and Modern Wealth Management*, ed. Richard C. Nolan, Kelvin F.K. Low and Tang Hang Wu (Cambridge: Cambridge University Press, 2018).
78. Lionel Smith, 'Give the People What They Want? Onshoring of the Offshore,' *Iowa Law Review* 103 (2018), 2155.
79. Lionel Smith, 'Massively Discretionary Trusts,' 53.

The problem with doctrinal critique is that it comes from a position of legal dogma: it asserts the true law against a supposed imposter. As Cotterrell and others have demonstrated, the 'true law' itself is a relatively recent development and indeed there may not be one true law but a fragmented laws of trusts. Like a critique of financial capitalism that rests on a return to the 'real economy,' it may be that there is no 'pure' trusts to which to return. Secondly, to rest a critique of modern developments in trusts law on a return to the one true trust is to suggest that the 'original' trust was unproblematic, when just like the so-called 'real economy' (that is, the productive economy rather than the financial markets) the true trust contributed deeply to inequality.[80] Cotterrell's critique of the trust as hiding property-power and inequality was a critique of the orthodox trust form underpinning Smith's criticisms of contemporary developments in trusts law.

It may nevertheless be that this is considered an adequate critique of the trust. In their contribution to the 1987 special issue on critical legal studies, Paul Hirst and Phil Jones warned the emerging CLC to reject critique, at least radical critique, of liberal law; they cautioned against throwing the baby out with the bathwater and pointed to what they called 'the critical resources of established jurisprudence.'[81] It may be that Smith's 'doctrinal critique,' coming from the position of a 'true trust'—established jurisprudence—keeps the lid on the abuse of trusts. Indeed, Smith's critique might fall within Shaunnagh Dorsett and Shaun McVeigh's idea of critique as an 'ethic of responsibility for the forms that law takes on.'[82]

While I agree that a concern with the trust form is important, I do not consider a critique rooted in the 'true trust' to be adequate. Instead, following Cotterrell, a better starting point is contemporary trust doctrine (aberrant as it may be) and asking the very questions Cotterrell asked: why does this doctrine exist? What is it for? Why has it taken its particular form and content? Answering these questions, we may well discover that current manifestations of the trust idea are like a fish in water, coinciding with contemporary ideas (ideology) of property, ie mobile, fragmented and yet with strong ties to settlor-caprice. In other words, we may find that trust doctrine has simply moved with the times, with shifting ideas of property, power and wealth.

---

80. See Donatella Alessandrini, *Value Making in International Economic Law and Regulation: Alternative Possibilities* (Oxford: Routledge, 2016), 1–4.
81. Paul Hirst and Phil Jones, 'The Critical Resources of Established Jurisprudence,' *Journal of Law and Society* 14 (1987).
82. Shaunnagh Dorsett and Shaun McVeigh, *Jurisdiction* (Oxford: Routledge, 2012), 23.

Empirical Critique

One problem in the critique of trusts is the lack of adequate information about trust practices. Two recent empirical studies have started to plug that gap. One, undertaken by Adam Hofri-Winogradow, conducted a series of mass, global surveys of trusts professionals to analyse trust reforms that constituted a 'stripping of the trust' or, as he later called it, 'the statutory liberalization of trust law.'[83] Hofri-Winogradow's intention was to understand the race-to-the-bottom and its distributive consequences. As he explained:

> Most aspects of the recent trust reforms reallocated costs and benefits so as to reduce social welfare, and that most of these welfare-reducing reforms either enacted into law positions earlier adopted by service providers in opting out of the then default law, or were adopted as one move in an ongoing inter-jurisdictional contest.[84]

His surveys suggested that certain reforms were enacted to retain trust business by pandering to users' interests, but that this did little to sustain or create a market in professional trust services.[85] Hofri-Winogradow's conclusion was that legislators need to think more carefully about social welfare. Whether or not that is sufficient is another question, but the evidence Hofri-Winogradow has gathered is essential to a critique of contemporary trust reforms. As Cotterrell stated, '*all* types of existing empirical social theory (and the empirical studies of social phenomena which they organise or attempt to integrate) are relevant to the project of critique.'[86]

While Hofri-Winogradow's empirical work is largely (although not exclusively) quantitative, Brooke Harrington's is qualitative. Harrington, a sociologist by training, undertook an ethnography of the wealth management industry by undertaking the training to become a qualified Trust and Estates Practitioner with the STEP.[87] This gave

83. Adam Hofri-Winogradow, 'The Stripping of the Trust: From Evolutionary Scripts to Distributive Results,' *University of Toronto Law Journal* 65 (2015) and 'The Statutory Liberalization of Trust Law across 152 Jurisdictions: Leaders, Laggards and the Market for Fiduciary Services,' *UC Davis Law Review* 53 (2020). Also see Adam Hofri-Winogradow 'The Demand for Fiduciary Services: Evidence from the Market in Private Donative Trusts,' *Hastings Law Journal* 68 (2017) and 'Trust Proliferation: a View from the Field,' *Trust Law International* 31 (2017).
84. Hofri-Winogradow, 'The Stripping of the Trust,' 570.
85. Hofri-Winogradow, 'The Statutory Liberalization of Trust Law.'
86. Cotterrell, 'Critique and Law,' 106 (emphasis in original).
87. Brooke Harrington, *Capital without Borders: Wealth Managers and the One Percent* (London: Harvard University Press, 2016).

Harrington the opportunity to undertake a series of interviews with industry insiders across multiple jurisdictions. Although the trust is just one tool in wealth management's armoury, Harrington has plenty to say about trust law, practice and industry.

Harrington's critique is from the perspective of a sociology of the professions and wealth inequality. A key insight from Harrington's work is the interrelationship between wealth accumulation, the wealth management industry and the laws that enable and sustain wealth:

> Trust and estate planning has contributed at multiple levels to enduring inequality worldwide, from building individual family fortunes to the creation of broader class institutions such as trust funds and charitable foundations. ... The work of trust and estate planners has made the 'leisure class' possible, and thus contributes to contemporary patterns of wealth inequality.[88]

As Harrington argues in another article, trusts are a privileged site of accumulation.[89]

Empirical work has been extremely helpful in shedding light on or confirming our suspicions regarding trust practice. Hofri-Winogradow and Harrington's studies remind us of one limit of Cotterrell's work and even recent concerns about the rising power of settlors: there has been little on the power of the trust industry. Harrington's work in particular suggests a need to turn away from a focus on 'the trust' and rather turn towards wealth management—the trust being one component of what we might call 'wealth assemblages' coding capital.[90]

Critical Trusts and Estates Scholarship in the US

A number of critical studies have emerged, many emanating from the US and in particular a group of scholars with a focus on trusts and estates law from the perspective of gender, race, class, and sexuality.[91] Much of

---

88. Brooke Harrington, 'Trust and Estate Planning: The Emergence of a Profession and Its Contribution to Socioeconomic Inequality,' *Sociological Forum* 27 (2012), 826.
89. Brooke Harrington, 'Trusts and Financialization,' *Socio-Economic Review* 15 (2017).
90. See Katharina Pistor, *The Code of Capital: How the Law Creates Wealth and Inequality* (Oxford: Princeton University Press, 2019).
91. Much of the impetus for this stems from the Biennial Critical Trusts and Estates conference, organised by Carla Spivack and first held at Oklahoma City University Law School in 2013. The only US trusts and estates casebook with a critical focus emerged from those associated with that conference: Deborah S. Gordon, Karen J. Sneddon, Carla Spivack, Allison Anna Tait and Alfred J. Brophy, *Experiencing Trusts*

this work focuses on inequalities produced by trusts and estates laws in the context of succession practices, a topic that has not had as much interest (in teaching or research) in English law schools.[92] While much of the doctrinal and empirical work discussed above focuses on high-net-worth individuals, this scholarship goes beyond the wealthy to consider trusts and estates in everyday succession practices. It isn't possible to do justice to this scholarship in this introduction, only to introduce trends in that scholarship.

Bridget Crawford and Anthony Infanti wrote of the need for a critical research agenda for wills, trusts and estates in 2014.[93] They argued that critical scholarship, far from being the 'internal' critique commonly associated with CLS, should take an 'outsider perspective' to examine the substance and structure of the law:

> It means examining why the law has developed in the way it has and considering what impact the law has on historically disempowered groups such as people of colour; women of all colours; lesbian, gay, bisexual, and transgender individuals; low-income and poor individuals; the disabled; and nontraditional families.[94]

Carla Spivack is another leading scholar in this burgeoning jurisprudence. Spivack's introduction to a special issue of the *Wisconsin Law Review* in 2019 on 'Wills, Trusts, and Estates Meets Gender, Race, and Class' provides some context to that work.[95] As she explains, much of this scholarship draws inspiration and insights from CLS, Critical Race Studies and Feminist Legal Theory and, as such, a central theme is 'a deep suspicion of legal formalism.'[96] A central aspect of this critique is to go

---

and Estates, 2nd ed. (West Academic, 2021).

92. Although that appears to be changing, as indicated by the recent publication of textbooks and edited collections: Daniel Monk and Daphna Hacker, eds., 'Wealth, Families and Death: Socio-Legal Perspectives on Wills and Inheritance,' *Oñati Socio-legal Series 4* (2014); Birke Häcker and Charles Mitchell, eds., *Current Issues in Succession Law* (Oxford: Hart Publishing, 2016); Brian Sloan, ed., *Landmark Cases in Succession Law* (Oxford: Hart Publishing, 2019); Brian Sloan, *Borkowski's Law of Succession*, 4th ed. (Oxford: Oxford University Press, 2020); Suzanne Lennon and Daniel Monk, eds., *Inheritance Matters: Kinship, Property, Law* (Oxford: Hart Publishing, 2023).

93. Bridget J. Crawford and Anthony C. Infanti, 'A Critical Research Agenda for Wills, Trusts, and Estates,' *Real Property, Trust and Estate Law Journal* 49 (2014).

94. Crawford and Infanti, 'A Critical Research Agenda,' 318.

95. The special issue arose from a Critical Trusts and Estates Symposium held at Wisconsin Law School in October 2018.

96. Carla Spivack, 'Introduction to the 2018 *Wisconsin Law Review* Symposium Issue: Wills, Trusts, and Estates Meets Gender, Race, and Class,' *Wisconsin Law Review* (2019), 161.

beyond formal equality in law, and consider the material effects of law—which chimes with Cotterrell's approach and could equally be called ideology critique. The various articles in the special issue address those who have been left out or excluded by traditional narratives. Another element that Spivack notes is the empirical grounding of the articles. As she observes, unlike other areas of law, 'the field of trusts and estates, with some notable exceptions, has lagged behind [the] intellectual curve' with respect to empirical evidence, but that 'one aim of Critical Trusts and Estates is to further this empirical direction.'[97]

Allison Tait's work continues these themes in the context of high-net-wealth individuals. In 'The Law of High-Wealth Exceptionalism' she demonstrates how high-wealth families escape traditional law and regulation:

> Capitalizing on ... the law of high-wealth exceptionalism, certain families are ... able to build walls around their fortunes and construct bespoke governance systems.[98]

Her later article 'Inheriting Privilege' demonstrates how 'the family trust ... is a mode of transfer that facilitates wealth preservation as well as wealth inequality.'[99] Drawing on the work of Bourdieu, Tait argues that the trust is a means of conveying not only economic capital across generations, but a family's cultural and social capital.[100] Tait's work is a clear example of how US critical trusts scholarship has escaped the 'intellectual ghetto' of the law school, and exemplifies the important work that critical and social theory can contribute to a critique of trust law and practice.

Reading Roger Cotterrell: an Overview of This Collection

As the chapters in this collection are oriented around the work of Roger Cotterrell, there is an inevitable continuity with Cotterrell's themes, methods and conceptual framing. As such the 'critical trusts law' represented in this collection is only one possible trajectory for critical trusts scholarship.

---

97. Spivack, 'Introduction,' 164.
98. Allison Anna Tait, 'The Law of High-Wealth Exceptionalism,' *Alabama Law Review* 71 (2020), 983. Similarly Jens Beckert has written about how trusts are a means of producing 'durable wealth': Jens Beckert, 'Durable Wealth: Institutions, Mechanisms, and Practices of Wealth Perpetuation,' *Annual Review of Sociology* 48 (2022).
99. Allison Anna Tait, 'Inheriting Privilege,' *Minnesota Law Review* 106 (2022), 1950.
100. Tait, 'Inheriting Privilege,' 1951.

In the first chapter, 'The Power of the Settlor,' Jonathan Garton continues the approach of Cotterrell by starting with a trust law orthodoxy: that the settlor drops out of the picture *qua* settlor. Garton argues that settlor-power is pervasive in trusts, whether through informal means, such as selection of trustees or the settlors' wishes being a relevant consideration in the exercise of discretions, or formal means such as the reservation of powers or through the use of conditions. In doing so he demonstrates that the dominant discourse that the settlor drops out of the picture obscures the continuing power of settlors, much repeated in textbooks and lecture theatres.

In 'Trusts Law and the Problem of Moral Distance,' Michael Bryan also takes issue with the view that the settlor drops out of the picture, but does so through a reconsideration of Cotterrell's concern with moral distance in modern trusts. While for Cotterrell moral distance was largely a problem of size, expertise and trustee discretion, for Bryan the problem is far more pervasive. Many modern trusts—particularly commercial trusts, including pension trusts—are what Bryan describes as 'limited duty trusts': trusts set up with a corporate trustee which has very limited powers, often to be exercised as directed by third parties, where beneficiaries have very limited scope for redress because there is little or no exercise of discretion that can be challenged, the corporate trustee is barely capitalized (its only real assets are the trust assets themselves), and it is difficult to bring an action against the directors—not to mention the prevalence of exclusion and exculpation clauses. For Bryan, these developments stem from an uncritical acceptable of the contractualisation of trusts law, and the only viable response can't lie with doctrine—these developments have, after all, all been sanctioned by the courts—but rather with regulation as a means of narrowing the moral distance between trustee corporations and beneficiaries.

In her chapter, 'The Reproduction of Property through the Production of Personhood: The Family Trust and the Power of Things,' Johanna Jacques takes up the question of power from the perspective not of persons—settlors, trustees, beneficiaries—but things. Jacques argues that trust property is clothed with a power that legitimizes the withholding of that very property and knowledge of the property from beneficiaries. The concern is that having access to this property or information will negatively impact the self-development of the beneficiary. As with Garton, Jacques notes the ability of trusts to govern the behaviour of beneficiaries; but unlike Garton, the focus isn't on settlor-power as such, but rather the interests of property itself—that is, the interest of property in maintaining itself across generations, of self-perpetuation.

The context of Jacques' intervention is crucial: debates over access to trust information and the visibility/invisibility of trusts, which are increasingly traversed through the discourse of privacy.

While the beneficiary in Jacques' chapter might appear powerless, whether because they do not have access to trust property and information or precisely because they do, Carla Spivack in her chapter—'The Myth of the Powerless Beneficiary and Twenty-First Century Trusts'—critiques the ideology of the helpless beneficiary (especially when coupled with the ideology of testamentary freedom) in light of developments in asset protection trusts and dynasty trusts in the US. Spivack demonstrates how these trusts negatively impact third parties, including crime and tort victims and shift fiscal burdens from the wealthy onto the poor. Far from being 'natural' doctrinal developments, Spivack argues that they were brought about by state legislatures from lobbying from those with special interests who will benefit from such trusts, and argues that courts must respond to the democratic shortcomings in such legislation.

Adam Gearey's chapter, '"The More He Argued, The More Technical He Became": Trusts and Surplus Value,' takes up the question of how economic power informs legal doctrine in the context of leading cases in 'orthodox' trusts jurisprudence concerning formalities. On the face of it Gearey provides a contextual account of those cases and the intersection of trust law and tax law. However, his interest is more subtle: the intersection of production, surplus value and financial capital with the tax function of the state—what he calls the knotting together of economic and political power. For Gearey, what is of note is how trust law, through formalities, makes surplus value visible, and in doing so turns it into a commodity to be preserved, enhanced, traded, inherited and indeed taxed.

Mark Bennett and Adam Hofri-Winogradow reconsider the trust's obfuscation function. In 'Subversion as an Agenda for Critical Trusts Law Scholarship,' they argue that far from the trust hiding the property-power of the rich and powerful, it actually simultaneously allows property owners to subvert the law—in particular by avoiding the liabilities that usually attach to property—while publicly enjoying the benefits that come with wealth. Importantly they note that this subversive function of trusts is one that judges and scholars have long criticised, and is all-too-well-known in popular discourse, to the point that they consider that there was already a rich seam in 'critical' trusts scholarship work both before and following Cotterrell which they describe as the 'subversion agenda,' which should continue to be developed. But to fully understand the (subversive) use of trusts in practice, they note that further empirical work is necessary which might prove difficult in the absence of a publicly available register of trusts.

Andres Knobel's chapter, 'Tax Justice and the Abuse of Trusts,' picks up the call for registration. Many of the preceding themes—privacy, (in)visibility, the abuse of trusts and tax—coalesce in Knobel's chapter. Knobel, a researcher at the Tax Justice Network, provides examples of how trusts have been abused—from tax evasion to corruption and money laundering—and argues that trusts should be subject to the same beneficial ownership registration and disclosure requirements as companies.[101] With regard to the abuse of asset protection trusts, Knobel argues for the extension of the rights of creditors to access trust funds. Neither reform would significantly affect the legitimate use of trusts, but would go a long way to preventing the negative effects of the abuse trusts.

In 'Trusts Law and Structural Power' TT Arvind and Ruth Stirton use the pension trust as a case study for examining equity's relationship with power. While much scholarship concerning power focuses on instrumental or relational power, their focus is on structural power, which embeds within institutions certain ways of acting and thinking and which as a consequence shapes (and forecloses) actions, beliefs, and agendas. While they depart from Cotterrell's conception of power, they continue his method of starting with doctrine: for Arvind and Stirton, doctrine is a vehicle for structural power. They argue that although equity has the potential for limiting the influence of structural power, at present it reinforces existing power relations. This is exemplified in numerous equity cases where the demands of certainty, the market, commerce, and the primacy of contract are privileged—and no better illustrated than by the failure in trusts law to adequately hold pension fund managers to account. Like Bryan, they consider that trusts law has given too much deference to contractualisation; but while Bryan considers that regulation of trusts might resolve some of the problem (in the context of trusts on the financial markets), for Arvind and Stirton trusts law has also given too much deference to (state) regulation which,

---

101. The arguments for transparency have been met with particular vigour from trust industry, which has countered with arguments based on 'democratic ideals' and the human rights of their clients and clients' families which revolve around privacy. As this collection was going to press, the Tax Justice Network published a report countering those argument: Andres Knobel, 'Privacy-Washing and Beneficial Ownership Transparency,' *Tax Justice Network*, 26 March 2024, accessed 17 April 2024, https://taxjustice.net/reports/privacy-washing-beneficial-ownership-transparency.

as a consequence of structural power, privileges commercial motivations and systemic interests over powerless pension beneficiaries.

Henry Jones's chapter, 'Charity and Ideology,' takes up the question of ideology in the context of charitable trusts and the problems that a critique of charity entails. The chapter begins with an elaboration of 'ideology,' explaining that ideology is concerned with the relationship between ideas and the material conditions of society but beyond that care must be taken: ideology is not necessarily about false beliefs, nor is it necessarily about dominant political power; and ideology can be productive or repressive, but not necessarily in a fixed or predictable way. However, a key role of ideology is securing consent to existing structures—and this is Jones' main argument: charity is ideological insofar as it contributes to the maintenance of existing economic and political systems. Jones demonstrates this through an history of charity, in particular through the construction of the categories of the deserving and undeserving poor (which he relates to economic developments such as the agricultural and industrial revolutions) and the 'orthodox' charitable purposes—prevention and relief of poverty, advancement of education, and advancement of religion. A thread running through Jones' chapter is the relationship of charity and ideology with the state and state-power, and that what is 'hidden' by charity are finance, capital, and privilege such that what is rendered invisible is the politics of charity or, put another way, the possibility of systematic change.

Lisa Sarmas explores a different aspect of law's power: how trust law enacts or performs gender. In 'The Gendered Trust' Sarmas draws on Cotterrell's idea that the trust performs a 'distancing effect' to explore whether trust law's doctrines and conceptual debates exhibit 'male' or 'female' characteristics as manifested in ideas of 'distance' and 'intimacy.' The argument is not that trust law performs one or the other, but rather that the gender binary informs the form of trusts law, which has both distancing effects (for example, fixed-interest trusts concerned with hard-nosed property rights, trustees' duties concerned with financial maximisation of the fund at the expense of social investing, and institutional constructive trusts in England and Wales) and intimacy effects (for example, flexible family discretionary trusts governed by trustees with intimate knowledge of the family circumstances, the trust as a 'personal obligation,' and malleable remedial constructive trusts in Australia). Sarmas' conclusion is that it is the ability to 'flip' between these conceptions that gives the trust its flexibility; although the possibility of a non-binary, queer or transgressive trust is considered, Sarmas concludes that the trust is basically straight and 'metrosexual'—slippery, elusive, doing little to challenge received orthodoxy and well-fitted to neoliberal capitalism.

In 'The Bank of England's Directors as Trustees in Walter Bagehot's *Lombard Street*,' Iain Frame examines Bagehot's argument that the Bank of England's holds its reserves on trust for the benefit of the public. Frame suggests that Bagehot's argument can be understood as a solution to the problem of collective action that occurs when there is a run on the banks—the Bank of England, as trustee, could be understood as a collective agent.[102] This argument has a certain resonance with the idea of charity, and Cotterrell's argument that the public might be construed as a sort of collective owner under charitable trusts.[103] In this regard the trust might be understood as a means of giving effect to communal norms. However, as Frame makes clear, Bagehot's argument isn't that the public are conceived as the beneficiaries but rather the country's banks. Drawing on Cotterrell, Frame argues that the trust is another means of obscuring the property-power of banks; rather than conceiving them as holders of property-power, Bagehot presents them as vulnerable and in need of protection. While the chapter is historically oriented, it is important in demonstrating the limits and possibilities of the (rhetoric of) trust.

Towards a New Agenda for Critical Trusts Law

Some of the chapters in this collection explicitly make the case for an agenda in critical trusts law. For example, Arvind and Stirton call for an agenda around structural power, and equity as a possibility for ameliorating such power; Sarmas makes the case for analysing the material effects of trusts laws' enactments of gender; Bennett and Hofri-Winogradow argue that trusts laws' subversions of other laws need critique; Knobel and Gearey in their chapters make arguments about tax and transparency of trusts. In concluding this introduction I want to draw out draw out particular lines of research that critical trusts law might pursuc.

One line of research, already underway, pursues questions of inequality. Economic inequality is a significant issue, and in the contexts of trusts often thought to be resolved by a suitable tax regime. However,

---

102. Incidentally this is exactly how trusts are conceived when used as part of a bond issue (sometimes called indenture trustees), which Bryan in his chapter criticises as 'limited duty trusts.'

103. Also see Jones in this collection.

as Tait and Chang have demonstrated, trust law itself might perpetuate economic inequalities.[104] Similarly, questions of gender, race and sexuality have already been posed and must continue to be pursued.[105] The inequalities produced and perpetuated by trusts law have been intensified by what Knobel in his chapter calls the 'abuse of trusts,' that is, the use of 'innovative' trust structures to protect one's assets.[106] These are attempts to use the law to escape the law, a use that is sanctioned by law. Knobel's response is to bring trusts and corporations closer together, that is, to regulate trusts in a similar manner to corporations, perhaps making the very validity of the trust dependant on certain bureaucratic requirements (such as registration or reporting). This would be a sharp departure in the common law tradition from the trust's supposed separation from the state and conceptual distinction from corporation. It would certainly meet strong resistance from 'industry.' In this regard the involvement of trust industry in the promulgation of trust laws goes some way to answering one of Cotterrell's questions about law: 'why does this doctrine exist?' Spivack's chapter demonstrates that questions of inequality relate not only to the differential impact of the laws, but also the political processes themselves, ie how those laws are made. This is an area not only for critique, but also a possible site for practices of resistance whether through contributions to public discourse (challenging the 'commonsense' of hegemonic trust discourse) or through consultation responses to proposals for law reform.[107]

Another aspect of trusts that needs further consideration is the relationship between trusts and tax, both domestically and transnationally. The tax implications of trusts influences whether or not a trust might be used as well as the terms of such trusts, and has also influenced the development of trusts law itself, as Moffat and Chesterman noted in 1988:

---

104. See Tait, 'The Law of High-Wealth Exceptionalism' and Felix B. Chang, 'Asymmetries in the Generation and Transmission of Wealth,' *Ohio State Law Journal* 79 (2018).

105. See for example 'Wills, Trusts, and Estates Meets Gender, Race, and Class,' *Wisconsin Law Review* (2019).

106. These structures are also investigated by Spivack and Bennett and Hofri-Winogradow in their chapters.

107. For example, following Brexit the Law Commission for England and Wales' *Thirteenth Programme of Law Reform* included a scoping study for a project entitled 'Modernising Trust Law for a Global Britain' which would consider introducing more flexible trust and trust-like structures to enhance jurisdictional competitiveness: see Law Commission, *Thirteenth Programme of Law Reform* (Law Com No 377, 2017), paras 2.23 to 2.26. As of 19 March 2024 the project had not started: https://lawcom.gov.uk/project/modernising-trust-law-for-a-global-britain.

Even by the beginning of the twentieth century the incidence of taxation was influencing the development of the private express trust. It may be claimed that this influence has so increased that fiscal considerations now dominate the practice of trusts even if not directly the formal rules of trusts law. Whether trusts should be created, what types of trust should be adopted and where their administration should be located are all, in reality, decisions taken by property-owners only after carefully considering the discal implications.[108]

Likewise, developments in trusts law have influenced developments in tax law. Moffat and Chesterman, in commenting on Cotterrell's 1987 article, questioned the extent to which trust law could adapt to the challenges of the tax state, but also noted that

> it will be necessary to consider whether the framers of tax laws have, in fact, been constrained by a perceived need to treat the established doctrines of trusts law as more or less sacrosanct, and therefore to tailor tax laws to fit them. If this has been so, it would indeed represent a considerable tribute to the entrenched status of trusts doctrine and the ideological power of the legal concept of 'trust.'[109]

It seems though, at least insofar as Treasury and HMRC are concerned, far from the trust continuing to have ideological power that the opposite has happened. Numerous fiscal policies aim at discouraging certain trusts by taxing them at higher rates (in particular discretionary trusts) while accepting that other trusts may have benefits and aiming for a 'neutral' tax scheme (for example, disabled persons' trusts, immediate post-death interest trusts, bereaved minor trusts and 18-25 trusts). Since the Finance Act 2006 it appears that most trusts are now 'distrusted' by Treasury and HMRC and are treated with fiscal hostility. The tax framework as it applies to trusts can be understood as a regulatory tool. Whether or not trusts—or, rather, particular forms of trust—are to be 'encouraged' or 'discouraged' is at heart a political question, although perceived through the lens of hegemonic trust discourse is an assault not only on trust industry (which allegedly brings financial benefits to the community) but on settlor-autonomy in how they choose to structure their property entitlements and distributions.

Challenging hegemonic trusts discourse goes hand-in-hand with challenging discourses around tax. Critical trusts law implies critical tax law; one must understand the tax context of trusts and the trusts

---

108. Moffat and Chesterman, *Trusts Law*, 50. See also Gearey in this collection.
109. Moffat and Chesterman, *Trusts Law*, 49.

context of tax, along with the range of political and economic questions such interrelationships entail. And to get a proper handle on these questions would benefit from critical theory and theoretical inquiry. It is a shame in this regard that taxation of trusts continues to 'fall into a no-man's land between the separate domains of taxation and trusts.'[110] Indeed, the 7th edition of *Moffat's Trusts Law* has removed the chapters on tax.[111] This follows the removal of pension trusts in the 6th edition entailing both a reduction in the contextual content and a view that there is a core of trusts law with 'fragmented' trusts laws at the periphery being confined to specialist texts. This is not to blame the authors: the challenges in UK Higher Education and changes in legal qualifying requirements mean that 'Equity & Trusts' modules are smaller and 'thinner' than in prior years, such that the breadth and depth of learning has significantly narrowed.[112] But some understanding of the interaction of trusts and tax is essential to the critical trusts law project. What is required of critical trusts law is a better understanding of the interaction of trusts and tax laws—not only within a jurisdiction, but across jurisdictions—as well as trust laws' interaction with laws relating to the enforcement of judgments and insolvency.

In this respect, the authors of *Moffat's Trusts Law* have included a new chapter on the international dimension of trusts: an area that is also ripe for further critical research. This chapter will no doubt grow and develop, but at present it focuses on trusts and trust-like developments in individual jurisdictions, with a brief discussion of conflict of laws and the Hague Convention on the Law Applicable to Trusts and on their Recognition. Trusts in a global context—that the settlor(s), trustee(s), beneficiaries, and trust assets might be spread across multiple jurisdictions—needs further and more careful consideration, particularly the complex interactions of multiple laws across multiple jurisdictions. Such research would bring together private and

---

110. Moffat and Chesterman, *Trusts Law*, 50
111. Jonathan Garton, Rebecca Probert, and Gerry Bean, *Moffat's Trusts Law: Text and Materials*, 7th ed. (Cambridge: Cambridge University Press, 2020), xix-xx.
112. 'Equity & Trusts' modules were often 30 credit (ie full academic year) at level 6, but nowadays more often than not are 15 or 20 credit modules, often part of a property law module that focuses on land, and often at level 5. Obtaining a sufficient grasp of the basics of trusts is the focus, with the different contexts of trusts siphoned-off into optional modules of advanced trusts law or trusts in commercial transactions. In this context, introducing the difficulties of tax—let alone taxation of trusts—is simply not possible. This downplaying of the contexts of trusts is heightened by changes in the regulatory context, e.g. the Solicitors Qualifying Exam tests 'fundamental' knowledge rather than contextual or critical knowledge.

international lawyers, considering the questions from both micro- and macro- levels, as well as critical political economists.

The global nature of trusts also points towards a further underexplored area: that many jurisdictions are former colonies of the UK. In *Capital without Borders* Harrington discusses some of the difficulties concerning the interrelationship of wealth management and offshore jurisdictions.[113] These jurisdictions are now 'innovators' in trust law.[114] They do this with the desire of independence, becoming self-sufficient, but instead of being in the grasp of coloniser they're in the grasp of capital.[115] Often these offshore jurisdictions are highly repressive, particularly of local people: the same rights don't apply to all, especially if locals 'interfere with the preferences of transnational capital and its representatives.'[116] While there is some work on the role of the UK on the global and offshore context of trusts, such as the TJN's Financial Secrecy Index,[117] Nicholas Shaxson's *Treasure Islands: Tax Havens and the Men Who Stole the World*[118] and Kojo Koram's *Uncommon Wealth: Britain and the Aftermath of Empire*,[119] much work is needed on the imperial, colonial and postcolonial context of trusts.[120]

A further area for research is what might be called counter-hegemonic discourse. In recent years the power of the settlor has been elevated to what might be described as an 'hegemonic discourse.'[121] This discourse focuses on settlor-autonomy and upholding settlor intention and sees much of trust law as merely default that can be opted-out of—what is often called the contractualisation of trusts law. The difficulty that faces critical trusts scholarship though isn't identifying the hegemonic discourse, but rather providing sufficiently weighty theoretical

---

113. Harrington, *Capital without Borders*, 254.
114. Harrington, *Capital without Borders*, 254.
115. Harrington, *Capital without Borders*, 256.
116. Harrington, *Capital without Borders*, 261.
117. Accessed 24 March 2024, https://fsi.taxjustice.net.
118. Nicholas Shaxson, *Treasure Islands: Tax Havens and the Men who Stole the World* (London: Vintage Books, 2012). Also see the documentary film 'The Spider's Web: Britain's Second Empire' (dir. Michael Oswald, 2017), accessed 22 March 2024, https://spiderswebfilm.com.
119. Kojo Koram, *Uncommon Wealth: Britain and the Aftermath of Empire* (London: John Murray Publishers, 2023).
120. It isn't hard to think of aspects of imperial and colonial aspects of trusts law: Crusades and the *wacq*; the South Sea Bubble; offshoring, tax havens and capitalism (commonly exemplified through the Vestey family case law); and the influence of the Judicial Committee of the Privy Council.
121. See Garton and Bryan in this collection, and on hegemonic trust discourse see above.

and political responses to the argument supporting settlors' property-power. The hegemonic discourse needs an ideological, political, and legal response. Lionel Smith's work goes some of the way to providing a legal response, although for the reasons explained above, this approach might fall short on the basis that it entrenches the view that 'true trust' was—and is—unproblematic when, as Cotterrell has shown, this was far from the case.[122] The work of scholars like Piketty and activists like TJN are contributing towards a political response. Whether this is a sufficient ideological response is debatable; revolutionizing the 'commonsense' of the community is a more difficult task.

In order to adequately counter hegemonic trust discourse a return to critical and social theory is necessary. While many chapters in this collection are grounded in theory, most wear that theory lightly, and the 'critical theory' discussed in this introduction has focused on the contextual and sociological approaches adopted by Cotterrell and subsequent critical work undertaken in the context of trusts scholarship. But if one looks in the journals, conference proceedings, handbooks and edited collections on social theory, critical theory and critical legal theory there is a vast array of theoretical trajectories and critical theories yet to be explored in the context of trusts.[123] As Roger Cotterrell noted in his 1987 article, 'if we seek to develop rigorously critical legal scholarship as a political and moral critique, as well as a sociological critique founded in and contributing to social theory, we have no choice but to swim in [deep theoretical waters].'[124]

Conclusion

Cotterrell's contributions to the development of critical trusts scholarship cannot be overstated. He paved the way for much critical thinking about trusts, providing an orientation towards questions of power and inequality. His sociologically-oriented critique remains essential; indeed,

---

122. See above. It may be that we are seeing a judicial response in cases such as the Privy Council's decision in *Grand View Private Trust Company v Wong* [2022] UKPC 47.

123. For example, Reza Banakar and Max Travers, eds., *An Introduction to Law and Social Theory* (Oxford: Hart Publishing, 2002); Vanessa E. Munro and Margaret Davies, eds., *The Ashgate Research Companion to Feminist Legal Theory* (Routledge, 2013); Emilios Christodoulidis, Ruth Dukes and Marco Goldoni, eds., *Research Handbook on Critical Legal Theory* (Edward Elgar Publishing, 2019). On *equity* and the resources of critique, see the two special issues of *Pólemos: Journal of Law, Literature and Culture* 10 (2016) and 11 (2017).

124. Cotterrell, 'Power, Property and the Law of Trusts,' 81.

a return to critical theory—whether Critical Theory (in the Frankfurt School sense) or the many critical theories that have developed since—ought to be high on the agenda for critical trusts scholarship. The project of critical trusts law must be truly interdisciplinary, drawing not only on critical theory but also political economy and the humanities (for example around questions of meaning and ritual), without forgetting our own expertise (as lawyers) in the intricacies of legal doctrine, and must also be collaborative, because the power of the hegemonic trusts discourses and practices cannot be grasped—let alone 'critiqued'—by scholars working in isolation. There are many alternative critical accounts of trusts to be written, using different theoretical frameworks—and I hope the collection inspires them.

2

The Power of the Settlor

*Jonathan Garton**

Introduction

In his seminal article on the nature of power and property in the law of trusts, Roger Cotterrell identified how the trust mechanism can facilitate and obscure what he termed 'property-power.'[1] His particular concern was with the orthodox narrative of the trustee as the controller of trust assets, managing them on behalf of passive beneficiaries who are not permitted to interfere in their administration, and how this obscures the fact that the true power lies with the beneficiaries, who not only enjoy the real value of the assets but can also use the 'fluidity' of beneficial entitlements to stay hidden from sight.[2] However, both the orthodoxy and Cotterrell's resituated narrative overlook the fact that in many cases substantial power lies with a third actor. While it may be trite to observe that any power enjoyed either by the beneficiaries or the trustees is only ever at the behest of the person who originally settled the trust property, the settlor may, when creating a trust, reserve for herself significant administrative and dispositive powers without undermining the core concept of the trust. In the case of a private family trust, she may use the inherent flexibility of the trust and the variety of interests that can be created under it in such a way as to exert significant control over the lives of her beneficiaries. In the case of a charitable trust, she may shape the landscape of social welfare provision far beyond those directly affected by her bounty. And while Cotterrell is correct to recognise that one of the key manifestations

* University of Warwick, UK.
1. Roger Cotterrell, 'Power, Property and the Law of Trusts: A Partial Agenda for Critical Legal Scholarship,' *Journal of Law and Society* 14 (1987).
2. Cotterrell, 'Power, Property and the Law of Trusts,' 86.

of beneficiary power is the principle in *Saunders v Vautier*,[3] under which the beneficiaries have the right collectively to override the wishes of the settlor by collapsing the trust and distributing the assets as they see fit, there are numerous ways in which the settlor may limit their ability to exercise this right. By way of a corrective, this chapter draws out some of the ways in which a settlor may retain power over the trust in spite of the oft-repeated assertion that, once the trust is constituted, the power shifts to the new legal and equitable owners, and she drops out of the picture.

Informal Influence of the Settlor

The traditional narrative tells us that, once a trust is up and running, the settlor 'drops out of the picture' unless she has also cast herself as trustee or beneficiary.[4] The principal manifestation of this is that it is the beneficiaries, and not the settlor, who have standing to hold the trustees to the terms of the trust. It also forms the basis for the rule against non-charitable purpose trusts: in *Re Astor's Settlement Trusts*,[5] a trust purportedly established for a range of non-charitable purposes was held to be void in the absence of beneficiaries as no other person, including the settlor, could initiate proceedings against a defaulting trustee.[6] Even the settlor of a charitable trust, which lacks beneficiaries in the strict sense, does not have inherent standing, enforcement being instead a matter either for the Attorney-General, under the *parens patriae* doctrine, or, since 1960, the Charity Commission.[7] (And while successive Charities Acts have also granted 'any person interested in the charity' the power to enforce the terms of a charitable trust, even this is not something afforded to the settlor as a matter of course: in *Bradshaw v University College of Wales (Aberystwyth)* Hoffman J was not convinced that the founder of a charity was sufficiently 'interested' in its administration, observing that 'there is no authority for the retention

---

3. (1841) 4 Beav 115.
4. This phrase is commonly repeated in this context: see e.g. David Hayton, 'Developing the Obligation Characteristic of the Trust,' *Law Quarterly Review* 117 (2001), 96; Jonathan Hilliard, 'The Flexibility of Fiduciary Doctrine in Trust Law: How Far Does it Stretch in Practice?' *Trust Law International* 23 (2009), 121; James Penner, *The Law of Trusts* (Oxford: Oxford University Press, 2022), 19; Gary Watt, *Trusts and Equity* (Oxford: Oxford University Press, 2023), 23.
5. [1952] Ch 534 (Ch).
6. [1952] Ch 534 (Ch) 542 (Roxburgh J).
7. Today by virtue of the Charities Act 2011, s 114.

of any such interest in the charity by the founder in English law'.)[8] The narrative is simple: in placing assets on trust, the settlor has divested herself of any proprietary interest that she once had in the assets just as much as if she had made an outright gift of them. This is of course the reason behind the principle in *Saunders v Vautier*,[9] which Cotterrell rightly identifies as the basis for the beneficiaries' power: the settlor has made a gift of the asset to someone else, albeit structured rather than outright, and in doing so the principle of freedom of alienation, at least in its English form,[10] demands that the new owners of the equity in the asset are entitled to use it as they see fit, regardless of the wishes of the former owner. When the settlor drops out of the picture, she thus loses any right to influence or enforce the behaviour of the trustees or the beneficiaries in relation to the trust.

But this is not necessarily the case. In a subsequent article, 'Trusting in Law: Legal and Moral Concepts of Trust,'[11] Cotterrell revisits the power dynamics of the trust and considers briefly the extent to which the settlor may continue to exercise power once the trust is up and running. With regard to the administration of the trust, he suggests that the settlor's formal power is limited to the law's requirement that the trustee must respect the terms of the trust during its existence, tempered by the fact that it is the beneficiaries, and not the settlor, who enforce these terms, and by the various ways in which an established trust may legitimately be varied, interpreted or terminated.[12] As such, he continues the narrative of the settlor formally dropping out of the picture. However, he does suggest that she can retain some informal power through her choice of trustee, i.e. by selecting someone, such as a family member or trusted colleague, over whom she might hold influence.[13] In fact, the settlor's power to influence trustees is not as informal

---

8. [1988] 1 WLR 190 (Ch), 194.

9. (1841) 4 Beav 115.

10. Consider further the *Claflin* doctrine, adopted in many US states, which prioritises the freedom of alienation of the earlier property-owner over that of her successor, and prevents beneficiaries collapsing the trust if this would defeat a material purpose of the settlor: *Claflin v Claflin* 149 Mass 19 (1889). See Gregory Alexander, 'The Dead Hand and the Law of Trusts in the Nineteenth Century,' *Stanford Law Review* 37 (1985); Roger Cotterrell, 'Some Sociological Aspects of the Controversy Around the Legal Validity of Private Purpose Trusts,' in *Equity and Contemporary Legal Developments*, ed. Stephen Goldstein (Jerusalem: Sacher Institute, 1992); Paul Matthews, 'The Comparative Importance of the Rule in *Saunders v Vautier*,' *Law Quarterly Review* 122 (2006).

11. Roger Cotterrell, 'Trusting in Law: Legal and Moral Concepts of Trust,' *Current Legal Problems* 46 (1993).

12. Cotterrell, 'Trusting in Law,' 82.

13. Cotterrell, 'Trusting in Law,' 82.

as Cotterrell suggests. It has long been recognised that it is perfectly proper for the settlor to provide the trustees with a non-binding letter of wishes, extrinsic to the trust instrument but nonetheless to be taken into account when exercising their discretion. If such a letter is provided, then not only is it perfectly proper for the trustees to take them into account, in spite of their fiduciary duty of loyalty to the beneficiaries, it may actually be necessary: in *Pitt v Holt; Futter v Futter*,[14] in the course of considering the operation of the so-called rule in *Hastings-Bass*,[15] under which the act of a trustee is voidable if made without sufficient deliberation, Lord Walker held that 'the settlor's wishes are always a material consideration in the exercise of a fiduciary's discretions,'[16] citing with approval an earlier judgment to that effect by Lightman J in *Abacus Trust Co v Barr*.[17] It is true that, at least in theory, the trustees must still reach their own decisions when exercising any discretion under the trust, for the settlor's wishes, while a relevant consideration, are not binding upon them. However, Wilson LJ considered in *Charman v Charman* that a trustee 'will usually be acting entirely properly if, after careful consideration of all relevant circumstances, he resolves in good faith to accede to a request by the settlor,'[18] in the context of determining whether assets held on discretionary trust were a 'financial resource' to which the settlor, who was a member of the class of objects, had access for the purposes of his divorce settlement.[19] Moreover, the twenty-first century rise of what Lionel Smith has labelled 'massively discretionary trusts,'[20] whose trust instruments are drafted so as to give the trustees extremely broad dispositive discretions but little to no guidance as to how these are to be exercised, means that there will be cases where a letter of wishes becomes determinative simply because the trustees have 'nothing else to go on' when deciphering the purpose of a settlement.[21] If trust instruments and their associated letters of wishes were always created contemporaneously then, while the letters might be of interest in terms of their effect upon the balance of property-power between trustees and beneficiaries, as their disclosure to the latter

14. [2013] 2 AC 26 (SC).
15. *Re Hastings-Bass (deceased)* [1975] Ch 25 (Ch).
16. [2013] 2 AC 26 (SC) [66].
17. [2003] Ch 409 (Ch).
18. [2006] 1 WLR 1053 (CA) [12].
19. Matrimonial Causes Act 1973, s 25(2)(a).
20. Lionel Smith, 'Massively Discretionary Trusts,' *Current Legal Problems* 70 (2017). See also Hanoch Dagan and Irit Samet, 'What's Wrong with Massively Discretionary Trusts,' *Law Quarterly Review* 138 (2022).
21. Smith, 'Massively Discretionary Trusts,' 45.

is not generally required,[22] they would not necessarily undermine the narrative of the settlor dropping out of the picture once the trust is constituted. However, there may be no such requirement. The assumption of practitioners appears to be, absent any authority to the contrary,[23] that non-binding letters of wishes may be revoked and replaced by the settlor at any time during her lifetime.[24] Whereas the orthodox narrative can accommodate the trustees taking account of the settlor's non-binding wishes at the time of the trust's creation, it seems that the reality is that they may be required to take account of her subsequent wishes 'as they evolve from time to time.'[25]

Formal Influence and the Reservation of Power

Even if the trustees are, following Pitt v Holt, under a positive duty to take the wishes of the settlor into account when exercising their discretion, her continuing power would be rather anaemic if it were limited to this given that the trustees must still reach their own independent decisions in the best interests of the beneficiaries (granted that there may be some cases where there are no relevant considerations other than the settlor's wishes to take into account when making those decisions). But the settlor does not have to make herself either a trustee or beneficiary in order to retain more formal power over the trust assets: she may explicitly reserve certain powers for herself in the trust instrument. Article 2 of the Hague Trusts Convention, incorporated into English law by the Recognition of Trusts Act 1987, specifically recognizes that 'the reservation by the settlor of certain rights and powers ... [is] not necessarily inconsistent with the existence of a trust,' and the modern reality is that many settlors—particularly, it has been suggested, entrepreneurs and those from civil law jurisdictions who are uncomfortable entrusting the management of family assets to others[26]—are only willing to set up a trust if they can retain significant control over the assets. The settlor dropping out of the picture is merely the default position, not an immutable rule. If she attempts to reserve for herself such

---

22. See *Breakspear v Ackland* [2009] Ch 32, although disclosure was, in fact, ordered in that case.
23. In *Breakspear v Ackland* [2009] Ch 32 [5] Briggs J specifically left open whether subsequent letters of wishes have 'the same status' as contemporary letters.
24. See e.g. James Kessler, *Drafting Trusts and Will Trusts* (London: Thompson, 2014) [7.16]; Smith, 'Massively Discretionary Trusts,' 46.
25. Smith, 'Massively Discretionary Trusts,' 46.
26. See Christopher McKenzie, 'Having and Eating the Cake: A Global Survey of Settlor Reserved Power Trusts: Part I,' Private Client Business 5 (2007), 338.

wide powers that she effectively retains beneficial ownership of the property, then of course the only trust created will be a bare trust for her (assuming that legal title was vested in the trustee; in the case of a self-declaration then the settlor will simply remain the absolute beneficial owner). But the powers that the settlor may reserve without undermining the existence of a trust are wide-ranging, and certainly give the lie to Cotterrell's suggestion that the real power lies with the beneficiaries. It is useful here to recall the 'irreducible core' of the trust as articulated by Millett LJ in *Armitage v Nurse*:

> There is an irreducible core of obligations owed by the trustees to the beneficiaries and enforceable by them which is fundamental to the concept of a trust. If the beneficiaries have no rights enforceable against the trustees there are no trusts. ... The duty of the trustees to perform the trusts honestly and in good faith for the benefit of the beneficiaries is the minimum necessary to give substance to the trusts, but in my opinion it is sufficient.[27]

So long as this irreducible core is left intact, the settlor is free in English law to reserve very significant powers for herself.[28] Four are considered here: (a) the power to appoint or remove trustees; (b) the power to control the investment of the trust assets; (c) the power to revoke the trust; and (d) the power to appoint the trust assets.

Regarding the first, the settlor's informal influence over the trustees may be reinforced if she reserves for herself the power to remove them from office and replace them with new trustees, or to appoint additional trustees.[29] The former is rarely seen in practice, while the latter is relatively common, but it is uncontroversial that both are permissible.[30] However, there are two significant fetters. First, while the threat of removal, or of the augmentation of their number, may encourage trustees to follow the settlor's wishes, they must still act solely in the best interests of the beneficiaries when exercising their discretion, and failure to do so will open them to legal challenge by the beneficiaries (and could in itself, ironically, justify their removal).

---

27. [1998] Ch 241 (CA) 253.
28. Note that many offshore jurisdictions, beyond the scope of this brief chapter, have legislation specifically designed to ensure that the validity of a trust is not compromised by the reservation of settlor powers: see generally Donovan Waters, 'Trusts: Settlor Reserved Powers,' *Estates, Trusts and Pensions Journal* 25 (2006).
29. Either by express power or by nominating herself as the holder of the default statutory power to nominate additional trustees under s 36 of the Trustee Act 1925.
30. See Jonathan Garton, *Moffat's Trusts Law*, 6th ed. (Cambridge: Cambridge University Press, 2015), 521.

Any new trustees appointed by the settlor would, in any case, be held to the same standard. Second, unlike many of the other powers that a settlor may reserve for herself, the power to appoint and remove trustees is almost certainly always fiduciary in nature, even if the settlor does not otherwise hold any fiduciary office. The reason for this was laid down by Kay J in *Re Skeats' Settlement*:

> Could the person who has the power of appointment put the office of trustee up for sale, and sell it to the highest bidder? It is clear that would be entirely improper. Could he take any remuneration for making the appointment? In my opinion, certainly not. Why not? The answer is that he cannot exercise the power for his own benefit. Why not again? The answer is inevitable. Because it is a power which involves a duty of fiduciary nature; and I therefore come to the conclusion, independently of any authority, that the power is a fiduciary power.[31]

Accordingly, the settlor must exercise the power in good faith, and solely in the best interests of the beneficiaries, lest it be set aside as a fraud on the power. It also means that, save in exceptional circumstances,[32] she cannot use the power to insert herself as trustee if she is unhappy with the administration of the trust.[33] This does not prevent her from continuing to exercise power over the trust assets, but ought at least to ensure that her power is not exercised for illegitimate reasons.

If the settlor wishes to play an active role in the management of the trust fund then she may reserve for herself the power to make investments and other asset management decisions on behalf of the trust. Although by default trustees have extensive investment powers under Part II of the Trustee Act 2000, it is uncontroversial that these may be cut down or removed by the trust instrument. Yet attempts by the settlor to keep these powers for herself are sometimes treated as contentious. Despite not inherently compromising the beneficiaries' equitable ownership, one leading text suggests that the ability to control the investment of trust property is a power that will, if reserved by the settlor, 'give rise to a powerful argument that the trust is a sham.'[34] The reason for this unsubstantiated fear appears to be a misreading of the decision of the offshore case *Rahman v Chase Bank (CI) Trust Co.*[35] In this case

---

31. (1889) 42 Ch D 522, 526.
32. *Montefiore v Guedalla (No 3)* [1903] 2 Ch 723 (Ch) 726.
33. *Re Skeats' Settlement* (1889) 42 Ch D 522; *Re Newen* [1894] 2 Ch 297 (Ch).
34. James Wadham, *Willhoughby's Misplaced Trust*, 2nd ed. (Saffron Walden: Gostick Hall Publications, 2002), 14.
35. [1991] JLR 103.

assets were settled on such trusts as the settlor should appoint in his lifetime with the trustee's consent, and while the trust deed gave the trustees wide powers of investment it also provided that the settlor's consent was required for their exercise. In practice, however, the trustees did not make decisions that were then referred to the settlor for approval, but rather all decisions were made by the settlor; further, the defendant bank, with which trust assets were deposited, took directions directly from the settlor. The Jersey Royal Court held that the trust was both a substantive and a formal sham, as the trust instrument (a) did not reflect the reality of the arrangement but (b) even if it had, the terms of the trust deed reserved too extensive powers for the settlor.[36] But it is clear from the judgment that it was the extent of the settlor's combined powers in that case that was the real problem, along with the fact that the trust instrument did not represent reality, and not the reservation of investment powers per se. Reservation by the settlor of these alone should not ordinarily be sufficient for the trust to be declared a formal sham, even if she retains full control of investment decisions.[37] After all, there is nothing objectionable about limiting or even excluding absolutely the trustees' power of investment without undermining the trust's irreducible core; why should the position be different if, instead, the settlor restricts the power of the trustees by stipulating that investment decisions require her consent—taken as entirely acceptable by Buckley J in *Re Cooper* when amending such a restriction under the Variation of Trusts Act 1958[38]—or alternatively she reserves the power to decide directly herself. If the settlor does reserve the power of investment then, although there is a presumption that this will attract fiduciary duties, there are dicta to the effect that express words in the trust instrument could create a personal power, thereby enabling the settlor to pursue her own agenda and 'disregard' the beneficiaries' best interests if she wishes.[39]

---

36. Strictly speaking, the decision turned on the settlement's violation of the (now abandoned) Jersey law maxim *donner et retiner ne vaut*, i.e. 'to give and to retain is not possible'; however, the Royal Court confirmed in *Re Esteem Settlement* [2003] JLR 295 [67] that the application of the maxim is the same as the finding of a formal sham: 'For the maxim to apply, the settlor must retain 'the power freely to dispose' of the assets placed in trust.'

37. See John Mowbray, 'Shams, Pretences, Blackmail and Illusion: Part II,' Private Client Business 1 (2000), 110-111; David Harris, 'No Such Thing as a Sham Trust?' Private Client Business 2 (2004) 98.

38. [1962] Ch 826 (Ch).

39. *Lord Vestey's Executors v Inland Revenue Commissioners* [1949] 1 All ER 1108 (HL) 1114 (Lord Simonds). See also *Inland Revenue Commissioners v Schroder* [1983] STC 480 (Ch); *Commissioner of Stamp Duties v Way* [1952] AC 95 (PC).

The power to appoint the trust assets and the power to revoke, amend or vary the trust completely are more considerable yet, as each effectively amounts to the power to wipe out the beneficiaries' entitlements completely. The layman would be forgiven for thinking that they amount to the settlor retaining outright ownership of the asset in all but name. Yet trust law obfuscates this in its formal distinction between a property interest and a power. In the words of Fry LJ in *Re Armstrong*:

> No two ideas can well be more distinct the one from the other than those of 'property' and 'power'[.] A 'power' is an individual personal capacity of the donee of the power to do something. That it may result in property becoming vested in him is immaterial; the general nature of the power does not make it property. The power of a person to appoint an estate to himself is, in my judgement, no more his 'property' than the power to write a book or to sing a song. The exercise of any one of those three powers may result in property, but in no sense which the law recognises are they 'property.'[40]

The distinction between property and power formed the basis of the decision in *Morgan v IRC*,[41] which concerned a beneficiary who resettled his life interest plus a reversionary interest contingent on his father's death on a new trust, under which he retained his life interest but the contingent interest was held for those who would be entitled to his residuary personal estate upon his death. As part of this resettlement he reserved for himself a power of revocation with the consent of the trustees. When his father died, the Inland Revenue claimed estate duty on the basis that the contingency of the original settlement had materialized, making him the absolute owner of the assets, and that this should not be undermined by the resettlement given its revocability. A majority of the Court of Appeal held that estate duty was not leviable because the son continued to have merely a life interest, notwithstanding his power of revocation:

> The fact that the sub-settlement is revocable has the result that Peter's life interest in the income of the shares is capable of enlargement into an absolute interest in possession in the shares themselves in the future with the trustees' consent. But this enlarged beneficial interest will arise (if at all) when the sub-settlement is revoked. The possibility that some subsequent event may enlarge Peter's beneficial interest does not in my view

---

40. (1886) 17 QBD 521, 531.
41. [1962] Ch 438 (CA).

itself constitute a beneficial interest accruing or arising on the death of the deceased.[42]

More recently there have been attempts to chip away at the distinction, notably the Privy Council decisions in *TMSF v Merrill Lynch*[43] and *Webb v Webb*.[44] In the former case, where the issue was the ability of creditors to access trust assets when their debtor was the settlor of a revocable trust, the Privy Council held that as the power of revocation could not be regarded in any sense as fiduciary, and so the only discretion which the debtor had was whether to exercise the power in his own favour, the power was 'tantamount to ownership' for insolvency purposes and the creditors were able to access the assets.[45] However, the court was at pains to stress the importance of the context, confirming that there was 'no doubt' that in other situations the power to revoke a trust was distinct from ownership of the trust assets.[46] In the latter case, where, in addition to the power of revocation, the settlor of two trusts retained legal title as trustee, the Privy Council held that this represented 'a bundle of rights ... indistinguishable from ownership' and the trusts were invalid.[47] With regard to powers of appointment, rather than revocation, the courts have been somewhat readier to recognize that a settlor who holds a general—i.e. the absolute power to appoint the trust assets to anyone in the world, including herself—should be treated as the owner for all most all practical purposes.[48] Such a power is not even restricted to being exercised *inter vivos*, as assets over which a testatrix has a general power can be disposed of by will.[49] A distinction between power and property is still maintained, however: if the holder of the power dies intestate then the power will be extinguished and the assets dealt with as they would be in default of appointment.[50]

Just as Cotterrell argued that the conventional narrative of trustee control obscures the fact that real power lies with the beneficiaries, so too,

---

42. [1962] Ch 438 (CA) 455 (Diplock LJ).
43. [2012] 1 WLR 1721 (PC).
44. [2021] 1 FLR 448 (PC).
45. [2012] 1 WLR 1721 (PC) [62].
46. [2012] 1 WLR 1721 (PC) [33].
47. [2021] 1 FLR 448 (PC) [89].
48. See e.g. *Re Triffitt's Settlement* [1958] Ch 852 (Ch) 861 (Upjohn J); *Re Churston Settled Estates* [1954] Ch 334 (Ch) 344 (Roxburgh J).
49. Note that by virtue of s 27 of the Wills Act 1837, a general gift of the testator's real or personal estate, including a residuary gift, operates to execute a power of appointment in the absence of a contrary intention.
50. *Re Churston Settled Estates* [1954] Ch 334 (Ch) 344 (Roxburgh J).

then, does the conventional narrative of the settlor dropping out of the picture obscure the fact that there are several ways in which she can continue to enjoy real power over assets despite having formally relinquished ownership. Not only may her wishes legitimately be taken into account by the trustees when exercising their discretion, she may reserve for herself significant powers over the management and appointment of the trust property, including the power to revoke the settlement entirely.

Using the Trust Itself as Influence

The discussion has so far focused on the ways in which the settlor can retain control over the trust assets and, by implication, power over the new beneficial owners. Also missing from the orthodox narrative is the extent to which the settlor is able to exert power over the lives of her beneficiaries merely from the way in which the assets are settled, i.e. without any need to interfere in their subsequent administration. That narrative tells us that concomitant with the settlor dropping out of the picture is the precedence accorded by English law to the free alienability of property. Central to Cotterrell's analysis is the fact that *Saunders v Vautier* and associated cases give the beneficiaries the collective right to collapse the trust and take the assets absolutely, so long as they own 100 per cent of the equity and are sui juris.[51] But this obfuscates the numerous ways in which the settlor can carve equitable interests out of her property in such a way as to limit the ability of the beneficiaries to come together and collapse the trust in this way. She may also structure the settlement so as to make enjoyment of the assets dependent on obeying her specific wishes. This is something that Cotterrell himself briefly acknowledges in his later work when he notes that:

> especially in traditional family trust contexts, trust law allows extensive controls over beneficiaries to be created by settlors, as in the case of protective trusts, or allows settlors to devise trusts (especially discretionary trusts) that avoid the specification of fixed beneficial property entitlements.[52]

He does not go into detail, but there are many options open to the settlor. Discretionary trusts can do more than his suggested avoidance of the specification of fixed—and hence alienable—property entitlements. With the only limits being conceptual certainty and administrative

---

51. (1841) 4 Beav 115.
52. Cotterrell, 'Trusting in Law,' 83–4.

workability, the class of objects can, if cannily designed, make it difficult, or impossible, for the beneficiaries collectively to come together
and agree to collapse the trust: for example, by virtue of the sheer size
and diversity of the class, or by incorporating future members whose
interests have yet to vest and so preventing the exercise of *Saunders v
Vautier* rights until the end of the perpetuity period.[53]

Of course, discretionary trusts still ultimately turn on the exercise of
trustee discretion, and so to some extent return us to the question of
the extent to which the settlor is happy to leave the administration and
appointment of assets to the trustees or prefers to reserve key powers
for herself. Another option is to settle property on trusts whereby
the beneficiary's interest is subject to some condition precedent or
subsequent, enabling the settlor to exert real power over his life by
discouraging or requiring particular behaviour in return for her gift. In
one Victorian case, for example, the beneficiary's life interest was terminated for his failure to comply with the condition that he not marry a
domestic servant;[54] more recently, the House of Lords upheld a gift to
a son conditional upon him not converting to Roman Catholicism.[55] In
theory, there is a limit insofar as the court will strike down a condition
subsequent if it is 'repugnant' to freedom of alienation,[56] and so this
device cannot be used to restrict the recipient's right to dispose of
their property. However, this can easily be circumvented as, instead of
gifting property subject to a condition subsequent, the settlor can gift
a determinable interest, i.e. not a gift that stands 'unless' a criterion is
fulfilled but a gift that lasts 'until' a criterion is fulfilled. The latter is
not affected by the rule against repugnancy on the basis that, whereas a
gift subject to a condition subsequent is treated as an outright gift that
may be struck down prematurely, a determinable interest is one which
is inherently limited and merely comes to its natural end when the condition is met. As one judge opined, '[t]he distinction is not a particularly
attractive one, being based on form rather than substance,'[57] but it
means that while a settlor cannot, for example, settle property for her
children conditional upon them not getting married,[58] or transferring

---

53. Perpetuities and Accumulations Act 2009, s 7.
54. *Jenner v Turner* (1880) 16 Ch D 188.
55. *Blathwayt v Baron Cawley* [1976] AC 397 (HL).
56. See generally Glanville Williams, 'The Doctrine of Repugnancy — I: Conditions in Gifts,' *Law Quarterly Review* 59 (1943).
57. *Re Trusts of the Scientific Investment Pension Plan* [1998] 3 All ER 154 (Ch) 158 (Rattie J). See also *Re King's Trusts* (1892) 29 LR Ir 401, 410; *Re Sharp's ST* [1973] Ch 331 (Ch) 340 (Pennycuick VC).
58. See *Morley v Rennoldson* (1843) 2 Hare 570.

to someone else, or going bankrupt, she can make limited gifts until such time as they marry, attempt to transfer the property, or go bankrupt.[59] The devices available to the settlor can also be combined in numerous permutations, enabling increasingly precise and sophisticated settlor control, as in the case of the protective trust, mentioned in passing by Cotterrell,[60] which supplements a determinable life interest with a discretionary trust for the primary beneficiary and his immediate family that arises in the event that his life interest is determined.[61]

Power and Charitable Giving

Having focused largely on private trusts, with an emphasis on the traditional family settlement, we might end by considering briefly the settlor's power in the context of the charitable trust. Here the power dynamics are inevitably different, as there are no beneficiaries in the sense of equitable owners: a charity's trustees hold the legal title to the assets, but they are subject to a fiduciary duty to apply them for its charitable purpose enforced by the Attorney-General and the Charity Commission.[62] Nevertheless, the options for exerting power and influence over the trust considered above are probably all available to the settlor of a charity. There is no reported caselaw directly on point, but there is authority to the effect that a charitable trust may expressly grant its trustees the power to revoke, amend or vary its terms,[63] and one leading charity law treatise takes it as read that this power can be reserved by the settlor for herself.[64] Alongside the fact that there is nothing to prevent a settlor from making a restricted rather than an absolute charitable gift, this serves as a reminder that the conventional narrative, which states that once assets are dedicated to charity they shall remain dedicated to charity, does not paint the full picture.[65] There is no compelling policy reason why the settlor should not reserve

---

59. See Williams, 'The Doctrine of Repugnancy,' 357–8.
60. Cotterrell, 'Trusting in Law,' 84.
61. Trustee Act 1925, s 33.
62. See Jonathan Garton, 'Charitable Trusts: Locating the Beneficial Interest' in *Oxford Handbook of Comparative Trust Laws*, ed. Adam Hofri-Winogradow et al (Oxford: Oxford University Press, forthcoming).
63. *Re Holloway's Trusts* (1909) 26 TLR 62; see also *Trustee of Queensland as Trustee of Queensland Community Foundation* [2016] QSC 276 (Supreme Court of Queensland).
64. Hubert Picarda, *The Law and Practice Relating to Charities*, 4th ed. (London: Bloomsbury Professional, 2010), 379.
65. *Re Wright* [1954] Ch 347 (CA).

the right to remove or appoint trustees, particularly given the fiduciary nature of that power, and although there is again no reported caselaw,[66] the Charity Commission has registered charities whose trust instruments reserve investment powers to the settlor.[67] But the nature of the charitable trust is that the settlor's powers go far beyond this. She may, through her private bounty, shape the very landscape of public social welfare provision.[68] If a wealthy philanthropist settles a high-value endowment on a grant-making charitable trust with narrow purposes then this can encourage service providers to pursue these purposes over others in order to access its grants. Resource-strapped service providers in a related field may succumb to 'mission drift' and move away from their original objectives in order to secure the funding that they need to survive.[69] If there are other potential donors still willing to fund the neglected purposes, they may find that there are no longer any willing service providers.[70] The ramifications can extend beyond the third sector, as a strong charitable presence in a field may be presented as justification for reduced public sector investment.[71] And although there are limits in the form of statutory reforms to the cy-près doctrine, which enable the purposes of a charitable trust to be altered not just when they have become impossible to carry out but, inter alia, when they have 'ceased… to provide a suitable and effective method' of using the trust assets in light of 'the spirit of the gift' and changing

---

66. Though note the words of Cross J in Re Jewish Orphanage Charity Endowments Trusts [1960] 1 WLR 344 (Ch) 348: 'If a testator or settlor can himself empower his trustees to invest in forms of investment not authorised by law for the investment of trust funds, I do not see on principle why he should not be entitled to confer on someone else a power to enlarge the original investment clause.'

67. See e.g. the trust instrument of the Waterways Infrastructure Trust, which operates canals and towpaths for the public benefit and requires the consent of the settlor (the Secretary of State for Environment, Food and Rural Affairs) to sell any of its land: accessed 4 March 2024, https://assets.publishing.service.gov.uk/government/uploads/system/uploads/attachment_data/file/183234/Canals-rivers-trust-settlement.pdf.

68. On which see generally Kathryn Chan, The Public-Private Nature of Charity Law (Oxford: Hart Publishing, 2016).

69. See Brenda Zimmerman and Raymond Dart, Charities Doing Commercial Ventures: Societal and Organizational Implications (Ontario: Trillium Foundation, 1998), ch 3.

70. i.e. the phenomenon of 'philanthropic particularism': see Lester Salamon, 'Partners in Public Service: The Scope and Theory of Government-Nonprofit Relations' in The Nonprofit Sector: A Research Handbook, ed. Water W. Powell (New Haven and London: Yale University Press, 1987) 111–12.

71. See for example, the ill-fated 'Big Society' agenda of the 2010 Cameron government: see Cabinet Office, 'Building the Big Society' (2010), accessed 4 March 2024, https://assets.publishing.service.gov.uk/government/uploads/system/uploads/attachment_data/file/60548/building-big-society.pdf.

'social and economic circumstances,'[72] the settlor's power is magnified exponentially by the fact that there is no scope for a charitable trust to be collapsed under the principle in *Saunders v Vautier*, which lies at the heart of Cotterrell's beneficiary-centred narrative.[73] Together with the exemption from the rule against trusts of perpetual duration, the nature of the charitable trust is such that the settlor can continue to exert significant power not just for years but centuries after her death.

Conclusion

In shining a light on the property-power of the beneficiaries, Cotterrell provides a valuable corrective to our tendency to emphasise the formal legal control of the trustees. But the beneficiaries' power is not the only power obscured by the traditional narrative of trust law. Despite formally divesting herself of legal beneficial ownership, the settlor may retain a wide range of administrative and dispositive powers that enable her to exert real control over the trust assets while remaining largely out of sight. More than this, she may use the inherent flexibility of the trust and the variety of interests that can be carved out of her original beneficial ownership to influence the lives of her beneficiaries, who are not always quite as free 'to take the money and run' as we might be sometimes think. In the case of a charitable trust, where no-one is ever free to take the money and run, the settlor's vision can be imposed not only upon the direct objects of her bounty but also on wider society, and potentially in perpetuity. Just as Cotterrell challenges the orthodoxy of the unyielding power of the trustee, so too should we challenge the orthodoxy of the settlor as a background player who, having created the trust, relinquishes power and drops out of the picture, never to be heard from again.

---

72. Charities Act 2011, s 62(1), (2).

73. While *Saunders v Vautier* does not permit the termination of a charitable trust, it does have some limited application for charities: see e.g. in *Wharton v Masterman* [1895] AC 186 (HL), in which it was used to end an accumulation provision, and *Barton v Tod* [2002] EWHC 264 (Ch), in which a charity entitled to a residuary estate, less an annuity held by the testator's son, agreed with the son to convert his annuity to a lump sum.

3

Trusts Law and the Problem of Moral Distance

*Michael Bryan**

Conceptions of Trust and Trusting

One of the many contributions made by Roger Cotterrell to the study of the sociology of law has been to demonstrate how social theory illuminates doctrinal issues. An instructive case in point is his analysis of the connections between trusts law and the moral notion of trust as a basis of social relationships, published in 1993 as 'Trusting in Law: Legal and Moral Concepts of Trust.'[1] In this paper he examined shifts in conceptions of trusteeship, beginning with a moralistic conception which relies on a network of close personal relations of trust between settlor-trustee, trustee-beneficiary, and settlor-beneficiary. This conception is far from obsolete.[2] But it has increasingly given way to what Cotterrell terms the property-receptacle version which places greater emphasis on the property entitlements of the beneficiary. A specific application of the latter is the capital management model of the trust, characterised by large capital holdings held on a semi-permanent basis by trustees (or more commonly trust corporations) enjoying extensive managerial powers. Cotterrell's examples of this model, drawn from 'third way' capitalist welfare, are pension funds and large charities.

The shift away from the moralistic conception of the trust has resulted in what Cotterrell terms a widening 'moral distance' between trustee and beneficiary. Insights derived from the literature on the social

* University of Melbourne, Australia. Roger Cotterrell, Matthew Harding, Nick Piška, and Sarah Worthington have wittingly or unwittingly helped me to write this chapter. The usual disclaimer apples.
1. Roger Cotterrell, 'Trusting in Law: Legal and Moral Concepts of Trust,' *Current Legal Problems* 46 (1993).
2. *Paul v Constance* [1977] 1 WLR 527.

nature of trust can help us understand this development.[3] To trust another person is to take the risk of relying on the other's goodwill in circumstances which cannot be fully defined in advance. But, trusting though we may be in our everyday personal relations, this primal notion of trust is an inadequate basis on which to act as employees, consumers or in doing business. Increasingly, we place reliance, not on individuals, but on systems. The personal nexus of trust is replaced by reliance on abstract systems, such as the systems of human resources, consumer protection and financial regulation. The displacement from individuals onto systems is attributable to the increasing complexity of social and economic life. Passive trusting has replaced the active conferment of trust. Indeed, statutory regulation, for example of financial advisers, has made reliance on systems in some areas of economic activity inescapable.

Just as the social institution of trusting has been diluted by the substitution of systems for individual trust, so also the evolution of commercial applications of the trust has been characterised by a growing moral distance between the three parties to a trust relationship, namely settlors, trustees, and beneficiaries. The insertion of complex agency relationships into the trustee-beneficiary nexus has resulted in trustees often having little or no direct involvement in the distribution of trust money to the beneficiaries, or having much knowledge of their circumstances. Beneficiaries for their part do not meaningfully 'rely on' trustees, and are in fact very often ignorant of their identity. Moreover, increasing reliance on contractual exclusions in trust instruments has reduced the standards of fiduciary responsibility and professional competence expected of trustees, thereby underlining the limited role nowadays played by the moralistic conception of trusting.

If the main lines of Cotterrell's argument are accepted, the prospects for both the social institution of trusting and the moralistic conception of the trust look bleak. Effective systems help us to navigate the complexity of contemporary social and economic relationships, but systems also distance us from decision makers who affect our lives. Likewise, the trust on this analysis provides no more than impersonal facultative machinery for the allocation of income derived from the investment of accumulated capital. The historic distinction between legal and equitable ownership has, sociologically, less explanatory force

---

3. Niklas Luhmann, *Trust and Power,* trans. Howard Davis, John Raffan and Kathryn Rooney (Chichester: Wiley, 1979); Niklas Luhmann, 'Familiarity, Confidence, Trust Problems and Alternatives' in *Trust: Making and Breaking Co-Operative Relations*, ed. Diego Gambetta (New York: Blackwell, 1988).

today than the functional distinction between capital manager and income recipient.

Cotterrell's paper identified developments in trusts law which were then only just beginning to receive attention from trusts scholars. A quarter of a century later, the trend, at least in the commercial sphere, towards the 'contractualisation' of trusts is better understood though perhaps insufficiently critiqued. This chapter has two aims. The first is to carry Cotterrell's story forward and to demonstrate that his arguments have as much validity when applied to certain applications of 'small trusts', including trusts which underpin the securitisation of debt, as they do to large pension trusts. The second aim is to examine possible legal and extra-legal responses to the decline in personal entrusting.

Social Theory and Legal Doctrine Updated

When Cotterrell wrote his paper Western societies were on the cusp of the digital revolution. It is still too early to assess fully the transformative effects of that revolution but it is undeniable that the new modes of communication have reinforced the diminishing reliance on personal confidence and the corresponding dependence on systems. Most major contributions to the sociology of trusting since 1993 accept the distinction, drawn by Cotterrell, following Luhmann on this point, between personal confidence and reliance on systems.[4] The scholarship of trusting also draws on philosophy, economics and psychology, and some fusion of intellectual approaches can be discerned in the recent literature. The scholarship has also tapped into media debates on the extent to which technology has transformed the nature of human trust.[5]

As far as the law of trusts is concerned, the equitable principles governing express trusts have not changed since Cotterrell's paper was published. Drafting ingenuity has, however, spawned increasingly

---

4. Niklas Luhmann, *Risk: A Sociological Theory* (New York: Aldine Transactions, 2005); Diego Gambetta, 'Can We Trust Trust?' in *Trust: Making and Breaking Co-Operative Relations*, ed. Diego Gambetta (Oxford: Oxford University Press, 2000), 213; Barbara Misztal, *Trust in Modern Societies: The Search for the Bases of Social Order* (Cambridge: Polity Press, 1996). Adam Seligman, 'Trust and Sociability: On the Limits of Confidence and Role Expectations, '*American Journal of Economics and Sociology* 57 (1998) distinguishes 'trust' from 'confidence', the latter resting on reliance on the predictability of another's actions, while the former recognises the freedom of choice in the person trusted. Translated into the discourse of trusts law, the widening of moral distance between trustee and beneficiary has caused most trusts discussed in this chapter to rest on Seligman's concept of confidence, rather than on his notion of trust.
5. See, for example, Rachel Botsman, *Who Can You Trust?* (London: Penguin Portfolio, 2017).

complex trust structures to serve a variety of economic purposes.[6] The focus of Cotterrell's analysis was on so-called 'big trusts', such as large pension funds, charitable trusts, and discretionary welfare trusts. 'Moral distance' in these trusts is largely a function of the size and complexity of the trusts—just as the substitution of systems for individual trust is essentially a product of increasingly complex social and economic organisation.

But a feature of modern commerce has been the creation of 'limited duty' trusts inserted into commercial agreements. This is a trust created as a component of a commercial contract which imposes few, if any, duties on the trustee (usually a company) beyond the duties of holding capital and making distributions of capital and income in accordance with the terms of a trustee-beneficiary contract.[7] The 'limited duty' trust is often inserted into securitisation arrangements whereby rights to enforce debts are sold to investor-beneficiaries. But there are many other commercial applications. Trusts created by commercial lenders by imposing trust obligations either directly on borrowers, as under a *Quistclose* trust,[8] or on an intermediary solicitor retained to take a charge over the borrower's property,[9] also belong to this category.

Complexity in these cases inheres in the overall commercial arrangement. The terms of the 'limited duty' trust that lies at their heart are simple; they confer none of the extensive management powers that trustees of 'big trusts' enjoy. Many of the latter, such as pension trusts and large charitable foundations, are theoretically unlimited in duration. Their trustees must formulate long term investment and borrowing strategies and, in the case of pension funds, must balance inter-generational needs and expectations. In contrast, 'limited duty' trusts operate within the shorter, closed timeframes of debt issue or loan payout. Their corporate trustees are 'hold-and-distribute' trustees, for whom questions of investment performance are rarely relevant.

The 'limited duty' trust cannot, strictly speaking, be termed a capital management trust, within Cotterrell's meaning of the term, since

---

6. *Citibank NA v MBI Assurance SA* [2007] EWCA Civ 11; *Assénagan Asset Management SA v Irish Bank Resolution Corp Ltd* [2012] EWHC 2090, [2013] 1 All ER 495.

7. The 'limited duty' trust includes, but is broader than, the bare trust. The latter is typically defined as a trust under which a trustee holds property without any duty to perform except to convey the property upon demand to the beneficiaries or as directed by them: *Re Blandy Jenkins' Estate* [1917] 1 Ch 662. The trustee company of a 'limited duty' trust is typically controlled by third parties and the duties owed to the beneficiaries are primarily defined by contract.

8. *Barclays Bank Ltd v Quistclose Investments Ltd* [1970] AC 567.

9. *AIB Group Ltd v Mark Redler & Co* [2015] AC 1503.

the trustee's powers and duties focus on the collection and distribution of capital and income, rather than on ongoing management. It is really a discrete application of the property-receptacle version of trust. But it resembles many modern capital management trusts in that any 'confidence' reposed by the beneficiary in the trustee is highly conditional, being defined by the terms of the contract between the parties and overlaid by a measure of prudential regulation. The problem of 'moral distance', or impersonality, is not the problem of size or scale of operations, as it is for (say) pension trusts, but rather of the automaton-like role the 'limited duty' trust plays in commercial lending arrangements.

What is Moral Distance?

Trusts are, as Cotterrell notes, 'networks of interdependence',[10] involving relationships between trustee and beneficiary, settlor and trustee, and settlor and beneficiary. Complex commercial trusts, combining contract and trust, simultaneously enlarge the network of interdependence by contractually inserting other parties into the overall managerial scheme while simultaneously limiting both the trustee's obligations and its liability for breach of duty. What is moral distance and what is its impact on these networks of interdependence?

The Trustee-Beneficiary Nexus

Pension trusts raise issues of size and expertise. They are typically characterised by large capital holdings and numerous beneficiaries. Effective management necessitates the dispersal of trust powers among qualified professional agents. Interposing agents—investment advisers, custodians, insurers and bankers—between trustee and beneficiary is one cause of distancing. Agents are contractually responsible to the trustees, not to the beneficiaries, and the beneficiaries will usually have no input into establishing or monitoring their performance standards.

The problem of 'moral distance' for these trusts affects both trustee and beneficiary. The complexity of a large trust can conceal from the beneficiary the standard of performance being exercised by the trustee; it may simultaneously make it harder for a trustee to obtain relevant knowledge of the beneficiary's circumstances. From the perspective of both trustee and beneficiary, complexity is therefore a significant obstacle to informed decision-making.

---

10. Cotterrell, 'Trusting in Law,' 93.

A 'trusting' relationship between trustee and beneficiary does not mean that their interests are identical. A trustee who identifies too closely with the needs of an individual beneficiary may fall foul of the equitable proscription of unauthorised conflicts of interest, the purpose of which is to promote disinterested decision-making.[11] 'Trusting' is not inconsistent with disinterested decision-making. But 'trusting' does imply some understanding of the beneficiary's needs, and of how the duties and powers vested in the trustee can best be directed to meeting those needs. Trust size, as well as the multiplication of agency roles within trust administration, may complicate the trustee's task of assessing the claims of an individual beneficiary.

Trust size carries less explanatory force, however, when applied to a 'limited duty' trust. A trustee company inserted into a lending agreement as a vehicle for receiving and distributing payments usually has no investment duties to perform. Vast sums are held on the terms of these trusts, but the value of the units, or fixed interests, held by the investor-beneficiaries does not depend on prudent investment management but on ensuring timely and full payment of debt obligations. Although the collection and distribution of the proceeds calls for managerial proficiency, neither size nor expertise fully explain the moral distance separating trustee from beneficiary under these trusts. Complexity resides not so much in the structure of the trust as in the structure of the overall lending scheme of which the trust is only one integer.

'Limited duty' trusts resemble 'big' pension trusts, however, in that the relationship between trustee and beneficiary is, in both cases, contractual as well as equitable. The beneficiary is not a volunteer and the value of her entitlement will be defined by the terms of the trustee-beneficiary contract. The phenomenon of trusts having a dual contractual/equitable character has been inelegantly labelled the 'contractualisation' of trusts law.[12] Much of the widening moral distancing deplored by Cotterrell can be explained in terms of the proliferation of contractualised trusts which do not have at their core the notion of a trustee subordinating personal interest to the interests of the beneficiary. Trusts law presupposes that trustee's interests are identified with those of the beneficiary. In contrast, contract law presupposes the pursuit of separate interests. Classical economic theory assumes that a freely-entered into contract

---

11. Lionel Smith, 'Fiduciary Relationships: Ensuring the Loyal Exercise of Judgment on Behalf of Another,' *Law Quarterly Review* 130 (2014).

12. John H. Langbein, 'The Secret Life of the Trust: The Trust as an Instrument of Commerce,' *Yale Law Journal* 107 (1997).

optimises the welfare of parties having opposing interests.[13] Absence of trust is a presupposition of arms-length contracting. Assuming that a trust satisfies the basic preconditions of validity, equity has no role to play in regulating positions of power and dependence between the trusting and trusted parties under contractualised trusts.[14] Regulation is a matter for contract law. But contract law in practice reinforces, rather than regulates, the exercise of managerial power since the beneficiaries' freedom of contract will often be severely limited.

The authorities on the enforceability of exculpation clauses in trust instruments illustrate the extent to which formal considerations of freedom of contract permeate the practice of a great deal of contemporary trusts law.[15] Exclusion is not just a matter of limiting or excluding liability for negligent performance of duties. It can extend to authorising the trustee to act, in specific circumstances, contrary to the interests of any beneficiary. In *Citibank NA v MBIA Assurance SA*,[16] effect was given to a clause in a securitisation trust instrument providing that the trustee, when acting at the direction of the guarantor of notes issued to one class of investors, 'shall not be required to have regard to the interests of the Noteholders [beneficiaries]' in the exercise of its discretions, and must instead give effect to the wishes of the guarantor.[17] Only the trustee's duties to act in good faith and to comply with the terms of the trust instrument have proved in practice to be sufficiently 'irreducibly core' so as to be immune from emasculation by contractual exclusion.[18] It has been left to prudential legislation, enacting non-excludable obligations, to accomplish any reversal of dependency within the trust relationship.[19] The increasing relevance of prudential legislation to the supervision of trusts confirms an important

---

13. Robert Cooter and Thomas Ulen, *Law and Economics,* 6th ed. (Harlow: Addison-Wesley 2016), 283–287.
14. Contractualised trusts are subject to the application of the equitable principles governing review of a trustee's exercise of discretion, but even here contractual interpretation precedes the application of the principles: *Finch v Telstra Super Pty Ltd* (2010) 242 CLR 254 (HCA).
15. *Armitage v Nurse* [1998] Ch 241 (CA); *Spread Trustee Co Ltd v Hutcheson* [2012] 2 AC 174 (PC).
16. [2006] EWHC 3215 (Ch), aff'd [2007] 1 All ER (Comm) 475 (CA).
17. *Citibank NA v MBIA Assurance SA* [25].
18. *Clayton v Clayton* [2015] 3 NZLR 293 (CA) [51]–[56]. It is, however, arguable that the ratio of *Armitage v Nurse* is confined to a trustee's managerial discretions and is inapplicable to the duty to distribute.
19. See the statutory segregation of trust assets rules for managed investment funds made under Financial Services & Markets Act 2000 considered in *Re Lehman Brothers International (Europe)* [2012] 3 All ER 1 (UKSC).

point made by Cotterrell, namely that the moral relationship of trust has increasingly been displaced from the trust and attached to the law.[20]

The Settlor-Trustee Nexus

Any analysis of personal trusting in trusts law must focus not only on the trustee-beneficiary relationship, but also on the settlor-trustee nexus. It is, after all, the settlor, not the beneficiaries, who initially places confidence in the honesty and skill of the trustees.

Classic accounts of trusts law give only a walk-on part to the role of settlor. They state that, once a trust has been constituted, there is no further part for the settlor to play in his capacity as settlor.[21] It is true that in construing the terms of the trust the court gives effect to the objective manifestation of the settlor's intention, which in a commercial trust often means construing contractual documentation. But the rules for terminating a trust under the rule in *Saunders v Vautier*,[22] and for varying trusts under the Variation of Trusts Act 1958, place limits on effectuating that intention.

This classic account of the settlor 'dropping out' of the trust after constitution needs modification.[23] Settlors often continue to exert influence over the administration of a trust by a variety of formal and informal techniques. Cotterrell rightly draws attention to ongoing influences practised by settlors, for example by communicating a letter of wishes to the trustees,[24] or by retaining a role as trust protector.[25] To these examples of settlor involvement should be added the fact that under many contractualised trusts settlors play a dual role—as both settlor of a portion of the fund and as a beneficiary of the invested proceeds. The pension contributor, commercial lender or investor under these trusts is both the settlor of her contribution to the fund and simultaneously a beneficiary. The trust may, for example, be constituted by the formal settlement of a nominal sum by an originator having no further managerial involvement. That originator truly 'drops out.' The effective settlors will be pension contributors or investors in a securitised loan

---

20. Cotterrell, 'Trusting in Law,' 79.
21. Geraint Thomas and Alastair Hudson, *The Law of Trusts*, 2nd ed. (Oxford: Oxford University Press, 2010) [1.37].
22. (1841) 41 ER 482.
23. See Jonathan Garton in this collection.
24. *Breakspear v Ackland* [2009] Ch 32.
25. The protector role can be found under various designations, e.g. 'Principal Family Member': *Clayton v Clayton* [2016] NZSC 29.

agreement who are also the beneficiaries of the scheme.[26] Both capacities are regulated by the terms of the pension scheme or investment contract, largely to the exclusion of equity. 'Contractualisation' has largely eliminated the role of personal confidence in regulating the relationship between trustees and settlor/beneficiaries.

In summary, while size and complexity are symptoms of moral distancing, the real causes are to be found in the substitution of a contractual regime of bargaining for the equitable principles premised on the identification of the trustee's interests with those of the beneficiary. Contract law also increasingly governs the settlor-trustee relationship, so that the settlor is no longer a legal actor who 'drops out' of the trust once it has been constituted.

The Recognition of Corporate Trustees and the Withering of Personal Confidence

This account of the evolution of trusts law in terms of a shift from the moralistic to the property-receptacle and capital management conceptions of trust might be criticised on the ground that, resembling some Toynbeean history,[27] it is over-schematic. It would be fallacious to assume, for example, that the 'moralistic trust' has been superseded. As previously noted, trusts founded on a conception of personal entrusting remain a popular mode of property-holding, even if the informality with which many such trusts are created means that they defy precise quantification.[28] This is not, however, a fallacy of which Cotterrell is guilty. He is aware of the dangers of schematic history, insisting that these conceptions 'do not represent an evolutionary scheme' and are better understood 'in terms of a tension between three different kinds of trust ethos, one of which is gradually coming to dominate.'[29] How is the gradual dominance to be explained? It is not enough to point to contractualisation as a self-sufficient explanation of the diminution of the role of personal trusting in trusts law. Some account must be given

---

26. A party who adds capital to a trust previously constituted by a nominal settlor has been held not to be a 'creator' of a trust, for the purpose of income tax legislation: *Truesdale v Federal Commissioner of Taxation* (1970) 120 CLR 353 but the decision is context specific. Contrast *Tucker v Commissioner of Inland Revenue* [1965] NZLR 1027.

27. Arnold J. Toynbee, *A Study of History* (Oxford: Oxford University Press, 12 volumes, 1934–1961) describing schematically the rise and fall of twenty-three civilisations.

28. *Paul v Constance* [1977] 1 WLR 527 (CA).

29. Cotterrell, 'Trusting in Law,' 86.

of how and why contractual norms have come to prevail over equitable norms in the evolution of commercial trusts.

It is not the purpose of this chapter to expound the history of commercial trusts. It is nonetheless possible to identify several doctrinal developments facilitating the development of various models of the contractualised trust, with special reference to the 'limited duty' trust being considered here. One such development, traceable at least back to the seventeenth century, is the creation of markets in equitable interests.[30] Another development, noticed by Cotterrell, is the judicial recognition of companies as trustees. This latter development deserves more attention than it has so far received.

Cotterrell drew attention to the significance, in Lord Nottingham's time, of the recognition of corporate bodies as trustees.[31] In *Sterling v Wilford*,[32] Lord Nottingham approved the appointment of the Drapers' Company, a City of London livery corporation, as trustee, remarking that 'the whole power of the Chancery doth not rest merely in a personal coercion, as the old books speak.'[33] In addition to livery companies, it was by then well established that ecclesiastical and municipal corporations could hold property for charitable objects.[34] In these cases no great moral distance separated the corporation from the objects they were obliged to advance.[35] The possibilities of corporate trusteeship only began to be exploited on any significant scale after the enactment of legislation, culminating in the Companies Act 1862, facilitating the creation of limited liability companies.

The synthetic 'off-the-peg' trustee company is central to the structuring of 'limited duty' trusts. Effective control of the trust lies not with the directors of the company but with a third party on whom authority has been conferred by the trust instrument to compel the directors to act on

---

30. The mortgaging of interests by expectant heirs may well have been a catalyst for establishing markets in equitable interests: P.S. Atiyah, *The Rise and Fall of Freedom of Contract* (Oxford: Oxford University Press, 1979), 172–173. The enactment of s 9 of the Statute of Fraud 1677, imposing writing requirements on 'all grants and assignments of any trust and confidence' presupposes the existence of markets in equitable interests.

31. D.E.C. Yale, 'Introduction' in *Lord Nottingham's Chancery Cases: Volume 2*, ed. D.E.C. Yale (Volume 79 of Selden Society, 1961), 90.

32. (1676) *Lord Nottingham's Chancery Cases*, 447 (Case 579).

33. See also *Att-Gen v Landerfield* (1744) 9 Mod 286; 88 ER 456 (holding that St Bartholomew's Hospital had capacity to act as trustee).

34. Michael Chesterman, *Charities, Trusts and Social Welfare* (London: Weidenfeld & Nicolson 1979), 11–80, 204.

35. Michael Chesterman, *Charities, Trusts and Social Welfare*, 203–205.

that party's instructions.[36] Neither the directors of the trustee company nor its external controllers are readily amenable to supervision by the beneficiaries. Substantial obstacles stand in the way of bringing any claim for breach of trust. Since few discretionary powers are conferred on the trustee, the ordinary principles of reviewing the exercise of a powerholder's discretion will have only a limited application.[37] The directors of the corporation cannot be held directly liable to the beneficiaries for breach of trust.[38] They can be held liable for assisting the corporation to commit the breach, but only upon proof of dishonesty.[39]

Perhaps most significant limitation on the practical application of trusts law is that the trustee company has few, if any, 'free assets' available to satisfy a personal judgment for breach of trust. The traditional notion of the individual trustee liable to compensate the trust fund 'to the last penny in his pocket' has an air of commercial unreality when applied to the 'limited duty' trust. The holding structure of a company created as a special purpose vehicle effectively creates a corporate version of the 'man of straw', against whom a judgment cannot be effectively enforced.

If we shift our attention from the trustee company and its directors to the third-party entity controlling the trustee's exercise of discretions, the legal analysis is, from the beneficiaries' perspective, just as bleak. Legal obstacles to effective supervision of the entity by the beneficiaries include the absence of privity of contract between these parties as well as uncertainty as to whether the entity owes direct fiduciary duties to the beneficiaries.[40]

Although 'duty light' the corporate trustee of a 'limited duty' trust will nonetheless enjoy significant rights. The trustee's right of indemnity from the beneficiary for costs and expenses incurred in the management of the trust will usually be excluded by an express term of the investment contract.[41] But the trustee also has a right of indemnity

---

36. Cf the role played by MBI Assurance SA as the 'note controlling party' entitled give directions to Citibank NA as trustee of securities in *Citibank NA v MBI Assurance SA* [2007] EWCA Civ 11 (CA).

37. *Tempest v Lord Camoys* (1882) 21 Ch D 571. Cf the principles governing review of the exercise of a fiduciary discretion made under a misapprehension: *Futter v Futter; Pitt v Holt* [2013] 2 AC 108 (UKSC).

38. For an analysis of the special circumstances in which a director of a trustee company might owe fiduciary obligations to a beneficiary see *Snell's Equity*, 32nd ed. (London: Sweet & Maxwell, 2010), [7-003] n. 28.

39. *Royal Brunei Airlines Sdn Bhd v Tan* [1995] 2 AC 378(PC).

40. *Snell's Equity*, 32nd ed. (London: Sweet & Maxwell, 2010) [10-009], [21-011].

41. *Hardoon v Belilios* [1901] AC 118. Legislation in some jurisdictions limits or excludes the trustee's right of indemnity from beneficiaries: Nuncio D'Angelo,

for its expenses claimable against assets comprised in the trust fund and enforceable by an equitable lien over the assets taking priority over the beneficiaries' claims to the trust property.[42] If the trustee company owes debts to third parties which are unsatisfied because the company (as we have just seen) has no assets of its own from which payment can be made, the third party's claim will be subrogated to the trustee's right to be indemnified from the trust assets, which also has priority over the beneficiaries' claims.[43]

The trustee's rights of indemnity from beneficiaries and the trust fund are not confined to corporate trustees; they are equitable principles of general application. But the creation of companies as 'empty vessels', holding few if any assets beneficially to satisfy claims brought by the beneficiaries or by third parties, illustrates the unreality of any confidence reposed by investor-beneficiaries in the trustee. The trustee company is simply an artificial instrumentality inserted into a 'limited duty' trust in order to provide insolvency protection for scheme participants.

Responses to Moral Distance: Equitable Dead Ends and Public Law Possibilities

Systems are pervasive and it is tempting to assume that our forced reliance on their operations is inevitable. Cotterrell rightly protests against adopting a passive or despairing attitude towards the dominance of systems.

> It is as though banking systems, political systems, economic and financial systems have a life of their own in relation to which individuals must somehow orientate themselves... If the moral purposes for which trust relationships exist are not fully understood and respected, efforts at subversion may come from a range of sources, not excluding...those who have access to or influence over the use of trust funds.[44]

One manifestation of subversion identified by Cotterrell is that 'people vote with their feet, so to speak. They avoid reliance wherever possible

---

Commercial Trusts (Chatswood: LexisNexis Butterworths, 2014), 146–149.

42. *Bennett v Wyndham* (1862) 49 ER 1183; *Re Raybould* [1900] 1 Ch 199.

43. The creditor's claim is derivative on the trustee's right of indemnity: *Investec Trust (Guernsey) Ltd v Glenalla Properties Ltd* [2018] 2 WLR 1465. If the trustee's claim is barred or limited, for example on account of compensation owed to the beneficiary, the creditor's claim will be similarly affected: *Cherry v Boultee* (1839) 41 ER 171.

44. Cotterrell, 'Trusting in Law,' 94.

on structures or systems they no longer trust.'[45] But voting with one's feet is not always possible, for example where the law compels employees to join a pension scheme, or where tax law mandates specific corporate or trust structures for the pursuit of charitable activity.

If, as Cotterrell notes, the moral relationship of trust is displaced from the trustees and attached to the law, the critical question becomes: what law enforces the morality of trusting? Specifically, has equitable doctrine a role to play in enforcing the morality of trusting?[46]

Some doctrinal responses to moral distancing are easily identified. These are directed towards ensuring the reality and integrity of decision-making by trustees. First, there is the principle that an exercise of discretion by a trustee who does not apply his mind to the exercise, but who instead acts at the direction of a third party, will be void.[47] The principle has obvious application to a trustee company acting exclusively at the direction of a third-party controller, without any independent consideration by the directors of the company of the trustee's exercise of power.

Secondly, the doctrine of a fraud on a power applies to an exercise of discretion by a trustee which either disadvantages the whole class of investor-beneficiaries or amounts to an oppression of a minority of beneficiaries.[48] The doctrine is more familiar to company lawyers, obliging directors to act for 'proper purposes', but it is also a sanction in cases of abuse of office by trustees. An illustration of its relevance in contemporary trusts law is *Assénagon Asset Management SA v Irish Bank Resolution Corporation* where an offer to exchange notes held by investor-beneficiaries on unfavourable terms was accompanied by a resolution that, if the majority of beneficiaries accepted the terms, the notes held by the minority of investor-beneficiaries would be redeemed on even less favourable terms.[49] This 'exit consent' version of game theory was held to be a fraud on the minority investor-beneficiaries who did not consent to the offer of having 80% of the value of their interest destroyed. The principle is germane when trustees exercise

---

45. Cotterrell, 'Trusting in Law,' 94.
46. On the broader question whether trustees may exercise their administrative and dispositive powers in order to pursue social justice see Matthew Harding 'Trustees' Powers and Social Justice,' in *Private Law and Power*, ed., Kit Barker, Simone Degeling, Karen Fairweather and Ross Grantham (Oxford: Hart Publishing, 2017).
47. *Turner v Turner* [1984] Ch 100.
48. *Vatcher v Paull* [1915] AC 372. Richard Nolan, 'Controlling Fiduciary Power,' *Cambridge Law Journal* 68 (2009).
49. [2012] EWHC 2090 (Ch). Contrast *Azevedo v Imcopa Importacao, Exportacao E Industria De Oles Ltd* [2015] 1 QB 1.

their discretions for purposes which are inconsistent with the terms of the trust instrument. Its potency is proof against widely-drawn exculpation clauses found in commercial trust instruments: such a clause cannot exclude liability for fraud on a power.[50]

But these are limited grounds of equitable intervention, effective only against particularly egregious instances of trustee wrongdoing. If the view is taken that 'systemic trusting' has gone too far to replace personal trusting in commercial trusts, the assumption that trusts principles are subordinate to contractual principles of freedom of contract should be directly challenged. Upon close inspection, however, potential grounds of challenge turn out to be illusory.

It is sometimes asserted that a foundational aim of equitable doctrine is to relieve against the consequences of imbalances of power. But although it is true that equity has developed principles for relieving against the exercise of undue influence and unconscionable advantage-taking, the principles have no purchase in the enforcement of commercial trusts which, as we have seen, rest on formal notions of freedom of contract. Similarly, the concept of the 'sham trust' has no role to play in this arena since the true character of the arrangement created by the originators of commercial trusts is indeed a trust.[51] The creator of a trust inserted into a debt securitisation agreement intends to create the very trust that is evidenced by the terms of the securitisation agreement. There is no intention to deceive.

Another possibility is that of fashioning fiduciary principles so as to reinforce notions of personal trust and confidence, on the assumption that the principles have the prevention of acquisitive advantage-taking at their core. But this suggestion has some formidable doctrinal obstacles to overcome. As currently understood, fiduciary principles are proscriptive, and not prescriptive, in their application: they prohibit unauthorised conflicts of interest and profit-making but do not positively require trustees to act in the best interests of the beneficiaries. Moreover, the directors of a trustee company will generally owe their duties to the company, not to the beneficiaries.[52] If the directors are bound to act at the direction of a third-party controller it is, at best, doubtful whether the controller owes fiduciary duties to the beneficiaries of the trust.[53]

---

50. *Armitage v Nurse* [1998] Ch 241.
51. *JSC Mezhdunarodniy Promyshlenniy Bank v Pugachev* [2017] EWHC 24269 (Ch).
52. *Percival v Wright* [1902] 2 Ch 421.
53. Richard Nolan, 'Invoking the Administrative Jurisdiction: The Enforcement of

These are doctrinal objections, and like many such objections they may be distinguishable on the facts of a given case.[54] More intractable is the 'values' objection, namely that freedom of contract is prized more highly than equitable principle. The capitalistic model of the trust is ultimately premised on the assumption that trustees' obligations are amenable to modification or extinguishment by the terms of a well-drafted contract. As *Citibank NA v MBIA Assurance SA* demonstrates, contract can even exclude the trustee's duty to act in the interests of the beneficiary. Most scholarship on the contractualised trust has uncritically accepted the primacy of freedom of contract which is said to illustrate the 'flexibility' of equitable doctrine.[55] Equity is nothing if not plastic.

Cotterrell rightly argues that the substitution of system for personal confidence in our economic and social relations is not inevitable. Likewise, the moral distancing of trustees, including trust companies, from the concerns of beneficiaries is not a development that should be uncritically embraced.

Trusts doctrine has, however, only a limited role to play in restoring the morality of trusting. While an extension of the principles of review of the trustee company's exercise of discretion, bringing them into line with the principles of administrative law review, may be appropriate to pensions trusts, the extension is irrelevant to the corporatisation of trusteeship in securitisation arrangements where trustee discretion is severely circumscribed.[56] Similarly, trusts doctrine of itself cannot solve the problem of over-broad exculpation clauses which exclude a trustee's personal liability for any breach save for fraud. Contractual construction techniques may establish limits on the efficacy of such clauses, for example where a trustee's breach can be characterised as 'gross negligence',[57] but constructivism by itself cannot correct imbalances of power between trustees and beneficiaries that these exculpation clauses reflect.[58]

Modern Trust Structures,' in *Equity, Trusts and Commerce*, ed. Paul S. Davies and James Penner (Oxford: Hart Publishing, 2017), 155.

54. Fact specific fiduciary duties may be owed in some cases, for example where directors of a trustee company undertake to provide advice or information to the beneficiaries: *Coleman v Myers* [1977] 2 NZLR 225.

55. Langbein, 'The Secret Life of the Trust,' 183–185, cf Alexander Trukhtanov, 'The Irreducible Core of Trust Obligations,' *Law Quarterly Review* 123 (2007).

56. *Finch v Telstra Pty Ltd* (2010) 242 CLR 254 (HCA).

57. Cf the minority judgments of Baroness Hale and Lord Kerr in *Spread Trustee Co Ltd v Hutcheson* [2012] 2 AC 174 (PC).

58. Philip Sales, 'Exemption Clauses in Trusts' in *Defences in Equity*, ed. Paul S Davies

In the final analysis, only legislation can correct distortions to the trust relationship caused by uncritical acceptance in this area of laisser-faire contractual philosophy; equitable doctrine will never be adequate for this purpose. Any such legislation must recognise hard economic reality: the commercial objectives which limited duty trusts are created to serve, such as the securitisation of debt, will continue to be pursued.[59] It would be counter-productive for the law to proscribe entire categories of commercial trust. If the morality of trusting is to play a role in commercial trusts, it will be regulatory law, governing the application and enforcement of trusts in financial products, that offers the most promising way forward in narrowing the yawning distance between trustee corporation and beneficiaries in modern commercial trusts.

Cotterrell notes that trusts law displaces personal confidence onto the law.[60] This is true, but a hard question that needs answering is: *what* law provides the most adequate substitute for personal entrustment? The most efficacious legal displacement for the commercial trusts discussed in this chapter is one that is little examined by trusts scholars, namely administrative regulation.[61] The most robust response to the widening of moral distance between trustee and beneficiary may well be not a re-assertion of equitable doctrine but a subjection of trusteeship to more intensive statutory regulation than the law (including trustee legislation) currently requires.[62]

---

et al (Oxford: Hart Publishing, 2018).

59.   Andrew Haldane, 'The Age of Asset Management?' (speech given at the London Business School, 4 April 2014 available at https://www.bankofengland.co.uk/speech/2014/the-age-of-asset-management, accessed 29 February 2024), suggesting that 'lower risk securitisation might benefit from preferential regulatory treatment.'

60.   Cotterrell, 'Trusting in Law,' 79.

61.   Cf the regulatory regime considered in *Re Lehman Brothers International (Europe)* [2012] 3 ALL ER 1 (UKSC), n. 19 above.

62.   This is not a new idea in legal sociology. See Karl Renner, *The Institutions of Private Law and Their Social Functions* (London: Routledge & Kegan Paul, English language edn. 1949 with introduction and notes by Otto Kahn-Freund). Renner did not analyse the trust, but Kahn Freund's introduction at p. 24 includes a perceptive functional analysis of the trust.

4

The Reproduction of Property through the Production of Personhood: The Family Trust and the Power of Things

*Johanna Jacques**

Introduction

In 'Power, Property and the Law of Trusts' Roger Cotterrell describes the concept of property as 'ideological.'[1] Property, in Cotterrell's view, is ideological because it hides the private power that owning things confers and that is unequally distributed throughout society behind the equality of every person before the law. For this, Cotterrell blames the legal distinction between persons and things. The distinction, he writes, allows the law to separate and de-emphasise the side of the distinction associated with inequality—things—from persons when declaring their equality. *How much* a person owns simply does not count towards their legal personhood, which, stripped of all its concrete life aspects, is equal to that of everyone else's. Cotterrell concludes that it is through the legal concept of property that 'it becomes possible to banish almost entirely from the discourse of private law recognition of one of the most dominant features of life in a society of material inequalities—that of *private power.*'[2]

Cotterrell accords the trust a special place within this ideological construct. The trust, he claims, exacerbates the blindness of the property concept to private power by allowing the real owners of trust property,

* Durham Law School, University of Durham, UK.
1. Roger Cotterrell, 'Power, Property and the Law of Trusts: A Partial Agenda for Critical Legal Scholarship,' Journal of Law and Society 14 (1987), 82.
2. Cotterrell, 'Power, Property and the Law of Trusts,' 82.

the beneficiaries, to hide behind the legal owners, the trustees.[3] This creates the appearance of non-ownership on the part of the beneficiaries, when in reality they have the trust property at their disposal, which increases their private power. According to this understanding, the trust should be regarded as the private property instrument *par excellence*; it hides the private power of private property behind a shell of legal ownership.

In what follows below, this chapter analyses a development in trusts law—paradoxically, a development which concerns another layer of privacy—that turns this understanding on its head so as to expose Cotterrell's own continued prejudice in favour of the person side of the person-thing distinction. The chapter will claim that the trust can be used as a mechanism for providing things with interests and the control usually ascribed to persons, ultimately enabling them to produce the personhood of those who are said to own them. Far from allowing beneficiaries to hide their property ownership, such trusts hide the power of things to ensure, with the help of the beneficiaries, their own reproduction and accumulation. Cotterrell misses this power of things because his argument is based on the assumption that interests, control, and ultimately social power can only ever be the attributes of persons, never of things.

The analysis this chapter presents will focus on the concept of autonomy. This is because autonomy, despite its prominent status in the justification of property rights—the autonomy of owners is furthered by their access *to* things—is in the context of family trusts central to claims for withholding things *from* owners, be it access to the things they are said to own or knowledge about their own wealth. The withholding of knowledge in particular is justified on the grounds that the development of any children-beneficiaries into autonomous adults would be negatively impacted if they knew just how wealthy they were. In this context, however, seeking to protect and develop the autonomy of beneficiaries favours the trust property rather than its owners. That this is the intended consequence of these measures and not merely an unintended side effect becomes apparent from the case law.

V v T and Other Cases

The case of *V v T* concerned an application for a variation by the settlors of a large family trust.[4] Such applications are commonly made

---

3. Cotterrell, 'Power, Property and the Law of Trusts,' 85.
4. *V v T, A* [2014] EWHC 3432 (Ch). Strictly speaking, the case concerned three

where the law has changed and the current terms of a trust are no longer favourable to the interests of the beneficiaries due to tax or personal reasons. Where all the beneficiaries of the trust are *sui juris* and capable of consent, they can agree on a variation without the involvement of the court. However, if there are minor beneficiaries, only the court can provide consent on their behalf. This may involve a public hearing.

The settlors in *V v T*, who were the parents of the minor beneficiaries (the trust also included a number of adult beneficiaries), anticipated that this hearing would necessitate the disclosure of information about the trust assets. They wanted to prevent this information from becoming public knowledge. They therefore applied for a private hearing, and the case gives the court's judgment in this respect. Privacy was granted, albeit not through a private hearing. Instead, the judge imposed reporting restrictions.

The interest of *V v T* lies in the reasons given by the judge in support of his decision, which reiterate those given by the parent-settlors when making the application. The settlors had argued that information about the trust ought to be kept out of the public domain. However, other than is usual in applications for privacy where minors' property is concerned, their aim was not to keep the *public* in the dark and thus from interfering with the minors' property or normal life, but to keep this information from the *children themselves*. In this, *V v T* broke new ground in the law on trust privacy. In previous cases, such as in *JFX*[5] and *K v L*,[6] the concern with privacy had been strictly about protecting the beneficiaries from the actions of the public, and the claim was therefore made that knowledge ought to be kept out of the public domain. In *V v T*, on the other hand, the claim was made that it would be harmful for the children to learn of their *own* wealth.

In *JFX*, which concerned a compromise arrangement between a minor and a NHS Trust following negligence in the minor's hospital treatment, the minor's interests were deemed to lie in the continued availability of funds paid to him for his ongoing care. The payment was substantial, and despite his injuries the minor was expected

---

related trusts.

5. *JFX (a Child suing by his Mother and Litigation Friend KMF) v York Hospitals NHS Foundation Trust* [2010] EWHC 2800 (QB).

6. *K v L (Ancillary Relief: Inherited Wealth)*, also known as *K v L (Non-Matrimonial Property: Special Contribution)* [2012] 1 WLR 306. *K v L* is not a trusts case, as the wealth concerned was the parents' wealth. However, the case is included here because it also involved the claim that information should be kept out of the public domain for the benefit of children.

to reach full legal capacity and thus obtain control over the settlement in the future. The judge considered that this control over a large fund would make the minor more vulnerable to 'those who would wish to profit from his money or deprive him of it,' in short, 'fortune hunters and thieves.'[7] It was therefore held to be in the minor's interest that information about his compromise settlement was not made known publicly. The concern here was with the acts of third parties and their potentially negative effects on the beneficiary, and at no point was it suggested that knowledge about the trust property would need to be kept from the beneficiary himself. The same concerns about the potential acts of third parties were also determinative in *X (A Child) v Dartford and Gravesham NHS Trust*,[8] and they furthermore appear to underpin the exemptions from access to the beneficial ownership register under the 5th Money Laundering Directive,[9] even though the Directive is not entirely clear on what basis access to the information of minor beneficiaries is denied. Article 1(15)(g) allows member states to grant an exception from access to the information on a case-to-case basis where this 'would expose the beneficial owner to disproportionate risk, risk of fraud, kidnapping, blackmail, extortion, harassment, violence or intimidation, or where the beneficial owner is a minor or otherwise legally incapable.'

In *K v L*, which concerned the privacy arrangements for a hearing determining the division of property at the break-up of wealthy parents, the parents had striven to keep their wealth hidden not just from their children, but also from their friends. In giving his approval to an anonymity order, Wilson LJ considered that making information about this wealth public would destroy the normality in which the children were growing up, for example by necessitating their physical protection. He said: 'We concluded that, unless we made the order, the normality of the current lives of the children would be forfeit, with results likely to be substantially damaging, perhaps even grossly damaging, to them.'[10] Here, the court's concern was again with the acts of others whose behaviour might necessitate changing the daily routines of children-beneficiaries to protect them from possible harm (hiring security, restricting activities, etc.).

Other than in *K v L*, where the property in question was that of the parents and therefore under their control, the settlors in *V v T* had

---

7. *JFX* [9] and [11] (Tugendhat J).
8. [2015] EWCA Civ 96.
9. Council Directive 2018/843 of 30 May 2018 (EU).
10. *K v L* [26].

already given their property to their children by making them the beneficiaries of their family trust. Despite this intentional act, they now made
the claim that knowledge about their entitlements could prove harmful
to their children directly, without the involvement of third parties. It
was on this basis that Morgan J was willing to consider 'appropriate
steps to protect the children from the adverse effect on their upbringing
and personal development which might well result from an open court
hearing generating publicity as to their potential wealth.'[11] At first, the
decision to impose reporting restrictions appears to have been based on
the necessity, in accordance with the Civil Procedure Rules, 'to protect
the interests of any child or protected party.'[12] However, Morgan J
then stated:

> I was concerned about the special position of the minor beneficiaries. I
> inquired whether it would be appropriate to impose some restrictions to
> safeguard the children from *the adverse consequences of them becoming
> aware at too early an age of the extent of their likely wealth.*[13]

And later on in the judgment:

> There was detailed evidence that the parents had striven to create as
> normal a life as possible for the children. A modest and low-key unos-
> tentatious lifestyle was a core value of the family. The parents were
> determined that the children *should not know at too young an age of
> the extent of the family's wealth. It was considered that such knowledge
> could deter the children from taking full advantage of the educational
> opportunities open to them. Further, such knowledge at a young age
> could create a sense of entitlement which might discourage the children
> from making their own way in life and contributing to society.*[14]

Clearly, the parents were concerned about their children's future autonomy, wanting them to become independent and autonomous ('make
their own way in life'), not entitled (avoid 'a sense of entitlement'),
educated ('take full advantage of the educational opportunities'), and
productive ('contributing to society').

At first glance, these motivations seem entirely reasonable. After all, the
pitfalls of wealth, particularly when it comes to the development of autonomy, have often been remarked upon.[15] Hannah Arendt, for example,

---

11. *V v T* [24].
12. CPR 39.2(3)(d).
13. *V v T* [11], emphasis added.
14. *V v T* [23], emphasis added.
15. The negative consequences of wealth feature equally in law, law and economics,

writes about 'the apathy and disappearance of initiative which so obviously threatens all overly wealthy,'[16] while Adam Hirsch notes that 'apart from the psychological considerations already remarked [such as the propensity of beneficiaries to spend given wealth more readily than earned wealth], beneficiaries of sudden infusions of wealth may simply be unpractised money managers, easily victimized, and they may know no better than to terminate a terminable trust.'[17] Another commentator puts this rather shorter: 'Wealth is a problem. ... Lives can be ruined by poverty, but lives can equally be ruined by excess wealth.'[18] It is unsurprising, then, that settlors in America as well as elsewhere have increasingly 'begun to fear something other than the prospect that their children will not have enough: the possibility that they will have too much.'[19]

The reasonable thing to do in response to these concerns about the effects of excess wealth is still to give, but give less. Thus, the wish to leave *some* wealth to one's children is not surprising; already in antiquity, the necessity to labour for the satisfaction of one's natural needs was regarded as slavish and beneath the proper status of the human,[20] and to settle a moderate amount of wealth on one's children would alleviate this necessity without affecting their development into autonomous adults. On the contrary, it would increase their autonomy by putting them into a position where they could pursue their interests without having to worry about their basic needs. Leaving *excessive* wealth to one's children, on the other hand, would mean risking this autonomy. The realisation of this trade-off manifests itself in some parents paying only for their children's education but not their ongoing maintenance, and can be summarised as the recognition of the need for children 'to make it on their own,' a recognition which has proved lasting through times of economic change. In 1986,

---

and economics scholarship. See, for example, Adam J. Hirsch, 'Spendthrift Trusts and Public Policy: Economic and Cognitive Perspectives,' *Washington University Law Review* 73/1 (1995), Gary S. Becker and Kevin M. Murphy, 'The Family and the State,' *Journal of Law & Economics* 31 (1988), and Neil Bruce and Michael Waldman, 'The Rotten-Kid Theorem Meets the Samaritan's Dilemma,' *The Quarterly Journal of Economics* 105 (1990).

16. Hannah Arendt, *The Human Condition* (Chicago and London: University of Chicago Press, 1998), 70–1.

17. Hirsch, 'Spendthrift Trusts and Public Policy,' 40.

18. Geoffrey Shindler, 'Wealth and Safety,' *Trusts and Estates Law & Tax Journal* (2014), 3.

19. Joshua C. Tate, 'Conditional Love: Incentive Trusts and the Inflexibility Problem,' *Real Property, Probate and Trust Journal* 41 (2006), 446.

20. Arendt, *The Human Condition*, 81–4.

Fortune magazine thus quoted multimillionaire Eugene Lang as having said that '"to me inheritance dilutes the motivation that most young people have to fulfil the best that is in them. I want to give my kids the tremendous satisfaction of making it on their own,"' while Warren Buffett said that the right amount to leave one's children is 'enough money so that they would feel they could do anything, but not so much that they could do nothing.'[21] More recently, the entrepreneur Kevin O'Leary said in an interview with *CNBC*: 'I told [my kids] when they finished college, I was going to give them this: nothing. ... Because that is what my mother did to me. You have to go make it on your own, and I think that is a very important lesson.'[22]

The parent-settlors in *V v T*, however, did not adopt this attitude. What is surprising is that these parents not only wanted their children to be autonomous but *also* wanted them to be very wealthy, even though they knew that mere knowledge about this wealth (not to mention access to it) would prevent the very autonomy and independence they strived to instil in them, not least because the large amount of wealth settled upon them would inflate their need for consumption and thus create a dependence on that wealth.

The contradiction contained in this double gesture of giving yet withholding, of wishing to create autonomy and yet knowingly creating dependence, was recognised in the case *MN v OP*,[23] where an anonymity order in relation to a variation of a trust was refused.[24] Here, the court distinguished cases relating to personal injury claims such as *X (A Child)* by pointing to the fact that in variation of trust cases the settlors had *chosen* to include children in the settlement and could therefore not rely on a presumption that anonymity should be granted where children are concerned due to their involuntary involvement in the transaction. Albeit indirectly, the court made the settlors aware that it was their choice to make their children so wealthy in the first place, and that they should therefore bear the consequences of this wealth coming

---

21. Carol J. Loomis, 'Should You Leave It All to the Children?' *Fortune*, 21 November 2012, accessed 1 March 2024, http://fortune.com/2012/11/21/should-you-leave-it-all-to-the-children/.

22. A. Montag, 'Kevin O'Leary Flies First Class, but Makes His Kids Fly Coach–Here's Why' *CNBC Make It*, 6 July 2018, accessed 1 March 2024, https://www.cnbc.com/2018/07/06/why-kevin-oleary-makes-his-kids-fly-coach.html.

23. [2017] 3 WLUK 80, appeal partially allowed in *MN v OP and ors* [2019] EWCA Civ 679.

24. Before then, the specific reasons for the anonymity order given in *V v T* had been cited with approval in *Gestrust SA v Sixteen Defendants (Including three minors and one minor who has now attained majority)* [2016] EWHC 3067 (Ch).

to the public's—and consequently the children's—attention. In the appeal that followed, the settlors stressed that the minor beneficiaries 'should be brought up to appreciate the importance of education and hard work; to establish themselves in worthwhile careers; to make a positive contribution to society and to choose friends who respect them for their personal qualities rather than for the accident of their birth.'[25] That the fact of the children's wealth was no accident at all seems to have escaped their attention.

The Trust as a Means of Protecting Property

If this is a trend—in an unreported 2018 case in the Cayman courts,[26] the court indeed commented on the trend of very wealthy people to raise their children with neither the trappings nor awareness of that wealth[27]—how is it possible to resolve the incongruence at the heart of this trend? This incongruence is the fact that settlors may use a trust to confer wealth that they know will crush the autonomy of its recipients, yet insist on measures that protect the development of this autonomy—and protect this development not in order to enable its recipients to use the property for their own interests, but so that they will have no need to use it. In that case, why not simply give less and thus limit the risk of over-consumption and dependence in the first place?

An answer to this question emerges when one lets go of the view of the family trust as a species of gift and begins to see it as a means of protecting property—not for the beneficiaries or the family, which is the common view,[28] but for its own sake. The trust, as Cotterrell also realises,[29] gives a form and stability over time to something (often a fund) that in an absolute owner's hands would simply amount to dissipatable wealth. Together with the restrictions and obligations that trusts law places on beneficiaries and trustees during the time that the trust is operative, this form ensures that the trust property is maintained and accumulated rather than spent. The trust thus allows things

---

25. *MN v OP and ors.*
26. *In the Matter of a Settlement dated 16 December 2009* FSD 54/18.
27. Peter Steen and Emilia Piskorz, 'Privacy, Open Justice and the Turning Tide,' *Trusts & Trustees* 24 (2018), 1011. This article also mentions a further English case (*A v XYZ & Ors* [2018] EWHC 1633 (Ch)) in which the claimants similarly sought to protect their children from knowledge about their own wealth.
28. See, for example, John Langbein, 'Burn the Rembrandt? Trust Law's Limits on the Settlor's Power to Direct Investments,' *Boston University Law Review* 90 (2010), 382.
29. Cotterrell, 'Power, Property and the Law of Trusts,' 85.

to 'resist' the control and manipulation associated with the ownership of property. This makes it difficult to conceive of the trust as a species of gift, as which it is so often described.[30] Instead, the trust might sometimes be better described as a gesture of withholding rather than giving property.[31]

However, this view of the trust faces a difficulty of its own that has to do with the way in which the distinction between persons and things operates at the heart of the legal concept of property. In understanding the dynamic between these terms, Louis Dumont's principle of hierarchy may prove helpful.[32] Dumont sought to show how opposing terms employed within a culture stand in a relationship that, as Michael Houseman phrases it, 'is inseparable from a reference to the whole that orders them with respect to each other.'[33] The opposing terms reflect not just a simple opposition, but a value differential or asymmetry (one term attracts a higher value than the other),[34] which arises from their relation to the whole.[35] One term may also be identical with the whole, in which case it encompasses the other term.[36]

Applied to the opposition between persons and things within the concept of property, the following order emerges: The concept of property consists of the opposition 'persons' and 'things,' with all control and power accruing to persons, things being seen as merely passive and manipulable. While persons have interests, things possess neither interests nor the ability to achieve them. Persons, furthermore, have a higher value than things. This higher value arises from the association of persons with the whole, namely property (despite

---

30. See, for example, John Langbein, 'The Contractarian Basis of the Law of Trusts,' *Yale Law Journal* 105 (1995), 632; *T Choithram International SA v Pagarani* [2001] [2001] 1 WLR 1 (PC) [11] (Lord Browne-Wilkinson); F.H. Lawson and Bernard Rudden, *The Law of Property*, 3rd ed. (Oxford: Oxford University Press, 2002), 55.
31. For an in-depth discussion of this view, see Johanna Jacques, 'Property and the Interests of Things: The Case of the Donative Trust,' *Law and Critique* 30 (2019).
32. Louis Dumont, *Essays on Individualism: Modern Ideology in Anthropological Perspective* (Chicago and London: University of Chicago Press, 1986), 253. Also see Michael Houseman, 'The Hierarchical Relation: A Particular Ideology or a General Model?' *Hau: Journal of Ethnographic Theory* 5 (2015), 255. Neither Dumont nor Houseman refer to trusts.
33. Houseman, 'The Hierarchical Relation,' 252.
34. Greg Acciaioli, 'Distinguishing Hierarchy and Precedence: Comparing Status Distinctions in South Asia and the Austronesian World, with Special Reference to South Sulawesi,' in *Social Differentiation in the Austronesian World*, ed. Michael P. Vischer (Canberra, ACT, Australia: ANU E Press, 2009), 53.
35. Houseman, 'The Hierarchical Relation,' 253.
36. This, however, is not a necessary feature. See Acciaioli, 'Distinguishing Hierarchy and Precedence,' 53–4.

the linguistic use of the word 'property' to denote both the thing and the concept). Persons are associated with property because property, that is, the ability to own things, is what is 'proper' only to persons, if not essential to personality.[37] Property is thus always property-of-persons. The term person, then, encompasses its opposite, thing, in a very specific sense; to be a person means to be able to encompass things through possession or consumption, something that is not thought to be possible in reverse. The higher value given to persons also means that property is an arrangement that must always work for the interests of persons, and may only work for things if an ultimate human interest is at stake. A case in point is the notion of property as stewardship, whereby things are preserved and protected from human use, but ultimately for the human good. The presumption of human interests when it comes to property is so pervasive that James Penner writes that 'it would indeed be a funny turn of events if the norms serving our interest in property in essence gave the things a person owned a power over him.'[38]

This means that any view of the trust that regards it as an arrangement that works in the interests of things, not their owners, is difficult to place within the concept of property. Indeed, it may be easier to make sense of the trust by finding a human interest served by the arrangement beyond the immediate access to resources and information that the trust denies. In many cases, such an interest is not hard to come by; Langbein, for example, refers to a number of purposes he classifies as protective but that ultimately serve the interests of the beneficiaries, such as 'to postpone enjoyment until the beneficiaries are more mature [or] to shield potential spendthrifts by restraining their powers of alienation.'[39] However, where settlors entangle themselves in contradictions by settling vast amounts of wealth on their children, supposedly to further the latter's autonomy by providing them with independent means, but then *also* wish to shape these children into individuals who essentially have no need for these means, it becomes difficult to insist that this settlement of wealth upon them still serves the children's interests.

---

37. Hegel, for instance, regards private property rights as the recognition of an embodiment of human will in things that is essential to the attainment of freedom (Georg Wilhelm Friedrich Hegel, *Hegel's Philosophy of Right*, ed. Thomas Malcolm Knox (Oxford: Oxford University Press, 2015). Dialectics, however, represents in itself an alternative analytic principle to that of hierarchy (Houseman, 'The Hierarchical Relation,' 256–7).
38. James E. Penner, *The Idea of Property in Law* (Oxford: Oxford University Press, 1997), 79.
39. Langbein, 'Burn the Rembrandt?,' 382, footnote omitted.

Fortunately, Dumont's principle of hierarchy also accounts for a reversal of the terms that make up a distinction at a lower level of the concept.[40] This reversal affects attributes as well as values, and when applied to the family trust as a sublevel construct of property, it allows for both interests and control to be assigned to the 'thing' side of the distinction. Power is now associated with things, whose interests take precedence over the interests of those who are said to be their owners. Due to the inanimate nature of trust property, however, this reversal requires a further step, namely the recruitment or 'production' of persons who put the property's interests first, thus ensuring its protection.

The Trust as a Means of Producing Personhood

In a family trust where the current beneficiaries of the trust are children, the trust form offers itself not only as a means of protecting the capital of the trust from potential dissipation but also as a means to shape the beneficiaries' attitude to the property. The concern, as far as 'inherited' wealth is concerned,[41] is how to incentivise certain behaviour in beneficiaries. The question is for whose benefit this behaviour is ultimately intended.

Some trusts do not hide their purpose of directing and providing rewards for certain behaviour, as the increasingly popular incentive trust in America shows. Here, the behaviour encouraged through the trust mechanism is generally one that settlors think will contribute to the beneficiaries' well-being and success in life, such as the completion of educational programmes or self-restraint in matters of consumption, although sometimes (for example, where the settlors make any payments to the beneficiaries dependent on the number of offspring they produce)[42] the line between the interests of the settlors and those of the beneficiaries become blurred. Nonetheless, like most protective trusts and trusts for minors, the main purpose of these trusts is to prepare beneficiaries to approach wealth in a way that will be responsible to *themselves* (the person-owners), that is, enable their optimal use of the property in a way that will not lead to unhappiness or ill health.

---

40. Louis Dumont, 'Postface: Towards a Theory of Hierarchy,' in *Homo Hierarchicus* (Chicago: University of Chicago Press, 1980), 239–45.

41. 'Inherited' in the loose sense of not having been earned. Many family trusts are established during the life time of the settlor. They may also run far beyond either the death of the settlor or the maturity of the beneficiaries.

42. Tate, 'Conditional Love: Incentive Trusts and the Inflexibility Problem,' 458.

However, where parent-settlors like those in *V v T* wish for their children to become producers rather than users of wealth while at the same time making them very wealthy, this raises the presumption that the measures they take to prepare their children for this wealth are of a different kind. After all, these measures cannot have been intended to prepare them for the use of the property and the social power it confers. Here, the view offers itself that the responsibility that the settlors seek to instil in the beneficiaries is not to themselves but to *the property*; property which the settlors produced and accumulated over a lifetime and which they do not wish to see dissipated by their heirs in pursuit of their interests or through a lavish lifestyle. If it is the property and *its* interests that the settlors have in mind when establishing the trust, the trust then becomes a means to further these interests. Rather than telling their children what they would like to happen to the property and hoping that their wishes will be honoured, parents use the trust form to enshrine the interests of the property in law. As Richard Posner writes, trusts are 'based on mistrust.'[43]

While the trust form ensures the successful restriction of the use of property by the beneficiaries during the trust's lifetime, for example through enshrining the property's interests in the trust instrument (houses must be maintained and may not be sold off, money may only be invested in certain stocks etc.) and enforcing these interests through the parties to the trust as well as the courts, settlors have no control over what happens when the trust ends. As the law restricts the period in which trust capital and income may be withheld from beneficiaries,[44] sooner or later the attitude of the beneficiaries to the property will become of paramount importance if the property is to be protected on an ongoing basis.

How does the trust form allow for the shaping of this attitude? Here, the trust offers a solution that complements the other restrictions it already places on the access of beneficiaries to the trust property: privacy. Thus, under normal circumstances there is no requirement for parent-settlors or trustees to inform children-beneficiaries of the wealth settled on trust for them, and the general private nature of the trust means that often little, if any, information about the trust is known

---

43. Richard A. Posner, *Economic Analysis of Law* (New York: Wolters Kluwer Law & Business, 2014), 717. Despite this insight, Posner thinks that trusts are 'actuated by altruism' (Posner, *Economic Analysis of Law*, 717).
44. Perpetuities and Accumulations Act 2009; *Saunders v Vautier* (1841) 4 Beav 115, 49 ER 282.

by third parties or is in the public domain.[45] It is only when settlors or trustees wish to vary a trust or for other reasons apply to the court that this privacy is threatened and information about the trust may enter the public domain. At this point settlors like those in *V v T* ask for privacy in order to keep knowledge about their wealth secret from their children.

This claim to privacy can be seen as ensuring that beneficiaries do not develop needs of consumption proportionate to their wealth, needs which they may eventually seek to satisfy with trust property. Such consumption would run counter to the intended protection of the trust property envisaged by the settlors. It can also be seen as ensuring that beneficiaries develop independent means of producing wealth so that they add to rather than take from the trust property. The concern with the autonomy of the beneficiaries thus reveals itself as a concern with the protection of property. Only if beneficiaries become independent in their production of the means they need to attain their interests is the trust property safe from their hands even after the point at which the restrictions of the trust are no longer operative.

The autonomy aimed at by the settlors therefore cannot be an open freedom to determine one's life using the resources that one's wealth provides; it is a freedom that is already predetermined towards production, a freedom where, by the time the person begins to think about using a thing for his or her own interests, that is, as a consumer, that thing has already recruited the person for *its* interests, that is, as a producer. By the time the adult beneficiaries receive the trust funds absolutely, they will value their independence from the property and will want to show that they do not need it. And what better way to show this absence of dependence than to increase the value of the property, encourage its growth, and ultimately, 'give' it away by settling it on trust once again for the next generation? In this way, property survives intact over generations, being looked after, added to, and ultimately, passed on.

Conclusion

Roger Cotterrell writes that the '"disembodied", unowned property' represented by private purpose trusts is not accepted under English law

---

45. A fact which has, however, started to change with the introduction of the OECD's Common Reporting Standard and beneficial ownership registers under European legislation, even though these measures remain contested and are also subject to exemptions (see, for example, the text accompanying footnote 9).

because 'property necessarily represents in ideological form the attributes of power of someone or some collectivity' and therefore needs to reflect that power. He concludes that 'the law cannot comprehend property without any beneficial owner.'[46] This chapter has tried to show that the family trust can subvert this idea of a one-sided ownership relation by effecting a reversal in the hierarchical distinction between persons and things. Under the appearance of wealth, beneficial owners are serving the very things they own by ensuring their protection and continuous reproduction.

This creates precisely a 'disembodiment' in the sense that owning trust property as a beneficiary no longer entails the association of property with the interests of its owners. Instead, property comes to possess its own interests, which are enshrined in the trust instrument and protected and enforced by the mechanisms of the trust. But this is not all. As recent case law shows, settlors seek to use privacy to ensure that beneficiaries develop into persons who will not only have no need for the property they will eventually come to own absolutely, but will also add to this property, thus ensuring its growth over time. This constitutes a 're-embodiment' of persons in line with the interests of things. One way of describing this process would be to say that the trust property, through the rights and obligations assigned to it by the settlors and through the operation of the law, reaches beyond the duration of the trust and shapes its future owners in a way that is conducive to its continued existence. While in practice the line between a family trust that has the best interests of the beneficiaries at heart and a trust that hides a concern with the protection of the trust property behind these interests might be a fine one, the existence of contradictory gestures by the settlors indicates that all is not as it seems. Settlors wanting their children to both be excessively wealthy and to have no need for such wealth are one example of such a contradiction.

With this, the question of 'embodiment' becomes a question that is no longer about ownership but about the way in which the 'bodies' to which things are attached are shaped by the legal rules that govern this attachment in the first place. If things can co-opt the legal rules governing their use in such a way as to create for themselves a certain kind of owner, then not only does the question of the social power that property ownership is said to convey become secondary—the persons holding this power should in themselves be regarded as shaped by the property regime in which they partake—but the concept of the social

---

46.   Cotterrell, 'Power, Property and the Law of Trusts,' 88.

must also change: Rather than exclude them, it must include the very things that are the 'objects' of property law.

This means that even in the law of trusts, where terms such as 'ownership,' 'person,' and 'thing' are still often employed as if they had stable, definite meanings,[47] law can no longer be seen as the means for structuring human power through the production and control of things. Instead, it should be seen as the mesh in which different agents are caught struggling over who can produce and control whom, and who has the better tools to ensure their own continued existence. On this reading, the family trust is not only a tool that enables and enhances individual and familial existence over time but also a tool for the continued existence of things. The resulting growth in things could be called a growth in wealth if wealth were not always understood as the wealth *of* someone. Paradoxically for the family trust as an arrangement for hyper-private property ownership, it allows property to free itself from the interests of its owners. Beneath the overall concept of property, the family trust thus enables things to enter a regime of property-as-such.

In the final analysis, Cotterrell's critique of the trust is therefore short-sighted—not because it does not realise the private power at work in trusts but because it situates this power exclusively at one end of the person-thing distinction. Perhaps this is not surprising given that he does not question the stability of this distinction. If one accepts that things can be represented at law and that they can thus have control over their own fate, then the assumption that the ownership relation always works for the interests of persons needs to be abandoned. Who really owns whom will on this account need to be established on the facts.

This two-way understanding of property affects not only the narrative of autonomy with which private property rights are commonly justified (could one still justify property rights if persons were no longer able to exercise them to further their own interests?) but also the real existence of personal autonomy, as persons may be controlled by things even when they believe themselves to be in control. At its most cynical,

---

47. In other areas of property law the meanings of 'ownership,' 'person,' and 'thing' have in themselves been subject to discussion. Alain Pottage thus notes in relation to biotechnological patents that here 'property theory's ontological presuppositions about persons and things, or about nature and artifice, are dissolved, and ... the need for legal operations to coordinate economic, scientific, and political exp`ectations, each of which fabricates different interests and entities, works a profound transformation in the pragmatics of "property"' (Alain Pottage, 'Instituting Property,' *Oxford Journal of Legal Studies* 18 (1998), 340).

it could also show a paradoxical state of affairs where autonomy—the independence of the subject from determining structures and its capacity for self-mastery—is no longer sought for the ultimate human good but to further the interests of things.

5

The Myth of the Powerless Beneficiary and Twenty-First Century Trusts

Carla Spivack *

Introduction

In 1998, Kyle Krueger sexually assaulted a four year-old boy, video-taped the act and circulated the videotape on the internet, for which he was criminally convicted.[1] The boy's mother, Lorie Scheffel, filed a civil suit on behalf of both herself and her son seeking damages, and was awarded $551,286.25. Krueger's only assets, however, were in the form of a trust with a spendthrift clause, which barred the trust assets from attachment by creditors. The trust assets were worth about $12 million.[2] The law of the state upheld the validity of such clauses. Lorie Scheffel argued for a public policy exception to the law because it prevented tort victims, who, unlike voluntary creditors, had no choice in the matter, from being compensated for harm. This, she argued, contravened the state's strong public policy of having crime victims

* Albany Law School, Albany, New York. My profound thanks to Paula J. Dalley, whose insight and clarity of mind brought this article back to life; to my colleagues at Boston College, Oklahoma City University and elsewhere: Alfred L. Brophy, Bridget Crawford, Greg Eddington, Michael Grynberg, Adam Hirsch, Ray Madoff, Chad Pomeroy, William LaPiana, Kent D. Schenkel, and Robert Sitkoff. Aspects of this chapter draw on Carla Spivack, 'Democracy and Trusts,' *ACTEC Law Journal* 42 (2017).
1. *Scheffel v Krueger* 782 A 2d 410 (NH 2001). For criticism of the decision in this case, see e.g. Kent Schenkel, 'Exposing the Hocus Pocus of Trusts,' *Akron Law Review* 45 (2012), observing that outcomes like this increase insurance costs; John K. Eason, Developing The Asset Protection Dynamic: A Legacy Of Federal Concern,' *Hofstra Law Review* 31 (2002), 45 n. 94, noting the injustice of the spendthrift provisions when applied to involuntary creditors, such as tort creditors.
2. 1998 WL 35390969 (NH Super) (Plaintiff's Trial Motion, Memorandum and Affidavit).

get compensation from the perpetrator.[3] The court refused to make this exception, however, citing a long-held policy not to 'question the wisdom or expediency of a statute.'[4]

One might think that there is something wrong with a system of property law that allows such manoeuvres. And, indeed, spendthrift trusts like these, which shield assets from the beneficiary's creditors—whether voluntary or involuntary—have been controversial since their advent in the nineteenth century.[5] John Chipman Gray challenged the legitimacy of a gift that is not subject to the claims of the donee's creditors and thus allows the donee to 'indulge himself simultaneously in both luxury and indebtedness.'[6] Objections to the bar to recovery by voluntary creditors have subsided somewhat today, but criticism of the bar to recovery by tort creditors is alive and well: voluntary creditors can investigate the assets of potential debtors, the argument goes, but tort victims have no such opportunity, and thus should be able to reach trust assets to recover damages.[7] Whatever one thinks about this, the fact is that spendthrift trusts are well established in American law.

The Title Split Paradigm and the 'Powerless' Beneficiary

Spendthrift trusts exemplify the phenomenon Roger Cotterrell calls the concealment of the 'property power' of the beneficiary. In his article 'Power, Property and the Law of Trusts: A Partial Agenda for Critical Legal Scholarship,'[8] Roger Cotterrell demystified the trust concept and laid bare the ideological work that concept has done and continues to do. It obscures what Cotterrell calls 'property power'—the social power access to and use of wealth give the holder, i.e. the beneficiary.

---

3. 1998 WL 35390969 (NH Super) (Plaintiff's Trial Motion, Memorandum and Affidavit).
4. *Scheffel v Krueger*, 672–673.
5. John Chipman Gray, *Restraints on the Alienation of Property*, 2nd ed. (Boston: Boston Book Co, 1895), 247.
6. Gray, *Restraints on the Alienation of Property*, x.
7. See e.g. Laurene M. Brooks, 'A Tort-Creditor Exception to the Spendthrift Trust Doctrine: A Call to the Wisconsin Legislature,' *Marquette Law Review* 73 (1989), 133–41; Frank A. Gregory, 'Trusts: Tort Claims as an Exception to the Spendthrift Trust Doctrine,' *Oklahoma Law Review* 17 (1964) 237–38 (1964); William N. Antonis, 'Spendthrift Trusts: Attachability of a Beneficiary's Interest in Satisfaction of a Tort Claim,' *Notre Dame Law Review* 28 (1953), 515; Weston C. Overholt, Jr., 'Tort Liability of the Beneficiary of a Spendthrift Trust,' *Dickinson Law Review* 57 (1953) 221–22.
8. Roger Cotterrell, 'Power, Property and the Law of Trusts: A Partial Agenda for Critical Legal Scholarship,' *Journal of Law and Society* 14 (1987).

In the same piece, he calls on critical legal studies to confront and undermine 'the duality of the human subject and social object … and the alienation and oppression which result from this duality.'[9] This duality makes humans see themselves as separate from and powerless over society and social institutions. Critical legal studies can make the connection between human actors and 'those characteristics and attributes which give the [human] actor power.'[10] Showcasing the trust as an example of this duality, Cotterrell explains how the myths of title split and the powerless beneficiary serve to 'free[] the property owner from constraints which the ideology of property otherwise imposes on her or him through its logic.'[11] These myths hide the reality that the beneficiary has the power associated with access to property—'property power.' Through its ideology, the trust creates a property owner who is free of the obligations the law otherwise imposes on property owners—debts, liabilities, taxes.

Cotterrell explained that the mechanism of the trust—splitting title between a legal and an equitable owner, the trustee and the beneficiary—allows the equitable owner to 'share in property-power but remain invisible to law as [a property owner] as such.'[12] In the title split paradigm, the beneficiary appears to be passive, with little or no control over the distribution or management of trust assets, which appears to be the purview of the trustee. In fact, ideology constructs the beneficiary as in need of protection. Yet, Cotterrell points out, this appearance is misleading. It is the beneficiaries who actually have access to the power associated with the trust property. Ironically, then, the trust 'fails to impose moral obligations' on that power holder, but even 'encourages us to think of moral obligations owed to them because of their beneficial entitlements.'[13] As others have also pointed out, the trust with a spendthrift clause actually increases the beneficiary's interest because it cuts off the obligations of property ownership which normally attach to its enjoyment.[14] In this light, the ability of the settlor to protect her own assets from her creditors is a logical extension of ideological work the trust has done for centuries.

---

9. Cotterrell, 'Power, Property and the Law of Trusts,' 81.
10. Cotterrell, 'Power, Property and the Law of Trusts,' 81.
11. Cotterrell, 'Power, Property and the Law of Trusts,' 83.
12. Cotterrell, 'Power, Property and the Law of Trusts,' 88.
13. Cotterrell, 'Power, Property and the Law of Trusts,' 88.
14. See e.g. Kent D. Schenkel, 'Trust Law and the Title Split: A Beneficial Perspective,' *University of Missouri-Kansas City Law Review* 78 (2009).

The mystification of the beneficial use is almost as old as the trust itself. Early English ecclesiastics used it to evade the mortmain statutes, which forbade the conveyance of land to the Church: instead, religious orders would arrange for its transfer to a layperson who would hold legal title to the property 'for the use of' the Church.[15] The Franciscans made ingenious use of the device: sworn to poverty, they soon came up with what Maitland calls 'a remarkable plan:'[16] the would-be benefactor would convey a house to the borough for 'the use of' the friars.[17] Despite the legal technicality, the friars had full rights over the property they received in this way, including the right to give, sell or exchange it.[18]

Cotterrell's point does not contradict the fact that some beneficiaries are indeed in need of protection, vulnerable, or truly incapable of exercising financial power in any effective way. An important function of trusts is to protect such people—the mentally disabled, minors, for example—from exploitation and loss of wealth. Cotterrell's point is not to deny this; rather, he is describing the ideology of the trust form itself, regardless of the characteristics of the beneficiary. He might well agree that there are cases in which there is a truly helpless beneficiary, and many in which there are not.[19] His point is that this ideology obscures that difference. It paints *all* beneficiaries as by definition powerless, and it does so in order to separate property ownership from the obligations the law normally attaches to it. As a corollary, the beneficiary is often invisible as well: not specifically identified in the trust instrument except by class, because, without power, he might as well be invisible to creditors and the rest of the world as well.

The Beneficiary in European Jurisdictions

The ideological work of whitewashing the beneficiary's 'property power' has always been a feature of the Anglo-American trust, especially the spendthrift trust. Other legal regimes that recognize the trust in a more limited form have a trust jurisprudence less affected by this ideology. For example, the French *fiducie* is statutory (as of 2007) and narrow

---

15. S.F.C. Milsom, *The Historical Foundations of the Common Law* (London: Butterworths, 1969), 173.
16. F.W. Maitland, 'The Origin of Uses,' *Harvard Law Review* 8 (1894), 130.
17. F.W. Maitland, 'The Origin of Uses,' 130.
18. Gilbert Paul Verbit, *The Origins of the Trust* (Authorhouse, 2002), 209.
19. See Cotterrell, 'Power, Property and the Law of Trusts,' 87 on property as security.

in scope: it is available only to corporations and is invalid if formed with the sole intention of benefiting an individual beneficiary. Similarly, Dutch law is much more restrictive in its definition and allowed uses of the trust. This civil law 'distrust of the trust' may stem from the desire of the drafters of the 1787 French Civil Code to do away with all feudal forms of property, split title in particular: they defined property ownership as absolute and unitary.[20] The 1798 Dutch Constitution was a product of French influence, for example, and its drafters also sought to erase all traces of feudalism from the law;[21] this may account for a similar approach to these issues.

Another clear example of this difference between the common law and the civil law trust ideology regarding the powerless beneficiary is the EU Trust Registry. In 2011, the European Parliament passed an EU-wide Registry of trusts, which lists the identity of all those with beneficial interests—settlors, trustees and beneficiaries—in a particular trust.[22] The version that finally passed was slightly scaled down from the original proposal: instead of making the registry public as in the draft version, it made it available only to national regulators tasked with combatting money laundering. Nonetheless, perhaps expressing a particularly common law view, British lawmakers and financial industry professionals were enraged. 'We consider registration of trusts to be a disproportionate approach and, in particular, one which undermines the common-law basis of trusts in the UK,' stormed an MP.[23] This outburst reflects how central the ideology of the invisible beneficiary is to the common law trust.

At around the same time, both France and The Netherlands passed new trust taxation regimes which reflect a similar attempt to make visible—demystify—beneficial interests of trusts. Both of these regimes treat the trust as transparent for tax purposes, i.e. they tax either

---

20. Sjef van Erp and Brams Akkerman, *Cases, Materials and Text on Property Law* (Oxford: Hart Publishing, 2012), 54.

21. Jeroen Chorus, Ewoud Hondius, and Piet-Hein Gerver, *Introduction to Dutch Law* (Kluwer International, 2006), 8.

22. Directive (EU) 2015/849 of the European Parliament and of the Council of 20 May 2015 on the prevention of the use of the financial system for the purposes of money laundering or terrorist financing, amending Regulation (EU) No 648/2012 of the European Parliament and of the Council, and repealing Directive 2005/60/EC of the European Parliament and of the Council and Commission Directive 2006/70/EC [2015] OJ L 141/73.

23. Quoted in Andres Knobel, 'Trusts and the UK: Half a Step Forward, Three Steps Backwards,' 19 December 2017, accessed 5 March 2024, https://taxjustice. net/2017/12/19/trusts-uk-half-step-forward-three-steps-backwards/.

the settlor or the beneficiaries on the assets of a trust, whether they are receiving distributions from the trust or not.[24]

Together, these two European developments take aim at the very heart of the common law trust: first, the Trust Registry eliminates the secrecy of trusts, a central feature of the trust since its beginnings in medieval England. Second, the new tax regimes pull large sums of hitherto tax-free assets into the tax revenue stream, eliminating many of the tax advantages that accrue to the trust, especially in the United States. Both regimes, in effect, make 'visible' assets which were previously hidden from the tax authorities, and take seriously the importance of the beneficiary.[25] Indeed, the Dutch tax laws were a reaction to the effects of that country's ratification of the Hague Convention and fears that it would allow Dutch citizens to avoid taxes by setting up foreign trusts.[26]

New Branches on the Spendthrift Trust Tree: Asset Protection Trusts and Dynasty Trusts in the US

American trust law, however, has veered in the opposite direction, taking the notion of spendthrift protection—and hence the ideology of the helpless beneficiary—much farther. Current law in many states allows settlors to protect not only the beneficiary's assets, but their own, from creditors. These trusts are called 'self-settled asset protection trusts' or, when codified in US states, 'domestic asset protection trusts' (DAPTs). In a parallel development, more and more states allow so-called 'dynasty trusts' which allow settlors and beneficiaries to maintain assets in trust tax free for generations, overturning long-settled principles of the common law such as the rule against perpetuities. I focus here on these two developments, but it needs keeping in mind that DAPTs in particular are a branch of the spendthrift trust tree.

Today's new generation of American dynasty trusts and DAPTs carries the ideology of the powerless beneficiary to an extreme. American law adds to this mystification process by allowing the doctrine of 'testamentary freedom' to obscure the other property interests at stake in trusts. American law valorizes testamentary freedom to a much

---

24. Loi de Finances Rectificative of July 31, 2011; Art 2.14a PITA 2001, the so-called 'Afgezonderd Particulier Vermogen' [the Separated Private Fund].
25. On the theme of visibility of beneficial interests, see also the chapters by Gearey, Jacques and Knobel in this collection.
26. J.P. Boer, 'Summary—The Anglo-American Trust in Dutch Personal and Corporate Income Taxation,' (2011), accessed 5 March 2024, https://hdl.handle.net/1887/17699.

greater degree than most other systems of succession law. Unlike most European jurisdictions, for example, American law allows parents to disinherit children, even minor or disabled ones, as an exercise of this 'freedom.'

The American ideology of 'testamentary freedom'—the belief that a testator or settlor has the right to control the use of his property after death—contributes to this process by further obscuring the reality of the trust and the property-power of the beneficiary.[27] The ideology of testamentary freedom privileges the intent of long dead settlors of trusts to protect their family members from the constraints of property ownership.[28] In doing so, it also hides the obliteration of the property rights of others which is an integral part of the function of the trust. The ideology of testamentary freedom turns property rights which conflict with the trust—spousal shares, child support, creditors' claims—from property into 'public policy' concerns, often regarding the public purse, which have much less traction than rights to property.[29] For example, one court ruled that a decedent's transfer of most of his assets into a revocable trust with his daughter as the beneficiary did not constitute a fraud on his surviving spouse's property rights as long as it was a 'reasonable and legitimate estate planning arrangement.'[30] In essence, the court said an arrangement which deprived his surviving spouse of property rights under state law was legitimate as an expression of his testamentary freedom, as long as it was not explicitly designed to cheat her.

The ideology of testamentary freedom distracts from the property-power of the beneficiary by making him look like a passive victim of the settlor's whims. This obscures not only the beneficiary's property power, but also the property rights of third parties, which the trust eliminates. The law then relegates the rights of third parties to the realm

---

27.   Reid Kress Weisbord, 'Wills for Everyone: Helping Individuals Opt out of Intestacy,' *Boston College Law Review* 53 (2012) 896.

28.   See generally Schenkel, 'Exposing the Hocus Pocus of Trusts,' 76 referring to the nineteenth century Massachusetts case *Nichols v Eaton*, which justified the spendthrift clause on the basis that 'on the settlor's freedom of disposition of her property [and] supporting] a donor's desire to benefit loved ones, [Justice Miller] said quite simply that he found no reason to rule that a donor should not be able to give property away and make it exempt from the claims of the donee's creditors.'

29.   See e.g. *Shelley v Shelley* 354 P.2d. 281, 286 (Or. 1960), noting that 'public policy requires that the interest of a beneficiary of a trust should be subject to the claims for support of his children' because '[w]e do not believe it is sound to use the welfare funds of the state in support of the beneficiary's children while he stands behind the shield of immunity created by a spendthrift trust provision.'

30.   *Karsenty v Shoukroun* 959 A. 2d. 1147, 1174 (Md. 2008).

of 'public policy,' a vague area in which the interests of third parties appear to be idiosyncratic and limited impositions upon the settlor's freedom.[31]

In reality, every restriction placed on a beneficiary's interest—say, to withhold her assets from creditors—impairs a corresponding property right—here the creditor's right to payment. Third party rights in such cases have been lost in the shadow of the 'right' of testamentary freedom, but they are not lesser rights. DAPTs, which a settlor may create during life, may be the most egregious example of this: the settlor's right to keep his assets immune from spousal support claims—whether arising from divorce or death—impairs the property rights of the spouse, who can no longer claim what the law has defined as her property. Spendthrift clauses bar a tort victim from property the law has defined as hers—adjudicated damages—a right to property otherwise guaranteed by our civil justice system. More broadly, the settlor's right to keep her assets tax-free in a dynasty trust requires an unspoken redefinition of everyone else's property: the rest of us must either accept a new, reduced, definition of our property or drive on broken roads.

One might argue that voluntary creditors—banks, credit card companies, etc—who do business with trust beneficiaries are able to protect themselves through due diligence: surely they can investigate the resources of potential borrowers to ascertain the nature of their assets. and can ascertain the existence of trusts which might bar recovery. This is not always the case in reality, however: some states' statutes of limitations for raising fraudulent transfer claims are so short (120 days for transfers to DAPTs in Utah,[32] 30 days in Alaska[33]) that a debtor could quickly become judgment proof four months after sending notice to creditors.[34]

The property rights that disappear under these regimes are as 'real' as the rights the trust creates. The state's law defines property. When a court orders spousal and child support, or asset division, the law has defined those assets as property of the receiving spouse. While many states have traditionally made so-called 'public policy' exceptions

---

31. See e.g. *Ventura County Dept. of Child Support Services v Brown*, 117 CA4th 144, 154–155, 11 CR3d 489, 497 (2004), holding that it was against public policy to apply spendthrift clause to child support claims.
32. Utah Code Ann. § 25-6-14 (2007).
33. A. S. A. 6-26.790. But see *Toni 1 Trust v Barbara Wacker*, 2018 WL 1125033 (Alaska 2018.) infra p. 19.
34. Utah Code Ann. §25-6- 14(9).

to spendthrift trusts for certain so-called 'super creditors,' like ex-spouses and children with support orders, the new generation of DAPTs shrinks these exceptions considerably. Utah, for example, bars all claims against the assets of a DAPT including those for court ordered child and spousal support,[35] as does Nevada.[36] Similarly, Alaska law bars challenges to transfers made to a DAPT to avoid support claims,[37] and it only allows a child support creditor to reach trust assets if the payment is 30 days overdue at the time the trust is created.[38] This is also the case with Hawaii DAPT law.[39] Indeed, avoidance of child support and other forms of family obligations are one of the selling points of DAPTs: one website touts Nevada as the only state that includes ex-spouse and child support creditors in those who may not gain access to protected assets in an asset protection trust; it advertises its trusts as truly 'divorce-proof.'[40] In these states, private law trumps the state law's definition of property—usually unbeknownst to those whose rights disappear.

Trusts achieve this same result through means of decanting clauses. These clauses allow trustees to transfer—'decant'—assets threatened by competing property rights into new trusts drafted to eliminate those very rights. For example, in the case of *Ferri*,[41] a trust beneficiary undergoing divorce worried that the trust assets he was entitled to were at risk of being deemed 'marital property.'[42] To prevent this outcome, the trustee—the beneficiary's brother—decanted the trust assets into a new trust whose terms made the assets immune from spousal claims.[43] The Massachusetts Supreme Judicial Court ruled this decanting valid despite the spouse's conflicting right to marital property.[44] It based the holding on narrow grounds that ignored the beneficiary's 'property-power' in the trust assets: it ruled that because the trustee had legal title, and because the trust instrument gave him absolute discretion,

---

35. Utah Code Ann. §25-6-14(3).

36. Nev. Rev. Stat. §166.120 (2012).

37. Alaska Stat. §13.36.13(a) (2012).

38. Alaska Stat. §34-40-110(b)(4) (2012).

39. Haw. Rev. Stat. §554G-91 (2012).

40. American Academy for Certified Financial Litigators blog, 'Why Nevada Is a Popular Destination for Those Who Want a Divorce-Proof Trust,' posted 3 February 2021, accessed 19 March 2024, https://aacfl.org/why-nevada-is-a-popular-destination-for-those-who-want-a-divorce-proof-trust?doing_wp_cron=1710639295.976763963 6993408203125.

41. *Ferri v Powell-Ferri* 476 Mass 651 (2017).

42. *Ferri v Powell-Ferri*, 653.

43. *Ferri v Powell-Ferri*, 653.

44. *Ferri v Powell-Ferri*, 663.

he was authorized to decant the assets.[45] The ruling makes the beneficiary's obvious control of the assets through his brother trustee disappear into thin air by waving the magic wand of title split and the myth of the passive beneficiary.

As noted, dynasty trusts also impinge on third parties' property rights by redefining their proportion of taxation. These trusts avoid taxes in a number of ways: among other strategies, they are established in states that have no income tax, and they avoid Federal taxes by being funded with exempt amounts that can grow tax-free in the trust. The shift of the tax burden due to the rise in dynasty trusts is substantial. A 2003 study estimated that the amount of capital these trusts shelter from taxes was around one hundred billion dollars (then),[46] and, because of the invisibility of private trust companies, this may drastically undervalue the true amount.[47] What this means is that settlors and beneficiaries of these trusts avoid their obligations to participate in a progressive tax system, leaving others to foot the bill, or do without. Dynasty trust beneficiaries' 'right' to avoid taxes triggers an obligation on the part of everyone else to make up the difference, thus forcing a redefinition of what their property is.

So at the new millennium we have two new forms of trust which take the mystification of title split to an extreme. The original spendthrift trust served to protect the vulnerable from exploitation. The vulnerable today—the mentally incapacitated or disabled, for example—still may need this kind of protection, and if their families are able to offer it, it seems like a fair policy decision to allow it.[48] To allow this protective mechanism, however, to devolve into a sleight of hand to hide a transferor's assets from the consequences of his own wrongdoing or improvidence, is not. This has long been the limit of English law: the prohibition against the transfer of funds into a trust for the benefit of the transferor goes back to 1487, the reign of Henry VII.[49]

---

45. *Ferri v Powell-Ferri*, 663.

46. Staff of Joint Comm. on Taxation, 112th Cong., Description of Revenue Provisions Contained in the President's Fiscal Year 2012 Budget Proposal 522 (2011) at 526.

47. Ray D. Madoff, *Immortality and the Law: The Rising Power of the American Dead* (Yale University Press, 2010), 76–84, describing dynasty trusts and the evolving treatment of them.

48. Of course, this leaves families without means out in the cold. But with the entrenched privatization of care in the US, it seems unreasonable to tell people they can't use their assets to take care of their own, if they are able.

49. Austin Wakeman Scott and William Franklin Fratcher, *The Law of Trusts*, 4th ed. (1987), volume 2A §156, tracing the origin of this rule to the 1487 Statute of King Henry VII, Stat. 3 Hen. VII, c.4, which voided conveyances in trust for the use of the transferor.

The legal and financial obscurity of self-settled and dynasty trusts pushes this reality even further into the shadows. The majority of private trusts today consist of assets other than real property—money, stocks and bonds, etc.[50] Unlike deeds to real property and wills, which are publicly recorded, trusts are completely private instruments. If a settlor transfers her estate to a trust during life—a 'living trust'—the instrument will likely remain private. There is no public registry of trusts in the United States, as there is in the EU.[51] Federal law requires banks which manage trusts to make reports about the assets they control, but private trust companies, which represent a growing trend among the wealthy, are under no such obligations.[52] According to Hoover's Online, in 2016 there were 22,000 private trust companies in the United States.[53] Uncovering the interest holders and determining the terms of the trust under private management—important information for putative creditors—can be daunting, or impossible. Indeed, one of the main reason the wealthy create these companies in the first place is to keep their assets and affairs confidential.[54] This undermines the transparency norm of property law by making information about the assets—or even their very existence—costly to uncover.

How did these trusts come into existence? The myth of title split and the powerless beneficiary are extremely useful to those who wish to aggregate property power in invisible hands. The legislatures which have passed these forms of the trust are more responsive to the interests of those members of society with assets, connections and influence than to those of society at large.[55] The rush by state legislatures to repeal

---

50.   Iris J. Goodwin, 'How the Rich Stay Rich: Using a Family Trust Company to Secure a Family Fortune,' *Seton Hall Law Review* 40 (2010).
51.   It lists settlors, trustees and beneficial interest holders of EU trusts, and is open to national officials responsible for anti-money laundering and tax evasion efforts.
52.   Alan V. Ytterberg and James P. Weller, 'Managing Family Wealth Through a Private Trust Company,' *ACTEC Law Journal* 36 (2010).
53.   Last accessed 10 July 2016. The webpage is no longer available.
54.   Todd Ganos, 'Wealthy Families Create Private Trust Companies for Privacy, Protection, Tax Savings, and Control,' *Forbes*, 28 October 2015, accessed 5 March 2024, https://www.forbes.com/sites/toddganos/2015/10/28/wealthy-families-create-private-trust-companies-for-privacy-protection-tax-savings-and-control. See also Alan V. Ytterberg and James P. Weller, 'Managing Family Wealth,' 628.
55.   For investigations of the role of lobbying and money on legislatures, see e.g. Linda Powell, 'How Money Talks in State Legislatures,' *Washington Post*, 5 November 2013, accessed 5 March 2024, https://www.washingtonpost.com/news/monkey-cage/wp/2013/11/05/the-influence-of-money-in-u-s-politics, analyzing the mechanics of donor influence on the drafting and progress of legislation). See also Jesse Dukeminier and Robert Sitkoff, *Wills, Trusts and Estates*, 9th ed. (Wolters Kluwer Law & Business, 2013) 705, asserting that 'local bankers and lawyers, who stand to gain from an influx

the rule against perpetuities and pass dynasty trusts has been the result of lobbying by the wealthy, their lawyers, bankers, and trust managers,[56] at times in the face of explicit popular rejection of these innovations.[57]

Typically, the special interests who stand to benefit from these new trusts control the drafting, introduction and debate about them. For example, the Maine dynasty trust bill passed 'after a lopsided debate whose key contributors were members of the banking lobby and attorneys in private practice who stood to gain the most from its passage.'[58] Nevada offers another example of this lack of democratic process: when proponents of perpetual trusts in that state held a state-wide referendum to repeal the state constitution's anti-perpetuity provision, voters rejected it by a margin if 60 percent.[59] Nonetheless, the state legislature passed a law—drafted by a committee which included members of a Nevada trusts and estates law firm[60]—allowing trusts to endure for 365 years.[61] In Michigan, the Greenleaf Trust Company, represented by a local law firm, 'spearheaded' perpetual trusts passage in that state.[62] In Connecticut, local banks and lawyers argued that 'people who want to set up dynastic trusts for their grandchildren, great-grandchildren and down the line of generations, are doing them in other states.'[63] Indeed, the lawyer who headed the lobbying efforts in the Connecticut Legislature reported that the at the hearing on the bill 'a kind of bidding war ensued as legislators extended the time period from 90 to 100 to 360 years, finally ending at a 2000 year period limitations.'[64] The New

---

of trust assets, have lobbied for [DAPTs and dynasty trusts].'

56.   See e.g. Grayson M.P. McCouch, 'Who Killed the Rule against Perpetuities?' *Pepperdine Law Review* 40 (2013), 1295, noting in 2013 that In the space of less than twenty years, at least half the states, responding to intense lobbying by lawyers, bankers, and financial planners, have enacted statutes authorizing perpetual trusts, with the express goal of attracting trust business from other states.'

57.   Steven J. Horowitz and Robert H. Sitkoff, 'Unconstitutional Perpetual Trusts' *Vanderbilt Law Review* 677 (2014), 1773.

58.   Chris Stevenson, 'Maine's Dynasty Trust Statute: The Product of an Informed Judgment,' *Maine Bar Journal* 23 (2008), 230.

59.   'Election 2002', *Reno Gazette*, 8 November 2002 at 3C.

60.   Steven J. Oshins, 'The New Nevada 365-Year Dynasty Trusts: Nevada Becomes a Leading Dynasty Trust State,' *Communique* (March 2006).

61.   N.R.S. 111.1031(1)(b).

62.   Karen L. Kayes, 'Building a Dynasty: Michigan Law Now Allows Perpetual Trusts,' posted on Warner Norcross & Judd website 27 November 2008, available at: https://casetext.com/analysis/building-a-dynasty-michigan-law-now-allows-perpetual-trusts (accessed 5 March 2024).

63.   Thomas Scheffey, 'Is Immortality Just around the Corner? "Dead Hand" Trust Law Relaxes Its Grip,' *Connecticut Law Tribune*, 4 March 2002, at 10 quoting 'veteran estate tax specialist' Frank S. Berall.

64.   Sheffey, 'Is Immortality Just around the Corner?'

Jersey legislature passed the Trust Modernization Bill overturning the ban on perpetuities which was sponsored by the New Jersey Bankers Association.[65] There have also been efforts, so far unsuccessful, to repeal state constitutional bans on perpetuities in North Carolina and Texas.[66] As Sitkoff and Horowitz note, 'lawyers and bankers have lobbied for perpetual trusts to attract, or at least retain, trust business.'[67]

Conclusions

The law must swallow a spoonful of legal realism and face the true nature of these trusts. The expansion of the trust I have been describing is in effect an opt-out of property law by stealth.[68] Courts like the *Ferri* court must extricate themselves from the formalism which blinds them to the reality of trusts and the property-power of the beneficiary. This is a place where courts have a role: they can—and do—police the boundaries of the universe of property forms.[69]

Traditionally, the doctrine of 'property exceptionalism' has relegated decisions about property forms to legislatures and kept them out of the hands of judges.[70] This is because, for property forms to enjoy legitimacy, they must be the products of democratic 'co-authorship'— that is, legislation by elected representatives from all interest groups in society—and judicial decisions are not 'co-authored' in this way.[71] It's not clear that this rationale always holds up, however. Even proponents of legislative decision-making about property acknowledge the

---

65. Rachel Wolcott, 'New Jersey Poised to Allow Dynasty Trusts,' *Private Asset Management*, 17 May 1999, 6, 10.
66. For North Carolina see Act of 23 March 2011, 2011 N.C. S.B. 398, 2011 Gen. Assemb., Reg. Sess. (N.C. 2011); for Texas see Ashley Vaughan, 'You Can't Take it with You: Property Rights after Death and Rethinking the Rule against Perpetuities,' *South Texas Law Review* 47 (2006), 637–39.
67. Horowitz and Sitkoff, 'Unconstitutional Perpetual Trusts.'
68. On trusts and the subversion of law see Bennett and Hofri-Winogradow in this collection.
69. Thomas W. Merrill and Henry E. Smith, 'Optimal Standardization in the Law of Property: The *Numerus Clausus* Principle,' *Yale Law Journal* 110 (2000), 4. See generally Henry E. Smith, 'Community and Custom in Property,' *Theoretical Inquiries in Law* 10 (2009), 34-36; Thomas W. Merrill and Henry E. Smith, 'What Happened to Property in Law and Economics,' *Yale Law Journal* 111 (2001), 385–8.
70. Hanoch Dagan, 'Judges and Property,' in *Intellectual Property and the Common Law*, ed. Shyamkrishna Balganesh (Cambridge: Cambridge University Press, 2013).
71. Avihay Dorfman, 'Property and Collective Undertaking: The Principle of *Numerus Clausus*,' University of Toronto Law Journal 61 (2011), 510–513. This discussion ignores the fact that several states provide for the election of state court judges, a reality which seems to eliminate the distinction for these purposes between legislative and judicial decision-making about property, even under the tradition of exceptionalism.

possibility of a role for courts when 'the democratic process underperforms' due to interest groups or when it is 'incapable of performing at all.'[72] The problem of legislative underperformance of its democratic role due to interest group capture is a particular one in property law, due to the arcane nature of the subject and the attendant lack of popular interest or awareness of the issues it raises.

To some extent, courts are beginning to respond to the new trust forms at both the Federal and state level. The Federal Bankruptcy Code, and courts applying the Code, have viewed DAPTs with scepticism.[73] In *Battley v Mortensen*,[74] a case which, according to one estate planning attorney, 'reverberated throughout the trust and estate planning world,'[75] a Bankruptcy Court voided Mortensen's transfer of property to the DAPT under Section 548(e), the Code's fraudulent transfer provision.[76] In doing so, the Court noted that this section 'was enacted to close this 'self-settled trust loophole.'[77] This is a significant development: fear of bankruptcy is one of the main reasons people seek DAPT protection.[78] At the state level, significant precedent indicates that states hostile to DAPTs will decline to enforce spendthrift provisions in foreign DAPTs.[79] Recently, the Alaska Supreme Court ruled that the state's foreshortened fraudulent conveyance law would not apply in a case where another state had jurisdiction over the parties and the matter of the trust.[80]

This trend may be occurring in English courts as well. In *JSC Mezhdunarodniy Promyshlenniy Bank v Pugachev*, the High Court found a trust to be illusory because the settlor, Pugachev, retained significant control of the assets deeded to the trust.[81] The importance of this case, in my context, however, is debatable: the defendant was

---

72. Dorfman, 'Property and Collective Undertaking,' 510–513.
73. See generally Richie W. Taylor, 'Domestic Asset Protection Trusts: The "Estate Planning Tool of the Decade" or a Charlatan?' *Brigham Young University Journal of Public Law* 13 (1998), 175.
74. *Battley v Mortensen*, 2011 WL 5025249 (Bankr. D. Alaska 2011).
75. Neil Schoenblum, 'On *Mortensen* and Other Asset Protection Developments: Ten Questions for Barry S. Engel and John R. Garland,' *Probate & Property* (December 2012), 30–31.
76. *Battley v Mortensen*.
77. *Battley v Mortensen*.
78. Taylor, 'Domestic Asset Protection Trusts,' 175.
79. Stewart E. Sterk, 'Asset Protection Trusts: Trust Law's Race to the Bottom?' *Cornell Law Review* 85 (2000), 1051 listing cases which indicate that that courts in states that are hostile to self-settled spendthrift trusts are unlikely to enforce the spendthrift provisions in self-settled asset protection trusts, regardless of the effect that those provisions might have under the law of the trust situs.
80. *Toni 1 Trust v Barbara Wacker*, 2018 WL 1125033 (Alaska 2018).
81. *JSC Mezhdunarodniy Promyshlenniy Bank v Pugachev* [2017] EWHC 2426 (Ch).

a foreign national who had fled to England to escape prosecution in Russia for appropriating the assets of his failing bank, which had been placed in receivership. Respecting the Russian court's order, the High Court had issued its own order freezing Pugachev's assets and ordering their disclosure to the authorities. What was not at issue in this case was the validity of a trust which by statute allowed its settlor to prevent his creditors form reaching his assets.

These trends overall, however, are encouraging, but courts must go further. This means that when courts face a creditor seeking to attach assets of a spendthrift trust, for example, they must first realize they are facing an issue of competing property rights and not one of the reach of testamentary freedom. Second, they must discard the myths which have obscured the power of the beneficiary. As this example shows, such analysis implicates centuries-old forms of the trust, as well as more recent iterations like DAPTs.

I conclude with a return to Cotterrell's 'Partial Agenda for Legal Scholarship.' As part of this agenda, he calls for a 'moral and political critique of law' which will tell us 'what is wrong with the law and why' and force us to seek out 'a moral vision.'[82] Such a project in the area of trust law would allow us to re-evaluate what we as participants in a democratic property regime want from the trust. It forces us to face squarely the question of what types of property ownership we want to allow. For example, one of the original purposes of trusts was indeed to protect the truly vulnerable such as minors, the disabled and the mentally ill. We might agree that a property form which allowed such people to enjoy assets yet keep them out of reach of their creditors offered enough social benefits to outweigh its cost, and that we were willing, as a society, to sacrifice some property rights in that cause. Asking such questions would force a much more realistic evaluation of trust forms, one which would make their costs and benefits clear by stripping them of the ideology which has obscured their workings since their beginning.

---

82. Cotterrell, 'Power, Property and the Law of Trusts,' 80.

6

'The More He Argued,
The More Technical He Became':
Trusts and Surplus Value

Adam Gearey

Introduction

This chapter responds to a challenge thrown down by Cotterrell's work: create an approach to trust law that shows how economic power informs legal doctrine. We will argue that an appreciation of the court's articulation of a 'just' and efficient distribution of surplus value is central to critical trusts scholarship. The court mediates between claims to surplus value made by factions of capital and the state's revenue authorities. In this institutional and normative complex beneficial interests function as forms of surplus value that can be preserved, inherited, taxed and traded.

The law of formalities provides a focus through which this complex can be studied. To this end, it is necessary to re-read four key cases: *Grey v Inland Revenue Commissioners*,[1] *Oughtred v Inland Revenue Commissioners*,[2] *Vandervell v Inland Revenue Commissioners*[3] and *Re Vandervell's Trusts (No 2)*.[4] Our study must also take into account

---

* Birkbeck Law School, UK.
1. *Grey v Inland Revenue Commissioners* [1960] AC 1 (hereafter cited in text as *Grey*).
2. *Oughtred v Inland Revenue Commissioners* [1960] AC 206 (hereafter cited in text as *Oughtred*).
3. *Vandervell v Inland Revenue Commissioners* [1967] 2 AC 291 (hereafter cited in text as *Vandervell v IRC*).
4. *Re Vandervell's Trusts (No 2)* [1974] Ch 269 (hereafter cited in text as *Vandervell's*

recent issues thrown up by the trade in securities—issues that reflect a strange afterlife of the 'formalities' cases. In *Grey, Oughtred* and *Vandervell*, the court attempted to 'materialise' the traces of beneficial interests, enabling wealth to become visible and taxable. This approach was ultimately supported by an interpretation of revenue law that defended the state's 'just' superintendence of private capital. With the securities trade, the scene shifts. Public power seeks to regulate markets, balancing the interests of issuers and investors, whilst extracting its own portion of surplus value through an electronic registry.[5]

Surplus value describes profits derived from productive economy that can be shaped in different ways. These value forms are separated or detached from productive economy so that they can be inherited and/or serve as vehicles for investment: money magically producing money. Surplus value as inherited wealth or profits from industrial enterprises is at stake in the formalities cases. The shift from the issues of the formalities cases to the concerns of *SL Claimants v Tesco* and uncertificated securities illustrates the court's search for legal forms appropriate to the relationship between fictitious capital and surplus value.[6] A concern with beneficial interests—whether under a trust

---

Trusts (No 2)). The key actor in each of these cases is the state's taxation authority, the Inland Revenue. In April 2005, the Inland Revenue was renamed Her Majesty's Revenue and Customs (HMRC).

5. The key case is *SL Claimants v Tesco* [2020] Bus LR 250. The SL Claimants case brought together a group of institutional investors, coordinated by a US Hedge Fund. The SL claimants alleged that Tesco had artificially inflated its profitability, leading to significant losses for investors (Sarah Butler, 'Tesco Faces £100m Claim from Investors over Accounting Scandal,' *The Guardian*, 31 October 2016, accessed 29 February 2024, https://www.theguardian.com/business/2016/oct/31/tesco-100m-pound-claim-investors-accounting-scandal. Shortly before the action against Tesco began, the Groceries Code adjudicator held against Tesco in relation to delayed payments to suppliers and other sharp practices that had been used to boost profits (Sarah Butler, 'Tesco Delayed Payments to Suppliers to Boost Profits, Watchdog Finds,' *The Guardian*, 26 January 2016, accessed 29 February 2024, https://www.theguardian.com/business/2016/jan/26/tesco-ordered-change-deal-suppliers). The Serious Fraud Office also opened investigations into Tesco's finances. Agreeing to a fine of £129 million, the supermarket entered into a deferred prosecution agreement. The SFO pursued another case against senior staff at Tesco PLC, which collapsed in 2018, amidst criticisms of the SFO's handling of the prosecution (Emma Simpson, 'Tesco Trial Collapse Heaps Pressure on SFO', *BBC News*, 6 December 2018, accessed 29 February 2024, https://www.bbc.co.uk/news/business-46468228). The case reveals tensions between merchant capital and finance capital over division of surplus generated in the industrial mass production of food. The state endeavours to promote the integrity of market operators, even if the actions of its agents seem ineffectual.

6. The trade in dematerialised and uncertificated securities is a trade in forms of fictitious capital as it based on the speculation of future profits. For a working definition of surplus value and fictitious capital, see below.

or a sub-trust, whether litigated in the field of revenue, or at stake in the trade of uncertificated securities—runs through all the cases that we will examine.

The first section of this chapter provides a critical account of Cotterrell's work. The next sections looks at the formalities cases and *SL Claimants v Tesco*. A conclusion presents the trust as a vehicle for the enhancement and preservation of surplus value.

Trusts and Surplus Value: The Complex and its Doctrinal Knots

Cotterrell's article contained two essential insights. Firstly, it drew attention to the ideological significance of property as the substratum of the law of trusts. Secondly, it argued that legal doctrine is not a 'reflection or derivation of other social phenomena' but must be seized in its own complexity.[7] These points came together in his understanding of the trust as a legal form that makes 'invisible' questions of private power and material inequality.[8] Cotterrell offered an inspiring critique of the evasions and mystifications of property law, but for all its perspicuity, certain key points were left undeveloped.

Assuming that abstract value refers to the theory of surplus value, the question becomes: how does the trust articulate a legal form of surplus value? Surplus value is a complex term even within Marxist scholarship. One might want to think of surplus value as wealth or profit. Whilst this is not entirely inaccurate, it does obscure the precise way in which the term functions in Marx's critique of political economy. The concept's relevance can be demonstrated without getting bogged down by matters of detail.[9] Surplus value describes the capture by capital

---

7.   Roger Cotterrell, 'Power, Property and the Law of Trusts: A Partial Agenda for Critical Legal Scholarship,' *Journal of Law and Society* 14 (1987), 79.
8.   Cotterrell, 'Power, Property and the Law of Trusts,' 82.
9.   Marx argued that Adam Smith discovered surplus value. The term thus comes from within the classic account of political economy. Smith understood that 'the development of the productive powers of labour does not benefit the labourer himself': Karl Marx, *Theories of Surplus Value: Part One* (London: Lawrence & Wishart, 1969), 69. Value is generated in production, and the capitalist mode of production extracts value from the exploitation of labour power. Whilst value can be seen in money terms, and requires an analysis of price, rent, profit and investment, it has to be grasped as a class relationship. If one follows Marx in identifying labour power as the source of value, then surplus value articulates the different forms taken by the exploitation of labour power. Surplus value can therefore be measured in money terms, but as money obscures class relations this quantitative measure conceals as much as it reveals. Quantities of surplus value can take different forms. Fictitious capital is one of the most sophisticated forms that surplus value can take, and it is therefore a form of surplus value in which relations of exploitation are most effectively concealed, even to the extent of being almost made

of the value created by social labour in commodity production under conditions of competition and the private ownership of the means of production, distribution and exchange.[10] Different 'factions' of capital are involved in a 'struggle' over the distribution of surplus value.[11] Trust doctrine endeavours to articulate coherent principles that manage these distributional tensions. Law cannot be reduced to a mere structuring of a prior economic concerns. It is essential to the institutional normative complex that is itself an element of the socio-economic totality.[12] This totality cannot be understood on a base- superstructure model. Law and legal forms are not superstructures determined by an economic base. The more appropriate metaphor is that of a complex or metabolism in which law is fundamental to the articulation and transformation of value. We will focus on tensions inherent in this complex that brings together courts, the state, taxation, trust doctrine, investors, private capital and the dynastic control of wealth.

Acting through its revenue authorities, the state attempts to determine its own share of surplus value—even to the extent that it comes into conflict with the family as a holder of private capital. However,

---

invisible. Marx's critique of the 'fetishism' of bourgeois economics urges us to see that class relations are, nevertheless, still determinant of the value of finance capital and its 'products.' Thus, a proper sense of the theory of surplus value requires an appreciation of Marx's account of the global dynamics of capital accumulation. In very broad terms, Marx shows how claims to quantities of surplus value relate to the power of different factions of capital to extract a portion of total surplus value. Surplus value must therefore be related to the global division of labour, the international mobility of capital and the inherently conflictual nature of a capitalist mode of production on a world scale. The approach in this chapter roughly follows the 'value form' tradition of thinking that stems from the work of Isaak Illich Rubin, *Essays on Marx's Theory of Value* (Detroit: Red and Black, 1975). The version of value theory presented in this essay also draws on David Harvey, *The Limits to Capital* (London: Verso, 1999) and Alfredo Saad-Filho, *The Value of Marx* (London: Routledge, 2002).

10.   The cases that we will read below all concern profits made through successful business activities. *Vandervell* realised profit on the sale of motor parts. The family business in *Oughtred* manufactured and sold food products. The issue in *Grey* concerned shares in the Sun Engraving Co Ltd.

11.   The fundamental point is that the 'factions' of capital claim surplus value in relation to their relative strength to 'capture' profits of production. Thus, the relative strength of finance capital vis a vis commercial capital or landed capital means that finance capital can claim more surplus value than rival factions. This very basic sketch of the struggle over surplus value would, of course, have to take into account complexities occasioned by (for example) the investment of finance capital in realty. Complexities aside, the main point of relevance for this essay is that the surplus value is effectively detached or made so 'remote' from labour processes that capital appears to generate value from itself.

12.   See Adam Gearey, 'Equity in a Severe Style,' *Australian Feminist Law Journal* 41 (2015), 161 and 'Equity and the Social Reproduction of Capital,' *Pólemos* 11 (2017).

private ownership and inheritance of capital is not 'threatened' by the revenue raising powers of the state as the state is dedicated to the preservation of market society. At the same time, a zone of tension lies between dynastic control of inherited wealth and the state's claim to tax. The court endeavours to mediate between the revenue authorities and private capital. In the formalities cases the revenue regime was defined by the Stamp Act 1891. The Stamp Act was aimed at particular kinds of instruments, not 'transactions' as such: the state could therefore claim its share of surplus value through its validation of acts of transfer and the levying of a fee on the transaction to a percentage of its value.[13] Uncertificated securities takes us to a different context.[14] We need to think about uncertificated securities as a form of fictitious capital—a sophisticated articulation of surplus value. Trade in uncertificated securities is carried out through electronic registries that make records of transactions for taxation purposes. Thus, although a 'virtual' stamp might replace a physical one, the fundamental mechanism for the state's capture of a share in surplus value remains the same: taxation.

If one agrees that a beneficial interest can be understood as surplus value taking legal form, a number of points follow. Regimes of taxation must be able to locate and make visible the whereabouts of beneficial interests to enable the state to extract its own share of surplus value. The formalities cases are exercises in 'making visible' forms of wealth that would prefer to remain invisible to the taxation authorities. Hardly surprisingly, the court made use of various forms of writing and recording to trace transformations of surplus value contained in equitable interests. Uncertificated trading lifts these themes into a different key. Whilst the main theme is no longer the familial distribution of wealth,[15] the trust and the sub-trust are essential to the structuring of the market in this particular form of security. Our focus will be a recent case in which the court plugged a 'fundamental hole' in the market's regulatory scheme and articulated norms relevant to this trade in surplus value.[16]

---

13. The history of stamping as a source of government revenue can be traced back to the late 1600s and the need to raise revenues for foreign wars. Later Stamp Acts targeted newspaper publishers. The 1891 Act established the contemporary regime of levying taxes on certain documents. See Brian Green, 'Grey, Oughtred and Vandervell—A Contextual Reappraisal,' *Modern Law Review* 47 (1984), 400.

14. Taxation of electronic share transactions is made in accordance with rules for the levying of Stamp Duty Reserve Tax, introduced in 1986.

15. It has long been appreciated that these cases provide insights into 'taxation and family squabble[s].' See Brian Green, 'Grey, Oughtred and Vandervell,' 385.

16. We are concerned with a trading system that seeks to operate in a virtual world, moving beyond more restricted and material forms of transaction. Investors, through

Within the political organisation of contemporary capitalism, law articulates surplus value and courts endeavour to solve conflicts over its distribution. Doctrinal solutions must be fair and efficient. Legal solutions to distributional issues make use of norms relating to justice, fairness, state authority and the functioning of the market.[17] Legal doctrines are inherently indeterminate and ambiguous, animated by fraught and ongoing attempts to knot together solutions to general problems. If anything is 'hidden'—it is hidden in plain sight. How can we see what was always there?

The Grandchildren, the Dutiful Widow and the Awkward Divorcee

For many commentators, the key formalities cases, *Grey*, *Oughtred* and *Vandervell*, show a disturbed body of law where the courts made a 'hash' of the problems they were trying to resolve. Indeed, Penner concludes that the only way out of the mess is legislation.[18] Our analysis does not lead to suggestions for reform. The case law can be used as a laboratory to study the legal forms taken by surplus value. The prominence of this case law and the place of formalities within trust syllabi also makes it a good place to start.

The formalities cases show how taxpayers sought to transfer beneficial interests in order to limit or evade liability to tax. The articulations of surplus value at stake were shares in trading companies

---

intermediaries, buy securities in secondary markets (in other words, not the primary markets where securities are offered to major institutional investors). Securities trading is carried out on the basis of immobilisation and dematerialisation. Immobilisation describes the way in which the international 'depository or clearing system' operates. A central depository opens accounts in the names of the holders of securities, and effects transfers by making the relevant entries as debits or credits in cash or security accounts. The securities themselves are not moved, and the 'clearers' do not hold the assets themselves. The movements of title to securities are represented by electronic transfers. Immobilised systems of trading are also dematerialised as the clearing systems do not issue paper record of title. Thus, 'dematerialised bearer securities', can be issued 'directly to the screen' and entered in a register which also records any change of ownership without any paper record.

17. The general sense in which the courts approach matters of fairness in taxation can be gleaned from *WT Ramsay Ltd v Inland Revenue Commissioners* [1982] AC 300. Lord Wilberforce articulated the principle that 'a subject is only to be taxed upon clear words, not upon "intendment" or upon the "equity" of an Act.' However, the courts are not confined to the literal approach, and can look at context. This does not mean that all attempts to minimise tax are inherently suspect. The key issue is the relevant legislation and the facts of the case in hand. *Ramsay* shows the court operating within its jurisdiction, making use of 'the undoubted power and duty of the courts to determine' legal principles and 'to relate them to existing legislation.'

18. James Penner, *The Law of Trusts* (Oxford: OUP, 2012), 164.

and industrial operations. Dividends drawn from the ownership of shares are legal claims to surplus value derived from the ownership of economic resources.[19] Dividends can, of course, be held in trust. In *Vandervell*, the issues at stake were the distribution of surplus value and the control of a successful company. A similar issue about control of a family company lies behind the share swap arrangement in *Oughtred*. This point can also be very clearly established in *Grey*:

> The Hunters ... had no obvious succession in management in their own families and were anxious to secure for their daughters and families generally the wealth which they felt would be at too much risk in industry after the war, with the depressions that previous wars had made them anticipate.[20]

This passage, drawn from a brief history of the Sun Engraving Company, describes a problem of control. Edward Hunter had no successor. No one in the family was able to take over the management of the business and it was necessary to secure the family's wealth against the inevitable crises of capitalism. A claim on surplus value can be precarious. Surplus value requires the kind of protection that the trust can provide.

What, more precisely, is the link between beneficial interests and surplus value? Beneficial interests are like particles in a cloud chamber—identifiable only by the traces of their movement.[21] There is something dark, even ghostly about them: 'invisible entitlement[s]' concealed 'behind the veil of legal title.'[22] This striking metaphor is not quite correct. What does legal title hide? In *Grey*, *Oughtred* and *Vandervell*, beneficial interests (whether linked to the equitable estate or not) are material forms of wealth. The courts grappled in *Grey*, *Oughtred* and *Vandervell* with the slippery nature of these forms of wealth, attempting to make visible that which preferred to remain in the shadows: surplus value secured in trust and passed between generations.

---

19. Dividends can be paid to shareholders on the basis of a loan. Does this contradict the thesis that dividends require surplus value? Not necessarily. It is important to make a distinction between the general point that dividends are forms of surplus value, and the specific context in which a business entity might, for various reasons, rely on methods for raising funds in the absence of available 'profits'. I am grateful to Nick Piška for making this point. A proper analysis would need to engage with the problematic of the credit system as outlined in Marx's *Capital Volume III*.

20. Ernest Corp, 'A Brief History of the Sun Engraving Co Ltd,' accessed 29 February 2024, https://www.sunprintershistory.com/factcorp.html.

21. Green, 'Grey, Oughtred and Vandervell,' 386

22. Green, 'Grey, Oughtred and Vandervell,' 386.

The House of Lords had to determine whether or not the state was entitled to its share of surplus value. In doctrinal terms, these issues emerge as arguments about the application of section 53(1)(c) of the Law of Property Act 1925. Section 53(1)(c) imposes formality requirements on dispositions of subsisting beneficial interests. At the risk of distorting a subtle and complex set of problems, the fundamental problem is the status of oral directions. Can oral directions dispose of a beneficial interest and thus avoid the tax that would be levied on a document?

Grey concerned an oral transfer of shares from the settlor, Edward Hunter, to his grandchildren. As has been pointed out, section 53(1)(c) 'singl[ed] out … subsisting equitable interests' thus 'fixing' (in the absence of 'paper title' and/or 'physical possession') the whereabouts of an equitable right. Commentaries on the case stress that section 53(1)(c) updated certain sections of the Statute of Frauds 1677 that related to fraudulent transactions of beneficial interest. The imposition of written formalities on dispositions of equitable interests would make it more difficult to shift beneficial interests and help to preserve the integrity of trusts. This concern with fraudulent transactions obscures another issue. Fraud is at one end of a spectrum of dealings with beneficial interests that extends to tax evasion and avoidance. Edward Hunter was not engaging in fraud, but his oral direction to his trustees did test the interpretation of 'disposition' in section 53(1)(c). The House of Lords appeared to hold that a transfer of a beneficial interest had to take a written form and would be subject to tax. *Grey* asserts the need for a document: a trace of the worth of a transaction. Hunter's words could not conjure the movement of the beneficial interests.

Oughtred concerned shares in William Jackson & Son Ltd, a family company still trading today.[23] Mrs. Oughtred and her son Peter, held shares in the company. They entered into an oral agreement in which Mrs Oughtred undertook to transfer to Peter a holding of shares she owned in exchange for his equitable interest in the company's shares. After the transfer, Mrs Oughtred would be equitably entitled to the entire shareholding. This arrangement was motivated by a concern to achieve dynastic control of the business. If the transfer could be made without putting it in writing, there would be no liability to stamp duty. The House of Lords ruled against them.[24]

---

23. The litigation in question took place some years before the appearance of the celebrated Aunt Bessie's brand of Yorkshire puddings—a product that Jackson and Son were encouraged to develop by Butlin's.

24. The IRC argued that an arrangement made between two shareholders to swap

The majority argued that the transaction was subject to tax.[25] This was because it was possible to locate a document that corresponded to the value of the beneficial interest.[26] The Stamp Act context allowed the court to apply a robust piece of reasoning. The court fixed upon a suitable completion document to identify both the point in time and the value of the transfer. It did not matter, for the majority, whether the bare equitable interest remained vested in Peter, or had been extinguished by a deed of release. This reasoning might leave certain problems unresolved but *Oughtred* is coherent with the court's approach to surplus value. The whereabouts of the son's 'bare equitable interest ... shorn of all value and significance' is not the main concern.[27] The House of Lords focused on the value bearing element of the transfer.

What conclusions can be drawn from these cases? *Grey* cannot be seen as the court setting its face against a 'transparent attempt to avoid a taxing statute.' This is because, under the relevant stamp legislation the emphasis is on documents that are taxed, not the transactions themselves. Furthermore, the court does not begin with a 'predisposition against the taxpayer.' Rather, the revenue is under a 'heavy burden' to ensure that the transaction in question is covered by the legislation.[28] This doctrinal analysis draws attention to the legitimating nature of the court's work. The court knots together presumptions about the burden of proof between taxpayer and the revenue to justify writing requirements in the contexts in which the disposal of beneficial interests take place. To be legitimate this tracking of surplus value in the form of beneficial interests must respect the precise nature of the disposal. A similar point could be made with reference to *Oughtred*. The ruling in the case leaves questions unanswered: in particular, is there a sub-trust or a constructive trust at work in the case. It may be that a beneficial

---

their respective holdings of shares should be placed in writing and thus subject to taxation. The shareholders argued, on the contrary, that the transaction could be concluded orally and without writing. Their argument was that a constructive trust arose when the oral promise to swap the shares was made. As the relevant legislation allowed such trusts to be exempt from writing, the 'swap' of the shares was effected by the trust. The House of Lord asserted that the completion document, a deed of transfer, could be taxed. That the beneficial interest in the shares had passed prior to the completion was not a material issue.

25.   Lord Denning, in the minority, thought that the transaction gave rise to a constructive trust which, although exempt, by s 53(2) from written formalities, would be caught by s 53(1)(c) when the constructive trust gave effect to the agreement.

26.   Green, 'Grey, Oughtred and Vandervell,' 400.

27.   Green, 'Grey, Oughtred and Vandervell,' 401–2.

28.   Graham Battersby, 'Some Thoughts on the Statute of Frauds in Relation to Trusts,' *Ottawa Law Review* 7 (1975), 486.

interest can be moved without the need for writing.[29] The formalities cases provide a broad justification for written formalities that operate as a way of recording a trace of surplus value in the context of stamp duty.

Vandervell v IRC continued these themes. The case was focused on the 'opacity' of the 'shifting of [a] beneficial interest.'[30] Vandervell sought to provide a large charitable bequest to the Royal College of Surgeons (RCS). What was his motivation? One can speculate that, nearing the end of his successful business career, he thought it might be time to 'give something back.' Once Vandervell had made the decision to found a chair at the RCS, he 'had little interest in how it was done.'[31] Lurking in the background is Vandervell's 'difficult and obstructive' ex-wife. His advisers were also worried about death duties and Vandervell's own liability to surtax. Imagine the kind of conversation that might have taken place in a country pub or a golf course club house with rolling views and a distant prospect of a river. Conversation would have turned on provision for the children, the difficult divorce, and a profligate tax hungry government. The plan hit upon was to transfer a body of shares to the RCS. Vandervell Ltd would then declare a dividend on the shares, but the RCS would grant a company controlled by Vandervell, Vandervell Trustees Ltd, an option to repurchase the shares at a fraction of their value. The option was also important as Vandervell was considering a future public floatation of his company, and it would be awkward if the RCS was the owner of a block of shares. Thus, Vandervell was anticipating a further capitalisation of his wealth. The point of the scheme was to enable the gift to the RCS without attracting tax liability on the income in Vandervell's hands. The plan would also remove the shares from Vandervell's estate and thus reduce his liability to death duty and deprive the revenue of its share of Vandervell's capital accumulation.

Litigation over this scheme was complex and protracted. However, there is a key point that ties together Lord Upjohn's ruling on formalities requirements under section 53(1)(c) with Lord Wilberforce's argument about the ownership of the option to purchase the shares. Both resist the de-materialisation of wealth, and seek to make it visible. Behind Lord Upjohn's reasoning on formalities is the scene of the man of property dealing with his affairs in something like a face-to-face way. Vandervell, as the sole beneficiary under the bare trust of the shares, transferred

29. Battersby, 'Some Thoughts,' 494.
30. J.W. Harris, 'The Case of Slippery Equity,' *Modern Law Review* 38 (1975), 559.
31. *Vandervell v IRC*, 297.

the legal title of shares to the RCS, with the intention that his beneficial interest came to an end with the transfer.[32] There is no confusion over who owns what or the identity of the beneficiary. Therefore, it is not necessary to comply with formalities and ensure that the disposition of the equitable interest is in writing. Although some commentators are critical of this conclusion, as it seems out of line with *Grey*, it rests on the idea that the mysterious and invisible form that came into being behind a trust has become something that is owned absolutely.[33] As the IRC lost on this point, it might seem that the court had suddenly developed a sympathy for schemes that conceal surplus value. However, the ruling of the House of Lords is in fact consistent with the general principle that the court is fundamentally concerned with hidden forms of surplus value. Once a trust is no longer in existence, this particular way of concealing surplus value is no longer an issue.

Although Lord Wilberforce came to conclusions different from those of Lord Upjohn, a similar resistance to the mysterious movement of surplus value can be traced in his reasoning. In locating ownership of the option to purchase the shares, Lord Wilberforce did not engage in speculations over the arcane aspects of the resulting trust, or the question of whether or not Vandervell would ultimately benefit from the shares. Vandervell had never actually dispensed with the equitable interest in the shares which he effectively 'controlled.'[34] The equitable interest could not hang in mid-air, drifting like a ghost. It was given material form by an automatic resulting trust. Lord Wilberforce stresses that wealth must have an owner. As the option to purchase the shares resulted to Vandervell he was liable to tax.

As Vandervell was liable for surtax, his executors thought it prudent to begin proceedings against Vandervell Trustees Ltd in order to obtain the necessary funds to cover the liabilities that would fall on the estate.[35] However, as the IRC failed in their attempt to be joined to the action, does *Vandervell's Trusts (No 2)* contradict our thesis? The first point is that, had the executors won, the revenue's claim to surtax would 'effectively' be 'upheld.'[36] The second point is that in the background of the case is a 'family squabble.'[37] It is important to remember that

---

32.   Green, 'Grey, Oughtred and Vandervell,' 408.

33.   Although it is probably likely on the facts of the case that the RCS held the shares subject to Vandervell Trustees Ltd, see Penner, *The Law of Trusts*, 135.

34.   *Vandervell v IRC*, 329.

35.   Graham Moffat, Gerry Bean and Rebecca Probert, *Trusts Law: Text and Materials* (Cambridge: Cambridge University Press, 2009), 202.

36.   Moffat, *Trusts Law*, 202.

37.   Green, 'Grey, Oughtred and Vandervell,' 415.

Vandervell's will, made in contemplation of his marriage to his second wife, did not mention provision for his children. This suggests that the settlement in question in *Vandervell's Trusts (No 2)* was a way of providing for them. Perhaps Mrs Vandervell was indeed 'seeking to undermine the secure financial structure which her lately deceased husband had carefully constructed for his children.'[38] Bringing together these points, we can suggest that *Vandervell's Trusts (No 2)* falls well within our argument. The old protagonists are still ranged against each other. Behind the Vandervell squabble is the desire to control the transmission of surplus value. The revenue is clearly interested in the result of the case as a means to levying surtax—even if they are riding on the tails of the executor's litigation.[39]

Principles for the tracking of surplus value can be exhumed from the disturbed reasoning in *Vandervell (No 2)*. The key issue for consideration relates to section 53(1)(c). How did the Court of Appeal come to the conclusion that Vandervell had divested himself of all interest in the shares he settled for his children, and was thus not liable for surtax? As Stephenson LJ asserted, it was difficult to find the point at which Vandervell disposed of his interest in the shares in accordance with section 53(1)(c). Behind the troubled arguments in the Court of Appeal is a sensitivity to the travails of a man of property who tried to 'do his best' for his children. Perceptions of the role of that Mrs Vandervell played in seeking to undo the settlement were also significant. Lord Denning stressed that the court should not 'defeat the intentions of a dead man.'[40] Undoing Vandervell's settlement would perpetuate 'injustice on a large scale.'

The reasoning of the Court of Appeal has been rightly criticised, but commentators have not focused on the distributional struggle over surplus value that animates the case. Lord Denning's argument can be read as an apologetics for a transmission of surplus value. Vandervell is raised from the dead:

> If he himself had lived, and not died, he could not have claimed it back. He could not be heard to say that he did not intend the children's trust to have it. Even a court of equity would not allow him to do anything so inequitable and unjust.[41]

---

38. Green, 'Grey, Oughtred and Vandervell,' 415.
39. The Court of Appeal found against the executors, and thus brought an end to the revenue's claim.
40. *Vandervell's Trusts (No 2)*, 322.
41. *Vandervell's Trusts (No 2)*, 321.

In speaking for the dead man, equity ventriloquizes justice. We come upon the final element in the solution to the problem faced by the court. Whether or not Lord Denning's arguments are correct in principle, he achieves a *coup de theatre* in making Vandervell talk. This trick provides a justification for the assertion that the court has provided a just and fair solution to the case. The judges have granted an honest family man what he would have wanted if he was still alive. Whilst the technical arguments for the executors may have some purchase, Lord Denning understands that if the court accepted them, it would seem as if the Inland Revenue were robbing an honest man's grave. There are limits to taxation, even if they are not contained in the letter of the law.

Where does this leave us? Although the ruling in *Vandervell Trusts (No 2)* may be doctrinally flawed, it seems to provide a striking justification for a solution to distributional problems; a knotting together of doctrine, ideology and pragmatics. The case enables a patriarchal transmission of wealth on terms that most people would probably consider fair, and, at the same time justifies 'the right' of the state to its claim of surplus value through taxation. Whilst this may be an accurate reading of *Vandervell,* the consequences of the case suggest that the aftermath of the case might raise more problematic issues. One particular consequence of the case warrants attention.

As Nolan has pointed out, on the basis of *Vandervell,* a beneficiary may instruct a nominee to dispose of an asset without being compelled to put the transfer in writing. Title can thus pass 'free of the beneficial interest.' This is a useful state of affairs for nominees holding 'shares and securities' and dealing with them on the basis of 'unsigned instructions.'[42] Shares and securities can be traded quickly and efficiently through 'oral instructions, telephone instructions or … electronic instructions *via* the internet.'[43] Has the law given up on attempts to track surplus value in a world of electronic transfers? Nolan suggests that *Vandervell* needs to be read in a novel way—through the doctrine of overreaching—to clarify how the movement of beneficial interests can be tracked. This kind of doctrinal solution certainly offers one way forward, but the real issue is undoubtedly the problems presented by increasingly subtle ways of abstracting and trading in surplus value.

---

42. Richard C. Nolan, '*Vandervell v IRC*: A Case of Overreaching,' *Cambridge Law Journal* 61 (2002), 169.
43. Nolan, '*Vandervell v IRC*,' 169.

Formalities and Fictitious Capital

Surplus value reaches its most mature form in fictitious capital. Fictitious capital, seemingly detached from productive activities, can be transformed into financial interests that can themselves be traded. Whatever form a security takes, it can be seen as a claim on existing surplus value, or surplus value that will be created. This is why a security can be described as fictitious capital. A security is fictitious (in very simple terms) as it is a claim to profits that may be produced. Conventional understandings of the inherent risks involved in the trading of securities acknowledge that it is essentially a form of speculation. But an approach to regulation as the balancing of risks will not allow us to appreciate what is at stake.

Marx's analysis of finance capital suggests that at least one of the functions of a system for trading fictitious capital is to speed up the turnover time of capital, further the expansion of world markets through a greater volume and frequency of exchange. In other words, a more extensive trade in surplus value.[44] In 2004, when the Financial Markets Law Committee, began to examine the legal issues involved, the trade in securities amounted to 'a total value of £765,000,000,000 per day.'[45] Whilst finance capital seeks to enable flows of trade, it comes up against certain limits. Previous systems of electronic transfer required 'mountains of paperwork' which overwhelmed 'clearing and settlement system.'[46] It was as if the legal requirements for tangible records disabled the very trade they sought to facilitate. The finance industry put a great deal of money and effort into the development of computer systems such as CREST. CREST 'hold[s] and transfer[s] shares'. It effectively services international markets, and thus furthers the profitability of British finance capital.[47]

These technological advances necessitated a regulatory response. The market in immobilised and uncertificated securities takes a very specific form that relies on trusts and sub-trusts. The key point is that these equitable vehicles are central to the transfer of beneficial interests

---

44. And lucrative opportunities for various dealers and stock jobbers to cream off their own share.

45. Financial Markets Law Committee Report, *Property Interests in Investment Securities* (1 July 2004), 4.

46. Roy Goode, 'The Nature and Transfer of Rights in Dematerialised Securities,' *Journal of International Banking and Finance Law* 10 (1996), 167–176.

47. See Brian Smith, 'CREST: Its Recognition and Approval,' *Financial Stability Review*, 1 (1996), 51–58.

in fictitious capital. More specifically—rather than an issuer of securities dealing directly with investors—an immobilised account in the hands of an intermediary or custodian gives the investor equitable interests in the sub shares of the security that can, in turn, be transferred to others. The trade in uncertificated securities is therefore conducted through an exchange of beneficial interests. The problem is that this entire system would be profoundly limited if writing requirements were necessary to the transfer of securities that had already been decertificated. Section 38(5) of the Uncertified Security Regulations 2001/3755 explicitly provides that section 53(1)(c) of the Law of Property Act 1925 does not apply to 'transfer of title to uncertificated units of a security by means of a relevant system.' CREST counts as a relevant system. It is worth noting that the system is owned and run by a private company. The regulations effectively make the operation of the system subject to approval and oversight by the Treasury, the Financial Services Authority and the Office of Frair Trading. A system such as CREST must keep 'registers of securities' and 'records of securities.' This enables the state to extract its own share of surplus value through the taxation of transfers, whilst private capital enjoys a system that enables international trade. The court is central to this complex as it articulates and clarifies regulatory norms—not least the precise nature of the rights that exchange surplus value and whose trace is recorded by the CREST system.

In *SL Claimants v Tesco PLC* the court confronted these issues. The claimant investors argued that they had a claim for compensation against Tesco under the Financial Services and Markets Act 2000 (FSMA).[48] The investment schemes in questions were characterised by holdings structured through a chain of intermediaries. Under the FSMA, the claim would only succeed if the investment interests were equitable. Tesco argued that rights fell short of being equitable, and as such, the claimants had no cause of action. The court asserted that the investor at the end of the chain of intermediaries did indeed hold something

---

48. The investors were alleging that they had suffered losses as they had relied on misleading statements published by the issuer of the shares. It is worth stressing that the legal owner of the shares was the person who appeared on the CREST register. The claimants were not registered with CREST, but held their shares through various institutional custodians, who in turn, relied on intermediaries. Tesco admitted that those investors who held through one intermediary did have an equitable interest, but those further down the chain had no standing to sue, as they did not have an 'interest in securities' as defined by the FMSA. Tesco also put forward the argument that the claimants had not 'acquired' or 'disposed' of interests under the Act. The upshot of these arguments the rights of the investors were not equitable but personal, and, as such fell outside of the statutory definition of interests in securities.

that 'was, or could be equated to, an equitable property right.'[49] Moreover, the chain of sub-trusts was not a mere 'convenience' but a proper structure.[50] The equivocation ('was or could be') is interesting— the right 'could be equated to' an equitable right.[51] It is as if the nature of equitable rights returns to the ghostly form of beneficial interests that had been the subject of so much litigation in the formalities cases. The sub-trust is therefore similar to the charm that Carnacki uses to hold in place the veil between the material and the spirit world.[52] An equitable right held in a sub-trust—whilst not quite a right—is still a 'right to a right.'[53] This emphatic term functions as a kind of spell to keep the ghosts at bay: an enchantment to enable equitable forms of surplus value to remain visible, exchangeable and taxable.[54] The echo of Arendt's notion of a right to rights is intriguing.[55] There can be no refugee from the exchange of surplus value on markets. Even the most fictitious and dematerialised forms of surplus value can be articulated through equitable principles and traded. It is hardly a surprise that the 'right to a right' is the right to be commodified.

So, in *SL Claimants* the court rescued the regulatory regime for decertified securities. As Gullifer and Payne have stressed, this case proved a nervous or 'unsettling' moment.[56] If Tesco's arguments were correct, there was a massive 'hole' in the protection offered by the FSMA to investors.[57] The court approached the problem on the basis that the wording of the relevant sections of the Act 'did not ... strip away the rights of investors who chose that mode of holding their investment.'[58] We can relate Mr Justice Hildyard's reasoning back to the court's knotting together of norms for the distribution of surplus value. Mr Justice Hildyard cleverly squared two compelling principles:

49. *SL Claimants v Tesco* [79].
50. *SL Claimants v Tesco* [79]–[80].
51. *SL Claimants v Tesco* [79] and [85].
52. William Hope Hodgson, *Carnacki, the Ghost Finder* (London: Eveleigh Nash, 1913)
53. *SL Claimants v Tesco*, para 85.
54. The solution put forward by the court stressed that the equitable 'right to a right' was held in a 'chain of sub-trusts' that was capable of surviving the bankruptcy of an intermediary, and could therefore allow an 'ultimate' if 'indirect' enjoyment of the 'bundle of rights.'
55. See Hannah Arendt, *The Origins of Totalitarianism* (New York: Harcourt Brace Jovanovich, 1973), chapter 9.
56. Louise Gullifer and Jennifer Payne, 'Intermediated Securities and Investor Protection,' *Law Quarterly Review* 13 (2020), 201–205.
57. *SL Claimants v Tesco* [10].
58. *SL Claimants v Tesco* [88].

the solidity of the sub trust and the continuing relevance of the 'no look through principle.'[59] The chain of sub-trusts argument asserts the 'reality' of the equitable rights—allowing investors a right to rights— whilst the assertion of the no look through principle potentially cuts in the opposite direction: limiting the ultimate liability of the issuer. Mr Justice Hildyard's argument balances the interests of investors and issuers, whilst also stressing the locatable nature of beneficial interests. He employs an appropriate metaphor—a 'waterfall' of surplus value.[60] Whilst cascading, water, or surplus value is in free fall. However, this free fall is conditioned by the channel that exists before and after the cascade. The torrent of surplus value can only exist if the channels are maintained. The direction of flow requires the revision of the rules on formality, and the assertion of the authority of the state as the guarantor that the boundaries of the channel will keep surplus value flowing.[61] Given that the operators of the CREST system are a private company, the regulatory tracking of surplus value has been effectively divided between the state and private capital. The state retains something very important: the guarantee of title to property—no matter how fictitious. Markets are unimaginable without the state, and without the court's articulation of a public/private complex for the flow of surplus value.

Conclusion

So, has the analysis put forward in this chapter met Cotterrell's challenge? It would be easy to throw up one's hands: the complexities of the law of formalities are difficult enough. Reading the cases through

---

59. The no look through principle provides that an investor in intermediated securities does not have 'direct rights against the issuer' but has to enforce their rights against the party closest to them in the chain of intermediaries. See Joanna Benjamin, 'Stewardship and Collateral', *LSE Law, Society and Economy Working Papers* 7 (2017), 3.

60. *SL Claimants v Tesco* [85].

61. It is interesting that *Vandervell* re-appears as an authority, albeit mediated by *Akers v Samba Financial Group* [2017] UKSC 6, [2017] AC 424. In *SL Claimants*, Tesco argued for a narrow interpretation of 'disposal' to bolster the assertion that 'a purchase or sale by the legal owner of legal title does not constitute a purchase or sale of the beneficial interest' [96]. This position seemed to be supported by *Akers*. In *Akers*, a decision under the Insolvency Act 1986, the Supreme Court held that a sale of shares did not constitute a disposition of an equitable interest, even when the equitable interest was 'extinguished' by such a transfer [97]. This position was supported by *Vandervell*. These arguments were not accepted. Under the wording of the FSMA, disposal or acquisition had to be given a broad semantic interpretation and as far as the beneficial interest in securities being traded in the CREST system were concerned, once an issuer of shares consented to their being traded, they could be acquired, vested or subject of a disposition.

Marx's concept of surplus value is just too much. But have we gained any insights into the otherwise obscured forms of economic power in trust law? The main point is that Marx's *Capital* provides an education in method. What this method can tell us about the law is often misunderstood. Marx puts forward an account of the law's relationship to a mode of production: a mode of production whose extraction of surplus value from productive labour is itself obscured. If the 'secret' of the mode of production is difficult to bring into view, then the role of the law is doubly obscured. A correct understanding of law in a capitalist mode of production looks to production and the relationship between production and the distribution or exchange of forms of surplus value. Law articulates and obscures the centrality of surplus value to the chaotic, destructive genius of capitalism.

Marx's method of 'seeing' requires the view of a 'whole': most properly an appreciation of a capitalist mode of production as a structure in motion. It is precisely the transformation of surplus value that is at stake in understanding how 'the system' functions. Moreover, it is necessary to comprehend the immanent tensions, the connections and disconnections, that characterise the motion of capital. Thus the forms of law that attend on surplus value are themselves mobile. Surplus value must be tracked through its various transformations. So, what is value? Value is not money, profit, market price, cost price or production price. It is not dividends or dematerialised and uncertificated securities. These are just the forms that value takes. Value is surplus labour extracted in production. The fundamental class relationship on which the mode of production is founded. Cotterrell urged trust scholarship to grasp this relationship as the subject's fundamental concealed dynamic.

The judicial articulation of surplus value shapes a normative complex that knots together economic and political power. To some extent we may be dealing with 'slippery equity' but if the arguments above are correct, then the slippery qualities of equity are limited.[62] Trust law is focused on the definition and delimitation of beneficial interest so that equity can serve certain important functions in the management of surplus value. To understand the law of trusts in this way is clearly to depart from the underpinnings of orthodox trust law and to follow the path opened by Cotterrell's work. It is now also possible to appreciate the importance to capitalism of a vehicle like the trust. The trust is a way of effectively storing, exchanging and expanding surplus value, whilst endeavouring to protect it from the shocks inherent to its condition.

---

62. Harris, 'The Case of Slippery Equity.'

A beneficial interest is a form taken by surplus value once is has been 'removed' from direct production and made available for investment or market exchange. The fundamental link with productive activity may come in and out of focus, but, without the ongoing production of surplus value, a beneficial interest would become more or less worthless. Marx touches very briefly upon this point when he discusses the miser's hoard. The trust is not a hoard, because the latter removes money from the risks of production and investment, whilst the former makes resources available in order that they should be deployed to capture more surplus value.[63] Equity should be studied as a mechanism or knot that holds together the power and fictions of capitalism.

---

63. Karl Marx, *Capital Volume II* (London: Lawrence and Wishart,1954), 44.

7

Subversion as an Agenda for Critical Trusts Law Scholarship

Mark Bennett* and Adam Hofri-Winogradow**

Introduction

Trusts are a unique legal institution in many ways, three of which are captured in Maitland's well-known comment in his lectures on Equity:

> Of all the exploits of Equity the largest and the most important is the invention and development of the Trust. It is an 'institute' of great elasticity and generality; as elastic, as general as contract. This perhaps forms the most distinctive achievement of English lawyers. It seems to us almost essential to civilization, and yet there is nothing quite like it in foreign law.[1]

The trust is unique, then, in having developed in Equity, in thereby being endemic to English law, and in offering unparalleled flexibility in the disposition of property.[2] Maitland does not, however, note a further, problematic, aspect of the trust's uniqueness: trust law is a branch of private law that regularly serves injustice by facilitating the avoidance, or subversion, of the liabilities of ownership. While some conceptions of contract and property might be assailed as manifesting an ideology of (unjust) free market capitalism,[3] contract and property were not originally,

---

* Victoria University of Wellington, New Zealand.
** University of British Columbia, Canada.
1. F. W. Maitland, *Equity: A Course of Lectures* (Cambridge: Cambridge University Press, 1910), 23.
2. Maitland, *Equity*, 23.
3. See Barbara Fried, *The Progressive Assault on Laissez Faire: Robert Hale and the First Law and Economics Movement* (Cambridge: Harvard University Press, 2001); Justin Desautels-Stein, 'The Market as a Legal Concept,' *Buffalo Law Review* 60 (2012); Michael A. Wilkinson and Hjalte Lokdam, 'Law and Political Economy,' in

and are not now, substantially means of subverting other parts of the law. Just as common lawyers never wonder at the trust's other unique features due to their familiarity,[4] neither have they often dwelt on the characteristic use of trusts for avoidance; though some exceptions are discussed below. This chapter argues that the agenda for a critical legal analysis of the trust should begin by recognising that the trust is unique in having, as one of its several characteristic functions, subversion of the law.

Such recognition is evident in the reaction to recent events and the debates they have triggered. The transactional detail found in the Panama Papers confirmed how offshore trusts are used to hide or protect wealth.[5] In 2017, the Tax Justice Network (TJN) issued a report by Andreas Knobel entitled 'Trusts: Weapons of Mass Injustice?,' arguing that trusts are implicated in the current crisis of extreme inequality, being 'one of the primary vehicles used to create and perpetuate wealth concentration, enabling wealthy elites to escape tax, regulation and creditors.'[6] It found that although they sometimes serve legitimate purposes in business and for the protection of the vulnerable, trusts allow for impenetrable secrecy about the ownership of assets, for the manipulation of ownership rights, and permit people to 'control and enjoy trust assets while legally distancing themselves far enough from them' that the property is not seen as theirs for purposes of taxation, the claims of creditors and those of former spouses.[7] Wealth thus becomes ownerless, at least as regards key liabilities of ownership, while the settlor remains effectively in control.

The TJN's fundamental critique of trusts law and practice was soon met with counter-arguments by some trusts practitioners.[8] Geoff Cook,

---

Encyclopedia of the Philosophy of Law and Social Philosophy, ed. Mortimer Sellers and Stephan Kirste (Springer, 2019).

4. F. W. Maitland 'The Unincorporated Body' in *The Collected Papers of Frederic William Maitland: Vol 3*, ed. H.A.L. Fisher (Cambridge: Cambridge University Press, 1911), 272.

5. Reid K. Weisbord, 'A Catharsis for US Trust Law: American Reflections on the Panama Papers,' *Columbia Law Review Online* 116 (2016): 93, accessed 29 February 2024, https://columbialawreview.org/content/a-catharsis-for-u-s-trust-law-american-reflections-on-the-panama-papers; Arthur Cockfield, 'Big Data and Tax Haven Secrecy,' *Florida Tax Review* 18 (2016).

6. Andres Knobel, 'Trusts: Weapons of Mass Injustice?' *Tax Justice Network*, 13 February 2017, accessed 29 February 2024, http://www.taxjustice.net/2017/02/13/trusts-weapons-mass-injustice-new-tax-justice-network-report, 5.

7. Knobel, 5–6.

8. Geoff Cook, 'Review by Jersey Finance of *Trusts: Weapons of Mass Injustice?* Published by Tax Justice Network,' *Trusts and Trustees* 23 (2017), 730.

Chief Executive of Jersey Finance, defended trusts as legitimate wealth management devices, observing that '[p]reservation of wealth is ... entirely legitimate—outside centrally planned economies that reject private ownership.'[9] An editorial in *Trusts and Trustees*, written by distinguished trusts lawyers, specifically countered many of the criticisms in the TJN report, asserting that effective remedies already exist for the abuses identified.[10] However, the editorial then went on to identify and accept a key critique of the modern discretionary trust, namely that due to settlors' retained powers or de facto influence, 'the boundary between a proper trust and a nomineeship has become blurred.'[11] It suggests that the test for sham should be made more effective, or that judges should 'adopt a more worldly approach in considering what is really disclosed by the evidence before them.'[12] That is an admission of some of the criticisms in the TJN report.

Given some practitioners' rejection of the TJN's critique of trusts, the eminent trusts and taxation practitioner Tony Molloy QC's contribution to a recent volume entitled *Trusts and Modern Wealth Management* is striking.[13] Molloy drew on modern economists of inequality such as Piketty and Atkinson,[14] putting forward a remarkable warning to trusts practitioners and their clients, that in an age of rampant inequality they must consider the social effects of protecting their wealth from redistributive taxation.[15] Molloy observed that 'it is difficult to imagine that the trust will not come to be viewed as toxic: not just on the myriad occasions when it is being used abusively, but precisely in its proper role as a prime driver, and protector—within the law—of wealth accumulation.'[16] He then noted that inequality affects

---

9. Cook, 'Review,' 731.

10. David Russell and Toby Graham, 'Trusts: Weapons of Mass Injustice or Instruments of Economic Progress?' *Trusts and Trustees* 23 (2017).

11. Russell and Graham, 'Trusts,' 366.

12. Russell and Graham, 'Trusts,' 366.

13. Tony Molloy, 'High-Net-Worth Trusts in the Twenty-First Century: Confiscatory Taxes and Duties?,' in *Trusts and Modern Wealth Management* ed. Richard C. Nolan, Tang Hang Wu and Kelvin F. Low (Cambridge: Cambridge University Press, 2018).

14. Thomas Piketty, *Capital in the Twenty-First Century*, trans. Arthur Goldhammer (Cambridge, MA: Bellknap Press/Harvard University Press, 2014); Anthony B. Atkinson, *Inequality | What Can Be Done* (Cambridge, MA: Harvard University Press, 2015).

15. On the recent focus on inequality in economic and legal scholarship, see David Singh Grewal and Jedediah Purdy, 'Inequality Rediscovered,' *Theoretical Inquiries in Law* 18 (2017); Wilkinson and Lokdam, 'Law and Political Economy'.

16. Molloy, 'High-Net-Worth Trusts,' 555.

democratic government,[17] and that current levels of tax exaction from the wealthy may lead to social violence.[18] Molloy concluded that '[i]n this situation, the chances are high that trusts for the very wealthy may have to be reimagined as tax- and duty-neutral: useable, for example, for control of, and succession to, the family fortune, but possibly not for reducing tax and duty.'[19]

These recent contributions show that scepticism about the trust has reached mainstream legal discourse, and such concerns have also seen the trust become a question for public comment in the pages of newspapers and for more sustained commentaries on the causes of social inequality.[20] This chapter analyses the history of the critical legal analysis of trusts, from foundational cases and commentaries through to contemporary accounts. In doing so, it engages Roger Cotterrell's agenda for a critical legal analysis of property and trusts law, which identified the trust's key role as hiding the actual structure of power relations that property law holds in place behind the roles of trustee and beneficiary. We argue that the current scepticism about the trust demonstrates that it no longer fulfils this obfuscating function: both legal scholars and public commentators have laid bare how the trust itself furthers the power of the wealthy by allowing them to use and preserve wealth while avoiding liabilities of property ownership. Furthering this research is an important agenda for the critical scholarship of trusts law today.

Cotterrell's Critical Agenda: The Ideological Function of the Trust

In his path breaking article, Cotterrell set out an agenda for critical legal scholarship that focussed on how the fundamental ideas of an area of law have significance in the 'consciousness of ordinary citizens,' thereby being understood and applied by those citizens in their social lives.[21]

---

17. Molloy, 'High-Net-Worth Trusts,' 571–572.
18. Molloy, 'High-Net-Worth Trusts,' 559.
19. Molloy, 'High-Net-Worth Trusts,' 573.
20. Philip Knightley, 'The Big Chill; Vestey Family,' *The Times* [London, England], 16 November 1991; Ben Schneiders, 'Happy Families: Family Trusts Have Been "Manipulated beyond Recognition to Be Used",' *The Age* [Melbourne, Vic.], 8 April 2017; Zachary Mider, 'How Waltons Shield Wealth: Wal-Mart Heirs use "Jackie O." Trusts to Limit Estate Tax Bills,' *Chicago Tribune*, 19 September 2013; Nick Smith, 'Trusts Under Siege,' *The New Zealand Herald*, 17 June 2011; Deborah Dowling, 'Tax or Trust?; Critics Charge Family Trusts Are Nothing More than a Gift to the Rich at a Time Country Needs Tax Dollars,' *The Ottawa Citizen*, 30 January 1993.
21. Roger Cotterrell, 'Power, Property and the Law of Trusts: A Partial Agenda for

He claimed that property law has an ideological effect through concealing the existence of private power in societies that have significant material inequalities.[22] It underpins the fundamental liberal idea that individuals are free and equal, by conceptually separating persons from the things they own. This presents people as equal in the eyes of the law despite their 'grossly unequal powers and capacities' in reality due to their unequal access to things.[23] Thus,

> however much more one person may own than another, the general freedom of transactions and the equal security of property which the law affords to all subjects makes it possible for legal ideology to affirm that the equality of legal subjects is in no way compromised by inequalities in the nature and amount of assets which they are said (in legal doctrine) to own.[24]

Once unequal property is disregarded, the private power it bestows can be ignored by legal doctrine and ideology, which simply guarantees individuals the equal right to transact with one another.[25] This feeds into ordinary citizens' consciousness, providing 'the ideological foundation par excellence which justifies the inequalities of capitalist societies.'[26]

Against this background, Cotterrell presents the trust as extending the 'ideological separation of the human actor from those characteristics or attributes which give such an actor' power by freeing persons from the constraints associated with property.[27] The concept of property includes the idea of a person owning a thing; the idea of the trust confuses our understanding of ownership.[28] It does so by allowing the conjunction of

> permanent, easily identifiable property-owners (explicitly recognised as such by law) in the form of replaceable trustees, together with an indefinite range of beneficially entitled individuals or collectivities ... who, having beneficial entitlements guaranteed in equity, can share in property-power but remain invisible to law as property-owners as such.

Critical Legal Scholarship,' *Journal of Law and Society* 14 (1987), 82.
22. Cotterrell, 'Power, Property and the Law of Trusts,' 82.
23. Cotterrell, 'Power, Property and the Law of Trusts,' 82.
24. Cotterrell, 'Power, Property and the Law of Trusts,' 82.
25. Cotterrell, 'Power, Property and the Law of Trusts,' 83.
26. Cotterrell, 'Power, Property and the Law of Trusts,' 83.
27. Cotterrell, 'Power, Property and the Law of Trusts,' 83.
28. Bernard Rudden, 'Things as Things and Things as Wealth,' *Oxford Journal of Legal Studies* 14 (1994).

The trust presents the trustees as the owners of the property, and the beneficiaries as having little power.[29] Indeed, 'the very fluidity of beneficial entitlements which the trust makes possible hides from view even more effectively than the property concept in its simple form the actual structure of power which private law guarantees and perfects.'[30] Ultimately, the trust represents an extension of the concept of property, allowing 'far greater flexibility in the manipulation of property-power ... and a further "disguising" in ideological forms of the nature of that power,'[31] and a critical legal scholarship of trusts law should be developed against this background.

Subversion as the Key Ideological Role of the Trust

Cotterrell's agenda for the critical legal analysis of property and trusts is rich and powerful. However, this chapter identifies another critical approach to trusts law and practice, under which it is not the 'disguising' of the control and use of wealth—hiding its concentration from public consciousness—that is the most important ideological function of the trust. Rather, the trust's key ideological role is allowing persons who are, substantively, property owners, to avoid the liabilities that would otherwise attach to that ownership, all the while enjoying very visible property-power.

For example, the trust's use for subversion is apparent when a spouse has property he or she controls transferred to trustees so as not to own it for the purpose of spousal property division on divorce.[32] It is also apparent when persons create discretionary and/or spendthrift trusts with themselves as beneficiaries, rendering themselves poor so far as their creditors are concerned while retaining effective, if indirect, control over significant assets.[33] Even a 'classic' spendthrift trust can enable a felon to enjoy the benefit of assets while blocking his victim's attempts to collect a tort judgment.[34]

While our approach can coexist with Cotterrell's, we note that it casts some doubt on his claims about the efficacy of the trust as a mechanism

---

29. Cotterrell, 'Power, Property and the Law of Trusts,' 86.
30. Cotterrell, 'Power, Property and the Law of Trusts,' 86.
31. Cotterrell, 'Power, Property and the Law of Trusts,' 86.
32. *Clayton v Clayton [Vaughan* Road *Property Trust]* [2016] NZSC 29; *Minwalla v Minwalla* [2004] EWHC 2823.
33. *Tantular v Attorney General* [2014] (2) JLR 25; Stewart Sterk, 'Asset Protection Trusts: Trust Law's Race to the Bottom?,' *Cornell Law Review* 85 (2000).
34. *Scheffel v Krueger* 782 A 2 d 410 (NH 2001); see discussion in Carla Spivack, 'Beware the Asset Protection Trust,' *European Property Law Journal* 5 (2016).

for hiding power relations. Given that the fact of property owner-ship is often private, or noted on a register the contents of which are unavailable to, or seldom consulted by, the general public, the trust is unnecessary for hiding persons' wealth. But more importantly for present purposes, since information about trust structures is occasion-ally made public—in litigation, for example—and there is speculation that trust structures are commonplace amongst the wealthy, we believe that the trust may not effectively hide the power of beneficiaries. Not only are people not fooled by the concept of transactional equality into ignoring the obvious power differences created by differential access to wealth; neither are they fooled by the trust into thinking that beneficiaries have no power in respect of the trust property.

This is because many people are familiar with the subversion critique of trusts. Through a number of sources, they have learned that the trust provides at least some beneficiaries with the effective equivalent of ownership of the trust property, even though the law in many areas still fails to express that fact by imposing the liabilities of ownership on such de facto owners. Trusts have long been identified in the media and by politicians as mechanisms of tax avoidance—with the Vestey family being a prominent and long-standing example—[35] and even the Conservatives have made election manifesto promises to take a 'more proactive approach to transparency and misuse of trusts.'[36] The massive offshore data leaks of the past decade have brought the use of trusts in 'private client' practice into a sharp and public focus, leading to scandals around the world concerning the hidden wealth of politicians and other public figures. The way that trusts provide control and power to those who create them is often well explained in print media.[37]

This argument is essentially that made by the authors of *Moffat's Trusts Law*. Directly engaging with Cotterrell's argument concerning the ideological function of trusts law, they caution that although it is plain that the trust has been used to maintain the property ownership of the wealthy classes,

> [h]ow far the moral concept of 'trust' in fact helped to legitimize the power attached to such ownership is ... not easy to discern. ['P]roperty is still to this day heard as univocally expressive of autonomy and liberty[.']
> ... But we may need to distinguish here between the abstract appeal

---

35. Elizabeth Bailey, 'Britain's Vestey Affair,' *New York Times*, 2 November 1980.
36. Conservative Party, *Forward, Together: Our Plan for a Stronger Britain and a Prosperous Future* (2017), 16-17.
37. See full references at footnote 20.

of 'property' as an idea and an every-man or every-woman appreciation of the trust as an everyday legal form. Of course, it is conceivable, perhaps probable, that the notion of 'moral obligation owed to beneficiaries' and of a paternalistic regard for the protection of them are constituents of a dominant discourse amongst the propertied and the legal fraternity. But a degree of scepticism may be called for as to whether the trust carries similar connotations for the property-less or even the 'less-well-propertied'. Might we discover that 'the family trust' is inextricably harnessed in the public consciousness with 'tax avoidance' and, that that link engenders pejorative statements about the trust?[38]

In the absence of empirical sociological evidence of public knowledge and opinion, it is difficult to know whether Cotterrell is closer to being right or to being wrong about trusts law successfully hiding the power of beneficiaries from the public, although the media coverage noted above suggests that our and *Moffats'* alternative view may be correct.

Regardless, resolving that empirical question matters not for our claim that there is another agenda for critical trusts scholarship, focused on the subversion function of trusts. The balance of this article identifies that agenda in an important critical tradition running from the early history of legal scholarship though to burgeoning developments today, identifying how trusts enable the avoidance of liabilities of property ownership, in a way that increases the power of the propertied.

Earlier Critical Approaches

For centuries, judges and legal scholars have recognised the pervasive use of the trust to avoid legal liabilities. One of the motivations at the source of the medieval 'use,' the antecedent of early modern and current trusts, was avoiding liabilities consequent on holding land off of a feudal Lord.[39] Blackstone identified the use as beginning in the practices of 'foreign ecclesiastics' 'who introduced it to evade the statutes of mortmain, by obtaining grants of lands, not to their religious houses directly, but to the use of the religious houses.'[40] The Chancellors

38. Jonathan Garton, *Moffat's Trusts Law: Text and Materials*, 6th ed. (Cambridge: Cambridge University Press, 2015), 62.

39. Sir John Baker, 'Uses, Wills and Fiscal Feudalism,' in *The Oxford History of the Laws of England: Volume VI 1483–1558* (Oxford: Oxford University Press, 2003); and see a list of 'the chief custodial purposes of [medieval] uses' in Joshua Getzler, 'Duty of Care,' in *Breach of Trust*, ed. Peter Birks and Arianna Pretto (Oxford: Hart, 2002), 43.

40. Sir William Blackstone, *Commentaries on the Laws of England in Four Books,*

at that time, being clerics themselves, enforced the use as binding on the trustee's conscience. The use having proven to be effective, people began to settle property to the use of others as an alternative to bequeathing it, wills of land having been impossible until 1540.[41] Blackstone clearly saw this as subversive: with respect to the religious use, he says that 'this evasion was crushed in its infancy.'[42] Yet he noted that the subversion became legally institutionalized and commonplace:

> The idea being once introduced, however fraudulently, it afterwards continued to be often innocently, and sometimes very laudably, applied to a number of civil purposes: particularly as it removed the restraint of alienations by will, and permitted the owner of lands in his lifetime to make various designations of their profits, as prudence, or justice, or family convenience, might from time to time require.[43]

Blackstone also noted the complaints against the use, namely that it prevented others from exercising their rights against the land in relation to the beneficiary; therefore an 'abundance of statutes' sought to nullify the subversion inherent in the use by treating the beneficiary as the owner of the estate.[44] He recounted how the Statute of Uses of 1536 was rendered ineffective by clever drafting and judicial confirmation of this drafting, so as to create the trust:

> To this the reason of mankind assented, and the doctrine of uses was revived, under the denomination of trusts: and thus, by this strict construction of the courts of law, a statute made upon great deliberation, and introduced in the most solemn manner, has had little other effect than to make a slight alteration in the formal words of a conveyance.[45]

Yet now, explained Blackstone, the equity courts were more careful to prevent subversion and 'wisely avoided in a great degree those mischiefs which made uses intolerable.'[46]

Similar reasoning can be found in the decision of Lord Mansfield in *Burgess v Wheate*. Lord Mansfield stated that trusts 'were founded

---

19th ed. (Philadelphia: J.B. Lippincott Company, 1893 [1765]), 648.
41.   Until the Statute of Wills 1540 (32 Hen 8 c 1), freehold land passed by primogeniture, or escheated to the decedent's Lord, or to the Crown.
42.   Blackstone, *Commentaries*, 648.
43.   Blackstone, *Commentaries*, 648.
44.   Blackstone, *Commentaries*, 650.
45.   Blackstone, *Commentaries*, 655.
46.   Blackstone, *Commentaries*, 655.

in fraud to avoid the statute of mortmain,'[47] quoting Bacon's *Use of the Law*, which noted that the use 'which grew first from a reasonable cause, namely, to give men power and liberty to dispose of their own, was turned to deceive many of their just and reasonable rights.'[48] Yet soon they were 'innocently applied' to other purposes, such as making a will of land.[49] The trust was therefore created 'for a reasonable cause,' namely 'the convenience of families' ... '[t]his was the only motive that made mankind endure uses and trusts.'[50] These classical passages recognize that from the very first the trust was at least partly about avoidance and subversion of legal rules.[51]

Jumping ahead a few hundred years, the subversive function of trusts also featured prominently in a 1922 essay entitled 'The Trust as an Instrument of Law Reform' by Austin Wakeman Scott, author of *Scott on Trusts* and the first and second Restatements of American law on the subject. Scott restated the key features of the historical development of the trust as a means of avoiding the incidents of estate-ownership, and as the means by which it became possible to make dispositions of land on death in ways not allowed by the primogeniture rules of feudal tenure.[52] This, he argued, caused the reform of feudalism as a legal regime, in a way that was perhaps far more effective and timely than would have otherwise occurred. Scott noted a number of other instances of trusts law and practice having a reforming effect on other law, and while his assessment was largely laudatory, he sounded a note of caution about the trust's reforming role being based on its use to avoid and subvert other legal rules:

> The trust has often served as a means of evading the law. ... The line between evasion and reform is after all a difficult one to draw. The evasion which in the long run proves successful is usually a reform. ... A trust is a device for enabling one to enjoy various rights, powers, and privileges in respect to property greater than those enjoyed by owners of property, for enabling one to enjoy the benefits of ownership without subjection to all the duties and liabilities resulting from ownership. The question with which courts of equity have been compelled to struggle

---

47. *Burgess v Wheate* (1759) 1 Eden 177, 218; 28 ER 652, 668.
48. *Burgess v Wheate*, 220; 669, quoting Bacon, 153.
49. *Burgess v Wheate*, 218; 668.
50. *Burgess v Wheate*, 195; 659.
51. For the avoidance function of equity more generally see, e.g., John Cartwright, 'Equity's Connivance in the Evasion of Legal Formalities,' in *Law and Equity: Approaches in Roman Law and Common Law*, ed. Egbert Koops and Willem Jans Zwalve (Leiden: Martinus Nijhoff, 2014), 112–21.
52. Austin Wakeman Scott, 'The Trust as an Instrument of Law Reform,' *Yale Law Journal* 31 (1922).

is how far it is possible to go without crossing the line which separates the legitimate use of the trust device from an illegal evasion of the letter or the policy of the law.[53]

Twelve years later, Arthur Nussbaum, a German legal academic who emigrated to the United States when the Nazis rose to power and settled at Columbia University, published an article on the sociological aspects of the trust that highlighted the subversion function, expressing a scepticism toward the trust that is perhaps attributable to his German legal training. Nussbaum observed that one of the functions of the trust is to allow persons to 'hide' their ownership of property:

> Thus the trust allows the real party in interest to hide, to disappear in an atmosphere of anonymity or at least of hazy remoteness. Equity, as it were, permits the owner voluntarily to subject himself to a guardianship carried out by the trustee. ... [G]etting rid of responsibilities on the one hand and concentrating benefits on the other, are at the foundation of the trust institution, and are its distinctive marks. They create a potentiality which multiplies the legal uses of property and, therefore, strengthens the dynamic force of capital within the social setting.[54]

Commenting on Scott's analysis of the double edge of the trust as an instrument of law reform, Nussbaum wrote that:

> More recently the trend of 'evasiveness', inherent in the trust, has found new fields of activity. What is evaded chiefly at present is statutory rather than common law, and the purpose is to circumvent modern restrictions or burdens imposed in the interest of the community rather than to avoid old and outmoded traditional rules which are generally felt to be ready for abolition.[55]

This is exactly the kind of analysis that, we suggest, should be central to the current agenda for a critical legal analysis of trusts.

The Current Critical Doctrinal and Sociological Literature

Recent years have seen an increasing volume of contributions from scholars, both legal and other, that point to the social functions and consequences of trusts law. Much of the recent literature focuses on the use of trusts for subversion. Often the analysis is written from

---

53. Scott, 'Trust as an Instrument of Law Reform,' 457–458.
54. Arthur Nussbaum, 'Sociological and Comparative Aspects of the Trust,' *Columbia Law Review* 38 (1938), 410.
55. Nussbaum, 'Sociological and Comparative Aspects,' 410–413.

the perspective of the particular non-trusts area of law being subverted; articles consider how trusts are used to avoid taxation, to avoid marital property sharing regimes, to avoid forced heirship regimes, to frustrate the claims of personal creditors, or even to hide criminal activities and their proceeds. In themselves, these contributions shed further critical light on the subversion function of trusts.

However, for a more sustained analysis of the characteristic use of trusts for avoidance, we turn to Kent Schenkel's article 'Exposing the Hocus Pocus of Trusts.'[56] This makes the general argument concerning avoidance clearly:[57]

> Trusts are often employed as tools in a kind of magic act where they make costs associated with certain activities undertaken by trust beneficiaries completely disappear. A trust beneficiary may receive substantial benefits to property and perhaps even virtual control over that property, yet the trust shields that property from costs associated with a beneficiary's commission of a tort, a default on unsecured debt obligations, or the failure to provide for the surviving spouse at death, to give a few examples. While the outright owner of property must hold that property subject to the valid claims of these other parties, no participant in the trust arrangement undertakes these burdens. Instead, in an act of hocus-pocus, they seem to simply vanish.

As Schenkel points out, the costs that are not borne by the trust beneficiaries are externalised to parties outside the trust.[58] By making the obligations associated with property ownership disappear, Schenkel argues, the trust effectively places costs on those who would otherwise have a claim against the person who would own the property if the trust did not exist.

Schenkel's main example is the US 'spendthrift' trust, which allows settlors to provide beneficiaries with vested, fixed entitlements to trust property that are inalienable either voluntarily or involuntarily, and therefore inaccessible to those beneficiaries' creditors. By analysing the normative justifications given for the recognition and enforcement of spendthrift trusts, Schenkel provides evidence supporting Cotterrell's ideology of property argument: the reasons given for the legitimacy of spendthrift trusts are grounded in the settlor's freedom to deal with their property however they choose, an aspect of the owner's

---

56. Kent Schenkel, 'Exposing the Hocus Pocus of Trusts,' *Akron Law Review* 45 (2012), 63–64.
57. Schenkel, 'Exposing the Hocus Pocus,' 63–64.
58. Schenkel, 'Exposing the Hocus Pocus,' 64.

absolute Blackstonian ownership.[59] Despite the weakness of this justification, particularly in light of the countervailing normative concerns about the trust's role in avoidance, and although on balance the normative arguments against the trust's use for avoidance would require the cessation of that use, path dependence stands in the way of such change. Schenkel thus identifies the power dynamics that uphold the trust's use for avoidance: trust providers and trust users derive large economic benefits from such use.[60]

Another general critique of the use of trusts to subvert other law is found in the work of Brooke Harrington, who has extensively addressed the use of trusts for wealth preservation and avoidance in her sociological *tour-de-force, Capital without Borders*. As she points out in a characteristic comment, '[a]mong high-net-worth individuals, perhaps the only figure as reviled as the tax collector is the debt collector. Historically, trusts have been the favored instrument for avoiding both. … For five centuries, trusts have been used to make "wealthy individuals effectively debt-proof"—impervious to creditors and to any judgments in creditors' favor.'[61] In an article entitled 'Trusts and Financialization,' she argues that 'experts found in trusts a ready-made tool to accomplish some of the tasks financialization requires, such as maximization of capital mobility and profits with minimum regulatory friction. This use of trusts thrives and depends on the gaps and conflicts among national legal systems, creating strategic disarray rather than convergence.'[62] As she also notes, 'trusts loosen the constraints of the law on assets and their owners … without trusts, there might have been no subprime mortgage crisis; because of trusts, the crisis spread globally.'[63]

The Further 'Perfection' of the Trust (for Avoidance)

Our proposed alternative agenda for critical trusts law scholarship, focused on the use of trusts to subvert other law, is also crucial for understanding the currently developing trajectory of trusts law and practice. Trust law itself has changed in the thirty years since Cotterrell's article,

---

59. Schenkel, 'Exposing the Hocus Pocus,' 95–96.
60. Schenkel, 'Exposing the Hocus Pocus,' 108–112.
61. Brooke Harrington, *Capital without Borders* (Cambridge, MA: Harvard University Press, 2016), 178–179.
62. Brooke Harrington, 'Trusts and Financialization,' *Socio-Economic Review* 15 (2016), 38.
63. Harrington, 'Trusts,' 42, 44.

with jurisdictions around the world racing to modify the traditional trust concept so as to satisfy the desires of trust service providers' clients. These changes are often aimed at perfecting the trust's utility for subversion, for example by bolstering settlor control or the trust's immunity from challenge. Among others, both authors of the present chapter have addressed some of the recent doctrinal changes, sometimes presented as brand-new legal 'products.'

Mark Bennett has addressed trust drafters' development of sett-lor-retained powers, allowing settlors to influence trusts they created without appointing themselves trustees.[64] Such powers run the gamut of interference with trustees' exercise of their own powers, from removing trustees, through dictating their administrative and dispositive choices, to removing and adding beneficiaries and revoking the trust entirely. Because many trust clients, actual and potential, are loath to lose control over the assets they pour into their trusts,[65] the ability for settlors to retain powers has proven popular with clients, and offshore jurisdictions, ever eager to please, have enacted detailed legislation declaring the retention of such powers valid.[66]

Adam Hofri-Winogradow provided a normative analysis of seven reform trends in trust law across jurisdictions, including curtailment of trustees' duty of care and liability consequent on its infringement, curtailment of beneficiaries' rights, elimination of the requirement that trustees own the trust property, the liberalization of trust investment law, the liberalization of trustee delegation, the abolition of the rule against perpetuities and rise of perpetual trusts, and the legitimation of self-settled spendthrift trusts.[67] He pointed out that

> comparing the consequences of recent reforms with the distributive justice and corrective justice implications of the pre-reform law of donative private trusts shows a marked deterioration from an already flawed baseline. ... Some of the reforms amplify the vigorously exclusionary effect

---

64. Mark Bennett, 'Competing Views on Illusory Trusts: The *Clayton v Clayton* Litigation in its Wider Context,' *Journal of Equity* 11 (2017), 55–59. See also Tobias Barkley 'The Content of the Trust: What Must a Trustee Be Obliged to Do with the Property?,' *Trusts & Trustees* 19 (2013) and Lusina Ho, 'Breaking Bad,' in *Trusts and Modern Wealth Management*, ed. Richard C. Nolan, Tang Hang Wu and Kelvin F. Low (Cambridge: Cambridge University Press, 2018).
65. Harrington, '*Capital*,' 120.
66. See, e.g. Bahamas Trustee Act 1998, s 3; Bermuda Trusts (Special Provisions) Amendment Act 2014, s 2A; Cayman Islands Trusts (Amendment) (Immediate Effect and Reserved Powers) Law 1995, s 14(1).
67. Adam Hofri-Winogradow, 'The Stripping of the Trust: a Study in Legal Evolution,' *University of Toronto Law Journal* 65 (2015).

characteristic of donative private trusts generally into a practice harming everyone except trust users and those legal and financial professionals providing trust services. Other reforms make trust relationships less beneficial for trust beneficiaries themselves, making trust administration more lucrative for the professionals supplying it at their clients' expense.[68]

Conclusion

As this chapter has made clear, there is a long and distinguished tradition of critical scholarship on trusts. Leading early modern English lawyers were well aware of the trust's subversive nature, as was the leading 20th Century US trusts scholar, Austin Wakeman Scott. Critical trusts scholarship was not born with the Critical Legal Studies movement of the 1980s, and did not disappear as that movement declined. It continues today, with scholars around the world responding critically to the recent twists and turns in the long history of the trust as enabler of law avoidance.

A key remaining challenge for critical trusts scholarship is the collection of credible empirical data regarding the use made of trusts in practice. While some efforts in this direction have recently been made,[69] these interview- and survey-based efforts leave room for improvement regarding validity. Progress in this regard may remain elusive until trust instruments become both registered and available to the public. But in order to understand the sociological and ideological functions of the trust, the subversion agenda should continue to be developed as a framework for understanding trusts law and its interaction with those other areas of law the avoidance of which it facilitates.

---

68. Hofri-Winogradow, 'Stripping,' 2. For further critical analyses of the reforms many jurisdictions have recently made to their trust laws see, e.g. Lionel Smith, 'Massively Discretionary Trusts,' *Current Legal Problems* 70 (2017); Lionel Smith, 'Give the People What They Want? The Onshoring of the Offshore,' *Iowa Law Review* 103 (2018); Stewart Sterk, 'Asset Protection Trusts: Trust Law's Race to the Bottom?,' *Cornell Law Review* 85 (1999-2000); Lusina Ho, 'Breaking Bad'.
69. Harrington, *Capital*; Adam Hofri-Winogradow, 'The Demand for Fiduciary Services: Evidence from the Market in Private Donative Trusts,' *Hastings Law Journal* 68 (2017); Adam Hofri-Winogradow, 'Trust Proliferation: a View from the Field,' *Trust Law International* 31 (2017).

8

Tax Justice and the Abuse of Trusts

*Andres Knobel**

Introduction

Opinions about trusts are sharply divided into two camps. On one side there are those who see them as legitimate, flexible, private legal arrangements to protect vulnerable people or to facilitate business and investment. On the other side, there are those who see trusts as secretive and potentially anti-democratic legal vehicles to protect wealth from taxes and from legitimate creditors, contributing to rising inequality and a range of illicit financial flows: tax evasion, tax avoidance, corruption or money laundering, and plenty more.

Both views seem irreconcilable, as if they are talking about different structures. As described in the next sections, the problem is that while many trusts can be and often are used for legal and indeed socially legitimate purposes, they are also deployed by lawyers, corporate service providers and other enablers of illicit financial flows to abuse their privacy and protective features, to protect wealthy and often criminal interests from rules and laws that bind the rest of society.[1]

This chapter will propose measures that would turn trusts into legal vehicles that address the concerns of protecting vulnerable people (e.g. elderly, minors, sick or disabled people) while preventing them from being exploited for abusive purposes. It summarises the explanations and proposals contained in the Tax Justice Network's publications:

---

* Lead Researcher on Beneficial Ownership for the Tax Justice Network.
1. See for example Hudson's description: 'clever practitioners have always drafted trusts so that property could be concealed from spouses and creditors, so that taxes could be avoided (often by leaving it unclear as to which potential beneficiary might take an equitable interest), and so that unknown mistresses and children could take secret benefits without the family knowing': Alastair Hudson, 'Law as Capitalist Technique,' *King's Law Journal* 29 (2018).

'Trusts: Weapons of Mass Injustice?'[2] and '"Trusts: Weapons of Mass Injustice?" A Response to the Critics.'[3]

Trusts may involve external conflicts—between those who use and benefit from them and the rest of society—and internal conflicts, between the settlors and beneficiaries or trustees of trusts.[4] This chapter focuses on the external conflicts, especially in relation to the abuse of trusts for corruption, tax evasion or to shield assets from legitimate creditors.

Apart from the issue of tackling secrecy, there is no better way to describe this chapter's proposals as an attempt to address and prevent the goals of some trusts, especially the kinds described by a lawyer in a recent Bermuda case:

> In addition to the preservation of existing and future tax benefits, important family wishes and objectives will also be attained.
>
> (A) The family looks upon its wealth as dynastic in nature and wish the Trusts to continue in perpetuity ...
>
> ...
>
> (C)(ii) Secondly, with the trust assets being held by the recipient generation, absolutely, the assets will not only be subject to the rigours of taxation noted above, but will also be exposed to claims of the recipient's creditors, spouses and others.[5]

Concept and Evolution

Trusts are usually associated with administering family assets during the life of the settlor or after their death, to take care of vulnerable minors

2. Andres Knobel, 'Trusts: Weapons of Mass Injustice?' *Tax Justice Network*, 13 February 2017, accessed 29 February 2024, http://www.taxjustice.net/2017/02/13/trusts-weapons-mass-injustice-new-tax-justice-network-report.
3. Andres Knobel, '"Trusts: Weapons of Mass Injustice?" A Response to the Critics,' *Tax Justice Network*, 25 September 2017, accessed 29 February 2024, https://taxjustice.net/2017/09/25/response-criticism-paper-trusts-weapons-mass-injustice.
4. This chapter refers to express trusts (those where the settlor deliberately created a trust, and not a trust inferred by the law from the conduct of parties). Most of the chapter's proposals do not refer to 'unit trusts' or other types of trusts used as investment entities that are subject to regulation and where investors have enforceable rights to income based on 'units' related to their investment in the trust.
5. *In the Matter of the G Trusts* [2017] SC (Bda) 98 Civ [29] (emphasis added), accessed 6 March 2024, https://www.gov.bm/sites/default/files/Reasons%20for%20Ruling-Re%20G%20Trusts.pdf.

or elderly, and for inheritance and succession planning. In addition, trusts became fully engaged in business, like companies. (For example, the legal field dealing with monopolies and cartels is called 'anti-trust' in the US because in 'the late nineteenth century, ... business trusts were used as the holding companies through which industrial oligopolies and monopolies were assembled—hence giving us the Sherman "Antitrust" Act of 1890.')[6] Currently, trusts are very much involved in the investment industry, where banks and other financial institutions set up trusts as special purpose vehicles,[7] or investment entities to pool money for investments. Trusts are also used for charitable purposes.

The uses described so far all seem potentially beneficial: trusts are flexible vehicles, a 'universal "fix-it"'[8] to solve a whole variety of problems in many different situations: caring for family members, supporting the work of charities or engaging in business and investments like any regular company.

So why do trusts get such bad publicity?

The Evidence against Trusts

The Financial Action Task Force (FATF) noted that corporate vehicles and trusts have long been identified by FATF as posing a risk for money laundering.[9]

In fact, FATF's forty anti-money laundering Recommendations include one (Recommendation 25) dealing specifically with trust transparency.[10] Trusts have also been mentioned by the US tax authorities (the IRS) in the 2019 'Dirty Dozen' list of tax scams.[11]

6. Henry Hansmann and Ugo Mattei, 'The Functions of Trust Law: a Comparative Legal and Economic Analysis,' *New York University Law Review* 73 (1998), 477 n 127.
7. See David Hayton, Hugh Pigott and Joanna Benjamin, 'The Use of Trusts in International Financial Transactions,' *Journal of International Banking and Financial Law* 1 (2002); Ewan McKendrick, *Goode on Commercial Law*, 4th ed. (Penguin Books, 2010), 161-162.
8. Tony Honoré, 'On Fitting Trusts into Civil Law Jurisdictions,' *Oxford Legal Research Paper Series* 27 (2008), 4, accessed 6 March 2024, https://papers.ssrn.com/sol3/papers.cfm?abstract_id=1270179.
9. Financial Action Task Force (FATF), *Laundering the Proceeds of Corruption* (July 2011) [47], accessed 6 March 2024, https://www.fatf-gafi.org/en/publications/Methodsandtrends/Launderingtheproceedsofcorruption.html.
10. FATF, 'The FATF Recommendations,' Recommendation 25 (previously Recommendation 34) as at 5 January 2019. The current Recommendations (updated November 2023) are available here: https://www.fatf-gafi.org/en/publications/Fatfrecommendations/Fatf-recommendations.html.
11. Inland Revenue Service, 'Abusive Tax Shelters, Trusts, Conservation Easements

There are many real-life examples of trusts being at the centre of major corruption, tax evasion and money laundering scandals: Sam and Charles Wyly's offshore trusts in relation to tax fraud in the US by shielding more than $1 billion in family wealth.[12] Ecclestone's family trust (related to Formula 1's Bernie Ecclestone) was involved in a bribery probe in Germany where 'it was revealed ... that the trust had made a payment to a German banker who Ecclestone claimed had threatened to report him to British tax collectors.'[13] This prompted the UK tax authorities to declare a previous agreement reached with the Ecclestone's trust void and to demand £1 billion in taxes and penalties.[14] Art dealer Guy Wildenstein's trust-based financial scheme was described as 'the longest and the most sophisticated tax fraud in contemporary France.'[15] The former President of Guatemala Portillo was accused of embezzlement and money laundering, where the money in a Swiss bank was held by a Liechtenstein trust.[16] Asif Ali Zardari and his late wife, Benazir Bhutto (former President of Pakistan), were accused of corruption involving the Rockwood Estate in Surrey in the UK whose opaque sale included as purchasers three Isle of Man firms owned by two local trusts.[17] Augusto Pinochet, the former Chilean dictator, accused of corruption and money laundering involved the use of Trilateral International Trading and the Santa Lucia Trust to keep

Make IRS 2019 "Dirty Dozen" List of Tax Scams to Avoid,' 19 March 2019, accessed 6 March 2024, https://www.irs.gov/newsroom/abusive-tax-shelters-trusts-conservation-easements-make-irs-2019-dirty-dozen-list-of-tax-scams-to-avoid: 'Changes in bank secrecy laws of foreign jurisdictions have revealed a plethora of foreign tax evasion schemes involving trusts, and the IRS is actively examining these cases, as well as a variety of tax evasion schemes involving the use of domestic trusts.'

12.   Peg Brickley, 'Judge Says Businessman Sam Wyly Hid Wealth Offshore,' *The Wall Street Journal*, 11 May 2016, accessed 6 March 2024, http://www.wsj.com/articles/judge-says-businessman-sam-wyly-hid-wealth-offshore-1462976141.

13.   Rozina Sabur, 'Ecclestone Fights £1 Billion Tax Bill,' The Telegraph, 22 May 2015, accessed 6 March 2024, https://www.telegraph.co.uk/news/uknews/law-and-order/11621126/Ecclestone-fights-1-billion-tax-bill.html.

14.   See Jane Croft, 'Ecclestone Settles with German Bank over Sale of F1 Stake,' *The Financial Times*, 27 January 2017, accessed 6 March 2024, https://www.ft.com/content/24b3e88c-e4b3-11e6-8405-9e5580d6e5fb.

15.   Doreen Carvajal, 'Billionaire Art Dealer Is Awaiting Verdict in Tax Fraud Case,' *The New York Times*, 20 October 2016, accessed 6 March 2024, http://www.nytimes.com/2016/10/21/arts/design/wildenstein-tax-trial-ends-with-art-dealers-fate-in-tribunals-hands.html.

16.   See the information available at the Stolen Asset Recovery Initiative (StAR) website, accessed 8 March 2024, https://star.worldbank.org/asset-recovery-watch-database/alfonso-portillo-switzerland

17.   David Pallister, 'Pakistan: Dropped corruption case may free up mansion cash for Zardari,' *The Guardian*, 22 September 2008, accessed 6 March 2024, https://www.theguardian.com/world/2008/sep/22/pakistan.

his bank account in Espirito Santo Bank in Cayman secret.[18] Vladimiro Montesinos, the advisor to the former president of Peru Alberto Fujimori, was accused of corruption involving the Hudson Trust and the Blue Ridge Trust, containing $6m between them.[19] Diepreye Alamieyeseigha, the former Governor of Delta State, Nigeria, accused of corruption, had settled a Bahamian trust—the 'Salo Trust'—for the benefit of himself and his family, to escape declaring the account in the required Nigerian Declaration of Assets.[20] Bloomberg's article 'China's Rich Rush to Shelter $1 Trillion From New Taxes' of December 2018 described that 'wealthy Chinese are rushing to shelter assets and income in overseas trusts before new tax rules go into effect.'[21]

As of January 2019 a search for the word 'trust' in the International Consortium of Investigative Journalists (ICIJ)'s offshore leaks database (including records from the Panama Papers and Paradise Papers) returns more than 9900 results as 'offshore entities.'[22] Cases involving political figures include Mudhar Ghassan Shawkat, former member of parliament of Iraq, where suspicions were raised internally by the employees at Appleby law-firm as reported by the ICIJ:

> Upon the incorporation of a not-for-profit entity, which was also a beneficiary of the trust, concerns ... emerged at the law firm. 'It is suspicious,' an Appleby employee wrote in an email, 'that they are setting up a charitable company offshore [Passion for Change S.A.] for funds coming out of Iraq—there does not seem any benefit other than lack of accountability in doing so.'[23]

---

18. See Committee on Homeland Security and Governmental Affairs United States Senate, *Money Laundering and Foreign Corruption: Enforcement and Effectiveness of the Patriot Act—Supplemental Staff Report on US Accounts Used by Augusto Pinochet*, 17 March 2005, accessed 6 March 2024, https://www.govinfo.gov/content/pkg/CPRT-109SPRT20278/html/CPRT-109SPRT20278.htm.

19. Redacción En Línea, 'El Colmo. Montesinos Envió Carta a Banco de Luxemburgo Para "Reinvertir" US$6 Millones en "Nuevos Mercados" [The Last Straw. Montesinos Sent Letter to Bank of Luxembourg to "Reinvest" US$6 Million in "New Markets"]' *En Línea*, 17 October 2010, accessed 8 March 2024, https://enlinea.pe/2010/10/17/el-colmo-montesinos-envio-carta-a-banco-de-luxemburgo-para-reinvertir-us-6-millones-en-nuevos-mercados.

20. Emile van der Does de Willebois et al, *The Puppet Masters: How the Corrupt Use Legal Structures to Hide Stolen Assets and What to Do about It* (Washington: The World Bank, 2011), 46, available at https://star.worldbank.org/sites/star/files/puppetmastersv1.pdf (accessed 6 March 2024).

21. Jinshan Hong, 'China's Rich Rush to Shelter $1 Trillion from New Taxes,' *Bloomberg*, 12 December 2018, accessed 6 March 2024, https://www.bloomberg.com/news/articles/2018-12-12/china-s-rich-rush-to-shelter-1-trillion-from-new-taxes.

22. ICIJ's offshore leaks database is available here: https://offshoreleaks.icij.org/search?utf8=%E2%9C%93&q=trust&c=&j=&e=&commit=Search (accessed 6 March 2024).

23. See ICIJ's page on Mudhar Ghassan Shawkat as part of its 'Paradise Papers—

The leaks also contain information about a trust settled by Shaukat Aziz, former Prime Minister of Pakistan (2004-2007) in favour of his family. The ICIJ article describes that Aziz was accused by the opposition of false declaration of assets, corruption and misappropriation of funds.

> Asked why Aziz's asset declarations in Pakistan didn't mention the Antarctic Trust, the lawyer told ICIJ that the 'legal owner' of the trust was Citicorp Trust Delaware N.A., not Aziz.[24]

Nevertheless, the number of trusts involved in corruption is very likely underestimated because trusts are generally far harder for investigators to penetrate than other legal vehicles like shell companies. The World Bank's 'Puppet Master' report on grand corruption cases explained that

> the grand corruption investigations in our database failed to capture the true extent to which trusts are used. Trusts, they said, prove such a hurdle to investigation, prosecution (or civil judgment), and asset recovery that they are seldom prioritized in corruption investigations ... Investigators and prosecutors tend not to bring charges against trusts, because of the difficulty in proving their role in the crime ... they may not actually be mentioned in formal charges and court documents, and consequently their misuse goes underreported.[25]

The 2018 report by FATF and the Egmont Group entitled 'Concealment of Beneficial Ownership' concluded that trusts may be used in major laundering schemes only when the stakes are high enough:

> The complexity and expense of establishing legal arrangements [meaning trusts] may limit their use when compared to the prolific exploitation of legal persons by criminals. ... The relative frequency of the use of legal arrangements in the cases analysed for this report (approximately one-quarter of all cases) may be due to the fact that many of the cases involved sophisticated predicate offences that yielded significant proceeds and thus warranted the additional investment.[26]

---

the Power Players,' accessed 6 March 2024, https://offshoreleaks.icij.org/stories/mudhar-ghassan-shawkat.

24. See ICIJ's page on Shaukat Aziz as part of its 'Paradise Papers—the Power Players,' accessed 6 March 2024https://offshoreleaks.icij.org/stories/shaukat-aziz

25. Emile van der Does de Willebois et al, *The Puppet Masters*, 15 16.

26. FATF, *Concealment of Beneficial Ownership* (July 2018) [51], accessed 6 March, http://www.fatf-gafi.org/media/fatf/documents/reports/FATF-Egmont-Concealment-beneficial-ownership.pdf.

Trusts are also involved in tax abuse. A study commissioned by the Australian Taxation Office (ATO) concluded that:

> The interactions between the trust and tax laws are being manipulated which could contribute to the sheltering of significant amounts of tax. At conservative levels this amount is estimated to be between $672 million and $1.2 billion per annum…Recent case investigations by the ATO reveal the ease with which wealthy taxpayers can utilise trusts in private groups and reduce their tax liabilities … In just these five cases alone, the tax leakage is estimated to be approximately $195 million.[27]

In the UK, the report 'Exploring the Use of Trusts' by Ipsos MORI Social Research Institute on behalf of HM Revenue & Customs (HMRC) described among others that UK's inheritance tax (IHT) 'was seen as a key motivator for taking out a trust. Settlors believed that by setting up a trust they would be able to avoid IHT on their death.'[28] In relation to this, in an article entitled 'Inheritance Tax: Why the New Duke of Westminster Will Not Pay Billions' *The Guardian* explained that 'the fact that Hugh Grosvenor's estate is held in a trust means that his £9bn inheritance is likely to remain largely intact.'[29] Similarly, in Argentina, billionaire Eduardo Eurnekian declared to the tax authorities that he had settled a trust in Cayman Islands and another one in Bahamas and had transferred millions to them. This way he avoided paying personal wealth taxes because the assets were no longer in his name. Initially, a court judgment found, in essence, that his assets should not

---

27. Australian Taxation Office, 'Current Issues with Trusts and the Tax System,' 24 January 2019, accessed 8 March 2024, https://www.ato.gov.au/about-ato/research-and-statistics/in-detail/general-research/current-issues-with-trusts-and-the-tax-system.
28. Katrina Leary and Helen Greevy, *Exploring the Use of Trusts* (Ipsos MORI Research Report 452, November 2018), accessed 6 March 2024, https://www.gov.uk/government/publications/exploring-the-use-of-trusts.
29. Juliette Garside, 'Inheritance Tax: Why the New Duke of Westminster Will Not Pay Billions,' The Guardian, 11 August 2016, accessed 6 March 2024, https://www.theguardian.com/money/2016/aug/11/inheritance-tax-why-the-new-duke-of-westminster-will-not-pay-billions. In relation to this, the Grosvenor estate made a statement declaring that other taxes are applicable to trusts in the UK, in place of inheritance tax: https://www.grosvenor.com/about-us/how-we-work/tax-policy/the-facts-about-our-ownership (accessed 6 March 2024). However, no information was provided about the actual taxes paid by the Duke's trust in place of inheritance tax. In addition, The Guardian suggested that the Duke's trusts could have benefited from other exemptions related to 'food-producing farms and for trading businesses that employ real people': Juliette Garside, 'Grosvenor Estate Structure Protects Fortune from HMRC,' The Guardian, 10 August 2016, accessed 6 March 2024, https://www.theguardian.com/money/2016/aug/10/grosvenor-estate-structure-protects-fortune-from-hmrc.

be considered as not belonging to him anymore, given that he controlled the trustees' decisions and that no distribution would take place before his death.[30]

A Little Bit from Column A, a Little Bit from Column B

The positive vision on trusts considers that their misuse for money laundering, corruption and tax evasion are just a few bad apples, and that companies are even more widely used than trusts to commit crimes. The negative vision on trusts considers that the privileges available to trusts are too broad, so while they may be used for legitimate purposes, nothing prevents them from being abused to engage in illicit financial flows.

Ideally, there should be a way to preserve trusts' socially positive uses while curbing or eliminating the harmful elements. This chapter explores two approaches to achieve this. The first concerns transparency. The second concerns trusts' special legal shielding effects, resulting from the separation of ownership over trust assets.

Proposal I: Transparency

Any legal vehicle that allows an individual to engage in business or control assets not under their own name can be exploited for criminal or abusive ends, especially if information on that vehicle, its owners and its assets is veiled in secrecy. The examples above show that trusts and other legal vehicles help criminals hide their identity and assets from authorities when engaging in illegal activities.

In 2014 the G20 group of countries established the 'G20 High-Level Principles on Beneficial Ownership Transparency,'[31] requiring countries to ensure availability of beneficial ownership information for companies and trusts.[32] The fourth round of mutual evaluations on compliance

---

30. Gabriel Gotlib and Walter C. Keiniger, 'La Causa "Eurnekian" Y Los Fideicomisos Constituidos en El Exterior [The "Eurnekian" Case and the Trusts Established Abroad]' Marval, 29 August 2003, accessed 6 March 2024, https://www.marval.com/publicacion/la-causa-eurnekian-y-los-fideicomisos-constituidos-en-el-exterior-4964.

31. Available here: https://star.worldbank.org/sites/star/files/g20_high-level_principles_beneficial_ownership_transparency.pdf (accessed 6 March 2024).

32. In the case of a trust, the FATF, the AMLD 5, and the CRS consider that all the parties to the trust (e.g. settlors, protectors, trustees, and beneficiaries) should be identified as 'beneficial owners.' Simone Wong considers that this may be over-inclusive and that it 'obscures the substantive nature of beneficial ownership in the context of trusts': Simone Wong, 'The New EU Anti-money Laundering Directive: Farewell to

with FATF Recommendations on anti-money laundering and counter financing of terrorism started in 2013 assessing countries not only on their availability of beneficial ownership information for legal persons and trusts, but also on their effective implementation of these measures.[33] In 2016, the OECD's Global Forum adopted new terms of reference to assess countries on their access to beneficial ownership information on legal vehicles, including trusts.[34]

While different legal persons exhibit differences in structure, liability, taxation and functions—for example, a company is different from a partnership, which is different from a private foundation, and there are also differences between legal persons and trusts[35]—*any* of these vehicles could be used to own or control assets and to operate in the economy or to become involved in illegal activities, as described above. So they should all be subject to the same transparency measures, such as requirements to disclose their owners or controllers. Nevertheless, when it comes to transparency the FATF anti-money laundering recommendations, and most countries' regulations including the European Union's anti-money laundering directives, distinguish between *legal persons* (such as companies) and *legal arrangements* (such as trusts), and transparency measures tend to be far more demanding for companies than for trusts—if there are any measures for trusts at all.

Legal persons (such as companies, some partnerships and foundations) usually have to incorporate and register with the commercial register in order to legally exist or at least to enjoy limited liability, and FATF Recommendations[36] require at least basic information on legal

---

Transparency of UK Trusts,' *Trust Law International* 31 (2017), 146. However, while the term 'beneficial ownership' may have different meanings depending on the context (e.g. treaties to avoid double taxation allow a 'beneficial owner' to be an entity), this paper refers to the FATF definition of beneficial owner on anti-money laundering (which is also referenced by the AMLD 5 and the CRS). This definition refers to all the natural persons who ultimately control or benefit from a legal entity or arrangement. This definition doesn't mean that a settlor or a beneficiary or trustee have the same rights or control, but it tries to cover all the possible persons who could have control or benefit from the trust so that at least authorities are aware of their existence.
33. FATF, 'An Effective System to Combat Money Laundering and Terrorist Financing,' accessed 6 March 2024, http://www.fatf-gafi.org/publications/mutualevaluations/documents/effectiveness.html.
34. OECD Global Forum on Transparency and Exchange of Information for Tax Purposes, 'Exchange of Information on Request: Handbook for Peer Reviews 2016-2020—2016 Terms of Reference,' accessed 8 March 2024, https://www.oecd.org/tax/transparency/documents/terms-of-reference.pdf.
35. Depending on the jurisdiction and the type of partnership, they may be considered legal persons or not.
36. FATF, 'The FATF Recommendations,' Recommendation 24 (as at 5 January

persons to be available to the public. In recent years more than 97 countries have approved or will be required to establish registries of beneficial ownership registries, where the 'beneficial owners' (the individuals who ultimately benefit or control these legal vehicles) will have to be registered.[37] Yet these regulations generally require more disclosure from companies than from trusts. For example, under the EU 5th Anti-Money Laundering Directive (AMLD 5), EU countries had to grant public access to beneficial ownership information for companies and other legal persons.[38] (The situation changed on 22 November 2022 when a ruling by the European Court of Justice invalidated public access to beneficial ownership information for the purposes of anti-money laundering.[39] EU countries responded differently to the ruling, some keeping their registries open, and others closing them or requiring access based on a legitimate interest.)[40]

Legal arrangements, like trusts, (which are treated more like contracts than like legal entities) are rarely registered with a government agency as a precondition for their existence, so for any outside party it may be impossible to know that a trust exists. In the cases where trusts *are* registered, this is often only with tax authorities, and even then only if the trust or any of its parties are liable to tax.[41]

Under the AMLD 5, trusts have to register their beneficial owners only if the trust is managed by a trustee located in the EU or if the trust engages in a business relationship or acquires real estate in the EU.[42] If an EU trust (that is, a trust created according to the laws of

2019). The current Recommendations were updated November 2023, and are available here: https://www.fatf-gafi.org/en/publications/Fatfrecommendations/Fatf-recommendations.html.

37.   Andres Knobel and Florencia Lorenzo, 'Beneficial Ownership Registration around the World 2022,' *Tax Justice Network*, December 2022, accessed 6 March 2024, https://taxjustice.net/wp-content/uploads/2022/12/State-of-Play-of-Beneficial-Ownership-2022-Tax-Justice-Network.pdf.

38.   See the factsheet provided by the European Commission, 'Strengthened EU Rules to Prevent
Money Laundering and Terrorism Financing,' 9 July 2018, accessed 6 March 2024, http://ec.europa.eu/newsroom/just/document.cfm?action=display&doc id=48935.

39.   *WM v Luxembourg Business Registers* (Joined Cases Case C-37/20 and Case C-601/20) [2023] Bus LR 611 (ECJ (GC)).

40.   Florencia Lorenzo, 'Split among EU Countries over Beneficial Ownership Ruling Mirrors Rankings on Financial Secrecy Index,' *Tax Justice Network*, 13 July 2023, accessed 8 March 2024, https://taxjustice.net/2023/07/13/split-among-eu-countries-over-beneficial-ownership-ruling-mirrors-rankings-on-financial-secrecy-index.

41.   See Tax Justice Network's Financial Secrecy Index that describe trust registration requirements in more than 110 jurisdictions: https://financialsecrecyindex.com/ (accessed 6 March 2024).

42.   Andres Knobel, 'The EU's Latest Agreement on Amending the Anti-money

an EU country) operates and is managed outside the EU, there may be no information whatsoever registered on that trust. In addition, even for trusts that do have to register their beneficial owners in the EU, access to information will not be to the general public but only to those that may prove a legitimate interest.

The first recommendation is that *trusts should be subject to the same beneficial ownership registration requirements that, under AMLD 5, applied to companies and other legal entities, where information is publicly available.* For instance, Denmark and Ecuador have been offering free online public access to trusts' beneficial owners.[43] In addition, one way to incentivise and enforce registration would be to require that any legal vehicle (including trusts) should be registered for them to be legally valid.[44]

Those who oppose transparency for trusts claim that they are different from companies because they are merely 'legal arrangements' not 'legal persons.' However, this difference is more theoretical than practical, for several reasons.[45]

First, while one of the main differences between legal persons (such as companies) and trusts involves the ownership of assets, there are practical similarities in the ways corporate and trust assets are treated as a distinct 'patrimony' (held in a different box) from the personal assets of a shareholder or from the parties to the trust.

Corporate assets are separated from the assets of a shareholder: the personal creditors of the shareholder may reach the shareholder's

---

Laundering Directive: At the Vanguard of Trust Transparency, but Still Further to Go,' *Tax Justice Network*, 9 April 2018, accessed 6 March 2024 https://www.taxjustice. net/2018/04/09/the-eus-latest-agreement-on-amending-the-anti-money-laundering-directive-still-further-to-go.

43.   See details in Andres Knobel and Florencia Lorenzo, 'Trust Registration around the World: The Case for Registration,' *Tax Justice Network*, July 2022, accessed 8 March 2024, https://taxjustice.net/wp-content/uploads/2022/07/Trusts-FATF-R-25-1. pdf.

44.   For more details, see Knobel, Harari and Meinzer, 'The State of Play of Beneficial Ownership Registration,' 55. Similarly, Alastair Hudson proposes consequences in case a trust isn't registered: 'A key reform of UK tax law to deal with trusts should be to require the withholding of preferential tax treatment for trusts unless those particular trusts are registered and their trust instruments lodged with HMRC.' Hudson, 'Law as Capitalist Technique,' 74.

45.   For instance, Hansmann and Mattei describe that for a Delaware business trust 'it is possible, under the statute, to organize an entity with all the attributes of a standard business corporation—including tradable shares with all the rights to earnings and control typical of common stock—simply by providing in the trust's governing instrument that the entity is to have those attributes.' Hansmann and Mattei, 'The Functions of Trust Law,' 475.

personal assets (which may include shares in the company, but not the corporate entity's underlying assets themselves), while the corporate creditors may reach the company's assets (but not the shareholder's personal assets).[46]

Unlike legal persons that may directly own assets, trust assets are legally owned by the trustee (not by the trust) but only under strong constraints: they do not belong to the trustee's personal assets (the trustee is not allowed to use them for his or her own benefit, nor can the trustee's personal creditors claim against the trust assets). Lionel Smith, for instance, rejects the idea of the common law trust as a separate entity,[47] but he acknowledges that the trust understood as a separate patrimony

> is the dominant understanding of the trust in Scots law. A trustee has his own private or general patrimony, containing his personal wealth and his personal liabilities. He also holds a special or trust patrimony, in which are found the assets of the trust and its liabilities. His personal creditors thus have access to the personal assets but not the trust assets, while trust creditors have access to the trust assets but not the personal assets.[48]

Second, trusts are for practical purposes already treated like legal entities. In many cases trusts have tax identification numbers and are subject to tax, just like companies. Trusts can directly own bank accounts. The OECD's Common Reporting Standard (CRS) for automatic exchange of banking information, for instance, treats a trust as an 'entity' when it owns a bank account.[49] In addition, case law and news

---

46. However, the personal creditors of the shareholder could eventually access the shareholder's interest in a company, and this way indirectly reach the corporate assets. See Proposal II, below.
47. Lionel Smith rejects the idea of the trust as a separate entity, mainly because he states that a trust cannot hold liabilities. The author appears to suggest that while the trustee 'is clearly seen to hold assets in separate "boxes" … all of the trustee's liabilities (both personal and trust liabilities) are liabilities of his own personal patrimony.' Lionel Smith, 'Trust and Patrimony,' *Revue Générale de Droit* 38 (2008), 386.
48. Smith' Trust and Patrimony,' 385.
49. While the CRS will increase transparency on trusts, many loopholes will prevent ensuring that all trusts will be covered or that all countries will receive information on those trusts. Not all countries are participating in the CRS (the most important outsider is the US). Trusts will only be covered if they are considered a 'financial institution' (depending on who manages the trust), and depending on the type of investment undertaken by the trust. For trusts that own bank accounts, all beneficial owners will be identified depending on the type of income and assets held by the trust. Even for trusts that will be within the scope of the CRS, access to information on trusts' beneficial owners will be confidential. For more details on CRS loopholes see Knobel, 'The EU's Latest Agreement on Amending the Anti-money Laundering Directive,'

articles often refer to 'the trust owning a house or shares in a company.'[50] In a September 2017 case regarding a dispute between a UK trust and the HMRC (the UK tax authority), the European Court of Justice concluded that trusts are to be considered legal entities when it comes to benefiting from EU's Freedom of Establishment available to legal entities.

As the court said:

> the trust and its trustees constitute an indivisible whole. That being the case, such a trust should be considered to be an entity which, under national law, possesses rights and obligations that enable it to act as such within the legal order concerned.[51]

Third, international bodies have recommended trust registration. For instance, the FATF 2014 Guidance on Transparency and Beneficial Ownership recommended that

> a centralised registry of trusts to which disclosure must be made of the information pertaining to all trusts (including information on the settlor and beneficiary) could be an effective mechanism as it would provide timely information on the trust and (if kept accurate) could provide competent authorities with access to necessary information for disclosure and international cooperation. Centralised trust registries would also ensure that beneficial ownership information is freely available to competent authorities across jurisdictions in a timely manner, without tipping off a trust under investigation.[52]

above, and Andres Knobel, 'OECD's Handbook for Implementation of the CRS: TJN's Preliminary Observations,' Tax Justice Network, 15 September 2015, accessed 6 March 2024, https://www.taxjustice.net/wp-content/uploads/2013/04/OECD-CRS-Implementation-Handbook-FINAL.pdf.

50. See e.g. Louse Story and Stephanie Saul, Streams of Foreign Wealth Flows to Elite New York Real Estate,' The New York Times, 7 February 2015, accessed 6 March 2024, https://www.nytimes.com/2015/02/08/nyregion/stream-of-foreign-wealth-flows-to-time-warner-condos.html or for instance the description that 'As part of a complex trust and corporate structure, the trusts own various assets located in the United States, the United Kingdom, Singapore, France and Hong Kong' (Peng and others v Rothschild Trust (Schweiz) AG and others [2017] NZHC 25 [10]).

51. Case C-646/15 *Trustees of the P Panayi Accumulation & Maintenance Settlements v Commissioners for HMRC* [2017] 4 WLR 210 [32]. The court added: 'That concept of "other legal persons" extends to an entity which, under national law, possesses rights and obligations that enable it to act in its own right within the legal order concerned, notwithstanding the absence of a particular legal form ... The assets placed in trust form a separate fund of property, distinct from the property of the trustees.' *Trustees of the P Panayi Accumulation & Maintenance Settlements*, [29]-[30].

52. FATF Guidance, 'Transparency and Beneficial Ownership,' October 2014, 32, accessed 6 March 2024, https://www.fatf-gafi.org/en/publications/Fatfrecommendations/Transparency-and-beneficial-ownership.html.

Another argument that has been mounted against trust registration says that requiring registration of all parties to a trust 'is unworkable, disproportionate, costly, and burdensome.'[53]

However, the FATF already requires trustees to obtain and keep all relevant information on the settlor, other trustees, protector, beneficiaries, classes of beneficiaries and any other person with control over the trust.[54] Therefore, relevant beneficial ownership information on all trust parties is already required to be collected. The only missing step—a simple, workable one—is to require that this information which the trustee already has, is registered with a government authority.

What is more, private foundations, which are usually offered in civil law countries as a tax/estate planning alternative to trusts,[55] are considered legal persons—so under FATF recommendations they must be registered just like companies. The EU's AMLD 5 (before the 2022 ECJ ruling) required EU foundations, as legal entities, to register their beneficial owners in public registries (Article 30), while applying the beneficial ownership definition that is applied to trusts—meaning that all parties to the foundation (who are very similar to the parties to a trust) must be registered: the founder (like the settlor), the protector and the foundation council (like the trustees), and the beneficiaries or classes of beneficiaries and any other person with effective control over the foundation/trust.[56]

In conclusion, there is no good reason why trusts should not be subject to the same beneficial ownership registration and public disclosure requirements as those that are applied to companies and private foundations. That is because trusts may create the same risks, and are in practice and effects very similar to legal persons already subject to those transparency requirements. Positively, according to the Tax Justice Network, more than 120 jurisdictions require some form of registration for some types of trusts, including 65 jurisdictions which require trusts' beneficial owners to be filed with a government authority.[57]

53. Geoff Cook, 'Review by Jersey Finance of "Trusts: Weapons of Mass Injustice?" Published by Tax Justice Network,' *Trusts & Trustees* 23 (2017), 735.
54. See FATF, 'The FATF Recommendations,' Recommendation 25 and Interpretative Note to Recommendation 10.
55. See e.g. Sterling Trust and Fiduciary Ltd's marketing and explanation on its website, under the heading 'Private Foundations vs Offshore Trusts,' accessed 6 March 2024, https://sterlingoffshore.com/knowledge-base/foundations/vs-offshore-trusts/.
56. Art 3.6.2.c of the EU AML Directive.
57. Knobel and Lorenzo, 'Trust Registration around the World.'

At the same time, the risks of facilitating illicit and abusive activity are large enough to mean that trusts cannot be considered only as 'private family matters.'[58] The UK authorities agree:

> While trusts can offer privacy in managing a person's affairs, there is a clear distinction between that privacy and keeping such arrangements deliberately concealed from a public authority such as HMRC for the purposes of tax avoidance or evasion.[59]

Lastly, it is important to remember that nobody is forcing anybody to set up a trust. Trusts confer privileges provided by society (asset protection, changing title to assets, possibility to engage in business)—and, just as with companies, society is entitled to ask for responsibilities in return for those privileges.

Proposal II: Access to Trust Assets by Legitimate Creditors

This section refers mostly to asset protection trusts, but as Matthews explains, 'in one sense, every trust is an asset protection trust. If it is fully effective, the assets held in trust are entirely cut off from the settlor's estate, and cannot be taken to satisfy the settlor's debts.'[60] For example, even a trust with a fixed beneficiary could achieve this if it allowed distributions only after the beneficiary turns 21 (until that time, trust assets would be protected). However, there are much more sophisticated trusts that achieve even higher protection from outsiders, for instance discretionary trusts and trusts that include spendthrift provisions.

Asset protection trusts are supposedly used to protect children or vulnerable people, based on the separation of ownership that they create. Instead of donating money or other assets directly to children or sick people who may be unable to manage them adequately, trusts allow settlors to transfer 'legal ownership' to trustees, who will hold the assets and manage them for the benefit of the beneficiaries.

---

58. For further detail see Andres Knobel, 'Beneficial Ownership and Disclosure of Trusts: Challenging the Privacy Arguments,' *Tax Justice Network*, 7 December 2016, accessed 6 March 2024, https://www.taxjustice.net/2016/12/07/beneficial-ownership-disclosure-trusts-challenging-privacy-arguments.

59. HMRC, *The Taxation of Trusts: A Review* (7 November 2017), para 4.2, accessed 6 March 2024, https://assets.publishing.service.gov.uk/government/uploads/system/uploads/attachment_data/file/754210/The_Taxation_of_Trusts_A_Review.pdf.

60. Paul Matthews, 'The Asset Protection Trust: Holy Grail, or Wholly Useless?' *King's College Law Journal* 6 (1995-6), 65.

This separation of ownership, which is at the heart of the trust concept, can also create unintended consequences against third persons, by putting trust assets in an 'ownerless limbo' where no single party has absolute rights over trust assets, making them unreachable by personal creditors of the settlor, beneficiaries, or the trustees.[61] This is in fact the *main goal* of asset protection trusts. They do this principally by giving discretion to the trustee to decide on what, when, how much and to whom to make distributions, so that until a distribution is finally made, nobody is entitled to anything in the trust, so there is no legal way for personal creditors to get at the assets inside the trust. As the saying goes, 'If you don't own it, nobody can take it away from you.'

Yet even if they do not *own* those assets in a trust, they may still have power to *enjoy* them. For example, Russian billionaire Sergei Pugachev created discretionary trusts in favour of his family, but the trust deed allowed him still to use the property:

> In respect of any residential property ... to permit SERGEI VICTOROVITCH PUGACHEV together with such other persons as he may from time to time permit personally to reside in the residential property and to use and enjoy the furniture and household effects in the residential property free of rent.[62]

As a *Harvard Law Review* paper described:

> All of these benefits can be coupled with essentially complete control allocated according to the grantor's [settlor's] wishes. ... This makes the total package effectively indistinguishable from property owned outright in terms of the benefits provided, but without important downsides property ownership entails, such as greater exposure to taxes, creditors, and vengeful ex-spouses.[63]

There are many examples where the legal separation at the heart of trusts have protected the assets of perpetrators of murder, sexual abuse, embezzlement and other crimes. For example, in *Re Wilson* the Internal Revenue Service (IRS, the US tax authorities) failed to access trust

---

61. If fraudulent conveyance actions are available (because the settlor transferred assets to a trust only to become insolvent and default on existing debts), personal creditors of the settlor may be able to access trust assets to repay their debt. But if the settlor created a trust many years ago, before having any debts, then fraud actions against the trust would not be available.
62. Quoted in *JSC Mezhdunarodniy Promyshlenniy Bank v Pugachev* [2017] EWHC 2426 (Ch) [118] (Birss J).
63. Note, 'Dynasty Trusts and the Rule against Perpetuities,' *Harvard Law Review* 116 (2003), 2604.

assets related to tax obligations owed by the trust beneficiary.[64] The court stated:

> At this time there is no property to which an IRS lien may attach. The Debtor/Beneficiary cannot compel distributions. Therefore there will be no property in the future against which the IRS may place a lien. The IRS must await a distribution from the Trustee.[65]

Scheffel v Krueger concerned a tort action to recover damages related to a criminal action where a male trust beneficiary was convicted of sexually assaulting a two-year-old boy and videotaping it.[66] When the boy's mother (the tort creditor) tried to attach the sexual abuser's interest in the trust to satisfy the tort judgment, the New Hampshire Supreme Court refused, stating that the trust's spendthrift provision barred a claim to satisfy a tort creditor, and that the trust qualified as a spendthrift trust even though the abuser-beneficiary exerted significant control over the trust: he could determine the frequency of payments, demand principal and interest after his fiftieth birthday, and dispose of the trust assets by will.

In *Duvall v McGee*, Katherine Ryon was beaten to death during a robbery at her home. After James Calvert McGee was convicted of felony-murder, Duvall (representing Ms Ryon's estate) tried to enforce a tort judgment against McGees's interest in an $877,000.00 spendthrift trust.[67] The court concluded that the victim of a violent tort may not attach a beneficiary's interest in a spendthrift trust.

A final example concerns Sheikh Fahad Mohammed Al Sabah, the former head of the Kuwait Investment Authority in London, who defrauded a Spanish company, GT, of hundreds of millions of dollars. When GT tried to collect in Jersey on an $800 million judgment against Fahad by accessing his interest in the Esteem trust (settled by Fahad, where he was also a beneficiary, and was even shown to effectively control the trust), the court rejected it because the trust remained valid.[68] As a law firm noted 'even though Sheikh Fahad had defrauded GT out of $800 million, the Court refused to let these 'bad facts' colour its judgment.'[69]

---

64. *Wilson v United States (In Re Wilson)*, 140 B.R. 400 (Bankr. N.D. Tex. 1992).

65. *Wilson v United States (In Re Wilson)*, 407.

66. *Scheffel v Krueger* 782 A 2d 410 (NH 2001). See also Spivack's discussion of this case and asset protection trusts in this collection.

67. *Duvall v McGee*, 375 Md. 476, 826 A.2d 416 (2003).

68. *Re Esteem Settlement* [2003] Jersey Law Reports 188.

69. Undated blogpost on JMV Law, 'Recent Decision Concerning Asset Protection

As if the 'ownerless limbo' resulting from separation of ownership into different parts did not create enough risks against outsiders (that is, legitimate creditors of the settlor or the beneficiaries), the separation of ownership may in some cases be completely fictional. Some trusts may allow a person to be not only the settlor but also a beneficiary, and in some cases also the trustee. The Cook Islands International Trust Act (as of 2004),[70] for instance, allowed a settlor to be the beneficiary, trustee or protector, among other means of control. Even the UK tax authorities describe this possibility: 'A trust is the legal obligation that results when a settlor appoints *themselves* and/or another person/s (the trustee/s) to hold and manage assets (the trust property).'[71]

Another way for the settlor to keep control is by establishing detailed instructions on the trust deed (or a 'letter of wishes') about how the trustees must manage and distribute trust assets. Alternatively, the settlor may retain a right to control or to remove the trustee (or appoint a 'protector' to control, remove or veto the trustee.) Furthermore, a settlor could establish a company to act as the trustee (a corporate trustee) and then control that company, in order to control the trust.

Indeed, it is this possibility of continued control over the assets that may explain why people prefer creating a trust for beneficiaries, rather than donating the assets to those beneficiaries. The Ipsos MORI Social Research report said

> settlors did not consider gifting as a viable option because this would not allow them to still be in control of the assets. They wanted to be able to pass on their assets but continue to be in control of how they were managed and used for a set period of time.[72]

In other words, a settlor may create a trust, not to care for children or sick people, but only to *give the appearance of doing it* in order to achieve the real objective: to protect assets against creditors, while retaining control. This was the judge's conclusion in the Pugachev case:

Trusts,' accessed 6 March 2024, https://jmvlaw.com/recent-decision-concerning-asset-protection-trusts/.

70. International Trusts Act 1984 (as amended 2004) (Cook Islands), s 13C: 'An international trust and a registered instrument shall not be declared invalid or a disposition declared void or be affected in any way by reason of the fact that the settlor, and if more than one, any of them, either: ... (g) is a beneficiary, trustee or protector of the trust or instrument either solely or together with others.'

71. HMRC, *The Taxation of Trusts*, para 3.1 (emphasis added).

72. Leary and Greevy, *Exploring the Use of Trusts*, 24–25.

At all material times he regarded all the assets in these trusts as belonging to him and intended to retain ultimate control. The point of the trusts was not to cede control of his assets to someone else, it was to hide his control of them. In other words Mr Pugachev intended to use the trusts as a pretence to mislead other people, by creating the appearance that the property did not belong to him when really it did. ... The whole scheme was set up to facilitate a pretence about ownership (or rather its absence) should the need arise.[73]

Asset protection trusts or trusts in general may be defended by invoking the idea of protecting vulnerable people. But no law requires trust beneficiaries to be vulnerable. Indeed many of the above examples describe trusts that protected debtors, criminals (including murderers, sexual abusers, and looters of national treasuries in poor countries) and other nefarious players. If countries genuinely want to protect vulnerable people—as they should—then that protection should be available to all vulnerable, not just those who can afford to set up a trust. Furthermore, the protections provided by trusts are not necessarily limited to cover the basic needs of the vulnerable, but may protect the entire capital.

The law usually has different solutions when a trust was created for the sole purpose of becoming insolvent and defrauding creditors, in which case fraudulent conveyance actions would apply; or if the trust is a sham, either because the settlor and trustee do not intend to operate according to what is written in the trust deed, or because the settlor is the trustee and sole beneficiary and has full control over the trust. However, for more sophisticated cases, when either the trust was created many years ago (so fraudulent conveyance actions would no longer apply) or when other persons are included in the trust as trustees and beneficiaries, it may not be easy for legitimate creditors to claim that the trust is invalid, so as to access trust assets.

The following proposal addresses the risks created by asset protection trusts,[74] without removing their legitimate roles, especially for cases

---

73. *Pugachev* [424] and [442] (Birss J).

74. These proposals are specific for asset protection trusts because other legal vehicles have other solutions to allow creditors to access assets. In the case of companies, if a person owning assets through a company becomes insolvent, their creditors could eventually get his shares in the company and then access the company's assets to repay their debt. In unit trusts (used for investments), investors have 'units' in the trust (similar to shares in a company) so the investor's creditors could also eventually get these 'units' to repay their debt (the units have a value based on the trust's assets and investments). Instead, in a typical asset protection trust (e.g. discretionary trust) used to administer family assets or care for children or vulnerable people, neither the settlor nor the beneficiaries have 'units' or fixed and enforceable interests or rights to dispose of trust assets.

where the asset protection trust is just a mechanism for the settlor to keep real control over the assets.[75]

This proposal involves 'appointing an owner' of trust assets held in an 'ownerless limbo' (assets put in the trust by the settlor but where beneficiaries have no rights to them yet), but only under certain conditions. This would be the case for example if an insolvent settlor has a legitimate creditor, but neither sham actions nota fraudulent conveyance actions are available.

In essence, when an insolvent settlor has legitimate creditors, those creditors should be able to access trust assets (transferred by the settlor any time in the past) as if those assets still belonged to the settlor's personal wealth—unless the beneficiaries have already received or become entitled to a distribution. In this situation, the trust would be treated as if it was a will, in the sense that the settlor would be indicating who should inherit the *remaining or surviving* assets (after all debts were paid), but the settlor would not be able to shield the assets from creditors only because they are mentioned in the will.

Instead, once assets are distributed to the beneficiaries, or once beneficiaries are entitled to receive them, only the personal creditors of the beneficiaries would have access to them (if the beneficiaries are insolvent). This would be similar as if the settlor had donated the assets to the beneficiaries.

If the settlor has died and insolvent beneficiaries have personal creditors, these creditors should have access to the trust assets, as if the assets had been inherited and belonged to the beneficiaries (regardless of whether the trust deed or the trustee would allow such a distribution).[76] The portion of trust assets that each insolvent beneficiary should be

---

75. This goal was also described by Mr Justice Snowden, quoting a claimant's skeletal argument: 'The settlors who own the assets to be put into the trusts are typically not the magnanimous patriarchs or plutocrats of old for whom the (onshore) discretionary trust was developed, but hugely wealthy individuals who at heart have no desire to relinquish their control or enjoyment of the assets intended to be transferred, and certainly have no intention that those assets should be advanced or appointed to others without their agreement.' Richard Snowden, 'The Use and Abuse of Trusts and Other Wealth Management Devices,' *Trust Law International* 31 (2017), 102.
76. This guiding principle should be subject to more exploration for unintended consequences. A judge, on a case-by-case basis, may decide not to apply these measures, if it considers that the trust is not an asset protection trust created to affect legitimate creditors. For example, a judge could decide not to apply these measures to a legitimate charitable trust, as long as the judge confirms that the trust is exclusively charitable, that the trust is not in reality accumulating wealth (instead of making substantial distributions), and that no distribution has been made to the settlor or its family members, but only to truly charitable causes.

considered to be entitled to (to repay personal creditors) would depend on the trust deed's provisions. For complex situations where the trustee had full discretion to determine who would get a distribution and how much, a judge could determine what portion of trust assets should belong to each insolvent-heir-beneficiary.[77] (The granting of extra rights to beneficiaries' or settlor's personal creditors would not, under this proposal, give any more rights to the beneficiaries or settlors themselves; and if there are no personal creditors or if debtors have other means to pay back their debts, trust provisions would remain intact.)

To address the risks of assets held in an 'ownerless limbo' this proposal considers treating trusts as if they were companies (in case there are personal creditors and if the debtor is insolvent). A company's *assets* are not directly reachable by a shareholder's personal creditors. However, if the shareholder becomes insolvent, those creditors may be able to obtain the shareholder's *shares* in the company (and thus reach their share of the corporate assets indirectly.) In this proposal, it is as if the insolvent settlor had 'shares' in the trust that would be reachable by the personal creditors. However, once the settlor dies or once beneficiaries become entitled to trust assets, it would be as if beneficiaries are now the owners of the 'shares' in the trust (which would then be reachable by the beneficiaries' creditors).

Although this proposal may sound radical to some, in fact countries already have ways to 'pierce' a trust to protect legitimate creditors. For example, access to trust assets will be granted in fraudulent conveyance actions (if the settlor transferred assets to a trust only to become insolvent), but also in cases of alimony, child support, public policy or unpaid taxes. In the US, for instance, under a 'grantor trust' where the settlor typically acts as trustee of his own revocable living trust, retaining the power to control its income and assets, the IRS may treat the trust's assets as belonging to the settlor for income and for estate tax purposes.[78]

---

77. This would require further exploration. One extreme proposal with the aim to discourage discretionary trusts would be to consider that the personal creditors of any (insolvent) discretionary beneficiary would have access to all trust assets. This extreme position would put a very high price in giving too much discretion to trustees, instead of predetermining what should be distributed to each beneficiary.
78. See Julie Garber, 'What Is a Grantor Trust?' blogpost on *The Balance*, 30 January 2022 (updated), accessed 6 March 2024, https://www.thebalance.com/what-are-grantor-trusts-and-how-can-they-be-changed-3505545.

Conclusion

Trusts may be used for legal and legitimate reasons. However, like any legal vehicle, they can be used for abusive and illicit purposes. To tackle the harms, while retaining their uses, this chapter presents two proposals. The first concerns transparency: for trusts to be legally valid, they should register their beneficial owners (settlors, trustees, protectors, beneficiaries, etc) in public registries, in the same way as legal persons such as companies and private foundations have to register their beneficial owners in public registries in some countries. The second proposal addresses the separation of ownership that can result in trust assets being enjoyed by settlors or beneficiaries, but unreachable by their personal creditors. Assets held in a trust created by an insolvent settlor with personal creditors should be accessible by those creditors, regardless of whether fraudulent conveyance actions apply, and regardless of when the trust was settled. However, the personal creditors of the insolvent settlor would no longer have access to the trust assets once they have been distributed to beneficiaries, or if beneficiaries become entitled (have enforceable rights, not contingent or discretionary ones) to access trust assets. In this moment, the personal creditors of insolvent beneficiaries should have access to trust assets. Nevertheless, as long as no personal creditor exist, of if the debtors have enough money to pay their debts, trusts would remain intact and no external party would have access to trust assets.

9

Trusts Law and Structural Power

T.T. Arvind and Ruth Stirton***

Introduction

Modern equity presents a paradox. On the one hand, much of its doctrinal apparatus is grounded in a past of dealing with the human and relational dimensions of transactions. The modern practice of equity, however, has drifted towards the domain of commerce and the market. This new, altered, context has subjected equity to a range of new demands—for certainty, for a recognition of the importance of contract, for the facilitation of commercial risk-management—which differ fundamentally from the social expectations, arising out of relations of trust and vulnerability, with which it historically dealt.[1]

These changes pose serious questions in relation to the role equity plays, and the role it should play, in the legal system. Should equity concede the demands of the marketplace, as private law in general has done, and embrace its role as a framework for infusing commercial structures with a certain degree of flexibility?[2] Or should it expressly seek to strike a different balance from the common law, grounded in the distinctive conceptual language of 'trust,' 'loyalty,' and 'conscience' in which its doctrines are expressed?[3]

* York Law School, UK.
** Sussex Law School, UK.
1. Peter Millett, 'Equity's Place in the Law of Commerce,' *Law Quarterly Review* 110 (1994).
2. See e.g. John H. Langbein, 'The Secret Life of the Trust: The Trust as an Instrument of Commerce,' *Yale Law Journal* 107 (1997); John H. Langbein, 'The Contractarian Basis of the Law of Trusts,' *Yale Law Journal* 105 (1995).
3. Margaret Halliwell, *Equity and Good Conscience in a Contemporary Context* (London: Old Bailey Press, 1997).

Our purpose in this chapter is to show that answering these questions requires a deeper consideration of the relationship between equity and structural power, and the role equity could play in dealing with structural power. The idea that equity is in some way connected with power is, of course, not new to socio-legal scholarship. It has underlain a significant body of work, including the seminal paper by Roger Cotterrell which inspired this collection.[4] Much of that work, however, has focused on what one might broadly call 'instrumental power'—the power of one individual to determine or alter the legal status or entitlements of another—and, in particular, on agent power arising out of property relations. Structural power represents a rather different phenomenon. As we discuss in greater detail in the next section, structural power is not simply the ability to exercise dominion over another, but a broader ability to embed particular dispositions within the functioning of institutions,[5] and to legitimise a given social structure by embedding a justificatory narrative for it into the ordinary functioning of social, cultural, and political institutions.[6] The role of argument in making law, and the role of doctrine in restricting the domain of permissible argument, make law particularly prone to becoming a vehicle for the exercise of structural power and, correspondingly, make it necessary for the legal system to incorporate mechanisms to identify and limit the influence of structural power. Although equity has the potential to provide such a mechanism, in practice it rarely engages with the task. Instead, it simply reinforces the power relations present in society without articulating, or seeking to articulate, any normative basis for doing so.

In the third section, we use a detailed case study of the pension trust to suggest that this reflects a deep conceptual fossilization within equity. Pension trusts embody a form of structural power which is fundamentally inimical to the interests of beneficiaries. Whilst equity could, in theory, provide redress, its deference to contract and regulation mean that it does not in fact do so. The final section builds on this analysis to argue for a new research agenda for socio-legal scholarship, focused on reviving equity's potential to ameliorate, rather than reinforce, the social impact of structural power.

---

4.   Roger Cotterrell, 'Power, Property and the Law of Trusts: A Partial Agenda for Critical Legal Scholarship,' *Journal of Law and Society* 14 (1987).
5.   Clarissa Rile Hayward, 'On Structural Power,' *Journal of Political Power* 11 (2018), 62–63.
6.   Rainer Forst, *Normativity and Power: Analyzing Social Orders of Justification*, trans., Ciaran Cronin (Oxford: Oxford University Press, 2017), 42.

Structural Power and the Legal System

What is Structural Power?

In legal theory as well as in the social sciences more generally, 'power' is typically discussed in terms of the dominion a legal actor has over another; their ability, to put it differently, to get someone to do something which they otherwise would not do, and which they might not wish to do.[7] As a result, this approach sees power as in terms of the ability of a person or group of persons to alter the position of another.[8] A trustee in a discretionary trust has power over the beneficiary because the trustee can determine the beneficiary's entitlements to proceeds generated by the investment of the trust property. Simultaneously, as Cotterrell pointed out, beneficiaries also have considerable power over trustees because they too can determine the trustees' legal entitlements—[9]for example through their ability under the rule in *Saunders v Vautier* to set aside the trust device.[10]

Structural power, in contrast, is a more subtle phenomenon. Unlike relational or instrumental power, structural power does not require the ability to exercise control over another's actions through direct dominion, nor does it require a conscious attempt to exercise dominion in the way instrumental power does. It refers, instead, to power that is conferred by the normative dimensions of social life. Rather than being a consequence of relations of *domination*, structural power is a consequence of relations of *justification*.[11] Structural power restricts the ability of an actor to freely determine their course of action by creating normative structures of justification that make it politically or culturally impossible for actors to pursue a particular practice or outcome to which they might otherwise have been inclined.[12] This impossibility comes, in part from, the normative dimension of structural power, which defines certain actions as normatively unacceptable while promoting, and creating arguments justifying, other types of actions.[13] But, equally and arguably more fundamentally, structural power functions

---

7. Robert Dahl, 'The Concept of Power,' *Behavioral Science* 2 (1957), 202–3.
8. See Wesley Newcomb Hohfeld, 'The Relations Between Law and Equity,' *Michigan Law Review* 11 (1912-1913).
9. Cotterrell, 'Power, Property and the Law of Trusts,' 86.
10. *Saunders v Vautier* [1841] EWHC 82, [1841] 4 Beav 115.
11. Forst, *Normativity and Power*, 49.
12. Forst, *Normativity and Power*, 17.
13. Forst, *Normativity and Power*, 17.

by creating conditions that make it difficult or impossible for actors to create or institutionalize practices that are grounded in other structures of justification.[14]

Structural power, in other words, functions as a form of closure that is *both* institutional *and* epistemic. Three of its manifestations are of particular importance to socio-legal analyses of law. The first, which has received particular attention in the study of organisations, is the ability to set agendas and determine the terms of debate. The classic example, which has particular salience in the post-crisis agenda, is the phenomenon where regulatory bodies define the challenges they face, and their task in relation to those challenges, in terms that are largely determined by the dominant thought style in the industry they regulate, and whose conceptual development and translation into actual policy agendas is frequently led by dominant firms in those industries.[15]

A second dimension of structural power, which has received particular attention from sociologists of power, is the ability to shape ideas, values, and beliefs in relation to the types of outcomes and conduct that are considered desirable, shift perceptions of whether and to what extent particular real or potential happenings constitute threats in relation to those outcomes, and establish accepted understandings of the types of actions and interventions—whether political or social—that will obviate those threats and increase the propensity of a society to achieve the outcomes in question. These typically operate in a self-reinforcing cycle between structural power and relational power where each element further supports the others,[16] and where the cumulative effect is to create social processes that are very difficult to displace or deflect.[17]

Underpinning both of these, and central to the success of both, is a third dimension of structural power, namely its entrenchment in and through the everyday practices of institutions. Structural power operates cognitively,[18] by creating and socially embedding schemas—dispositions to see the world in a particular way and to respond to events in

---

14. Forst, *Normativity and Power*, 40–47.
15. See e.g. Young's study of policymaking by financial regulators in the US: Kevin Young, 'Not by Structure Alone: Power, Prominence, and Agency in American Finance,' *Business and Politics* 17 (2015).
16. See e.g. Fairfield's analysis of economic reforms in Chile: Tashi Fairfield, 'Structural Power in Comparative Political Economy: Perspectives from Policy Formulation in Latin America,' *Business and Politics* 17 (2015).
17. See e.g. Hayward's analysis of the social entrenchment of discriminatory policies in the US: Clarissa Rile Hayward, *De-Facing Power* (Cambridge: Cambridge University Press, 2000).
18. Forst, *Normativity and Power*, 63 n. 6.

particular ways.[19] In institutions, these schemas create institutional propensities towards particular modes of operation and, in particular, propensities towards adopting particular ways of formulating questions, evaluating the likely consequences of particular courses of action, and considering the desirability of outcomes. As the work of Mary Douglas has demonstrated, these schemas, or 'thought styles' as she terms them, shape not just evaluative processes but also world views: the responses which they see particular stimuli as producing, the way in which they perceive or ascribe causal responsibility for events, and their perceptions of the desirability or undesirability of various risks.[20]

The institutionalisation of these schemas, and the shaping of institutional dispositions to accord with them, has a significant effect on social interaction. It means that social interaction is *habitually* characterised by particular patterns of incentives and disincentives which not only become a necessary basis of social interaction but also, because of the roots of structural power in relations of justification, are coupled with a powerful *legitimatory* basis for the resulting social order and for a 'frame of mind' in which the justificatory basis of that order is seen as being *objectively* legitimate and desirable.[21] For those *exercising* the power, the consequence is to create a 'second nature of functioning,' where the rules of the structures and the justifications for the patterns of outcomes they produce become part of what is seen as 'natural' rather than a choice which is potentially contestable, grounded in a particular ideology, or requires critical scrutiny.[22] For those *subject* to the exercise of the power, the consequence is to render certain types of social actions impossible or difficult, due to the social force of the schemas and the institutional structures they generate.[23]

The Power of Doctrine

As the previous subsection has shown, structural power, unlike instrumental power, can operate even where its beneficiaries did not themselves institute the constraints on social action, or even intend

19. Sally Haslanger, *Resisting Reality: Social Construction and Social Critique* (Oxford: Oxford University Press, 2012) 406–427.
20. See generally Mary Douglas, *How Institutions Think* (Syracuse (NY): Syracuse University Press, 1986).
21. Hayward, 'On Structural Power,' 23–24.
22. Forst, *Normativity and Power*, 44–45.
23. Hayward, 'On Structural Power,' 25.

them to come about.[24] This distinguishes it from standard, agent-based accounts of social power, such as the influential account advanced by Keith Dowding, which treats social power as consisting of the ability to achieve desired outcomes by deliberately altering other actors' incentive structures and, consequently, ties this to the possession of resources which enable the first actor to alter the second actor's incentives.[25] From this perspective, social power is never a useful tool for critically analysing judge-made law as an individual litigator rarely possess the ability to alter the judge's or the other party's incentive structures in a way that might influence the direction of the law. Structural power, in contrast, collapses the artificially sharp structure / agency dichotomy on which such accounts depends, by highlighting the extent to which agents may, whether consciously or routinely, exploit the power conferred by institutional predispositions.

This has obvious implications for how we study law. Equity, like other branches of private law, is dependent on rules and principles articulated in terms of concepts which are normative in form and open-textured in character. The law of trusts, for example, is expressed in legal rules such as 'the duty to take reasonable care,' 'the duty to avoid conflicts of interest,' or 'the duty of loyalty,' which use normative and evaluative language, but are open-textured in that nothing about the concepts carries any necessary implication in relation to when the duties come into existence, what they require legal actors to do, or what constitutes their breach. The answer to these questions is, instead, determined through accumulated institutional practice—the combined mass of judicial rulings, accepted interpretations, and other practices, that are collectively termed 'doctrine.'

The result is that doctrine embeds dispositions towards particular ways of formulating questions and evaluating competing options, as well as to particular types of outcomes, in the ordinary functioning of the legal system, precisely like the schemas dicussed above. The purpose of doctrine, as analytical legal theorists have long recognised, is to screen a sensitive decision-maker off from factors to which he or she would otherwise have had regard, by assigning a high evaluative weight to some factors, a low weight to others, and declaring still others to be legally irrelevant.[26] This is the exact role schemas play, and it suggests

---

24. Iris Marion Young, *Responsibility for Justice* (Oxford: Oxford University Press, 2011), 52.
25. Keith Dowding, *Rational Choice and Political Power* (Aldershot: Edward Elgar, 1991).
26. Frederick Schauer, 'Formalism,' *Yale Law Journal* 97 (1988).

that doctrine is best understood as comprising of structured sets of schemas. Much like schemas, doctrine does not *determine* an outcome. Instead, its primary effect is to rule out certain types of outcomes while also creating a predilection towards other types of outcomes. Doctrine may sometimes do so directly by declaring certain outcomes impermissible. More commonly, however, it does so indirectly by requiring courts or equivalent actors to take into account factors or ignore factors, the practical effect of which is to rule out or impose high bars to certain types of outcomes. Whilst doctrine is never conclusive, even a partial effect—for which there is considerable evidence—makes law particularly prone to becoming a vehicle for structural power.

That structural power is problematic is obvious. A fundamental tenet of socio-legal scholarship is that systems of law must be judged at least in part on whether they show some degree of socially responsiveness. To be socially responsive, a system of law must at a minimum show a conscious awareness that law has a socially relevant institutional function, as a 'facilitator of response to social needs and aspirations,'[27] and it must also show the ability and willingness to engage with that role in developing and applying the rules of law. Structural power, in contrast, not only precludes the law from doing so in relation to the social needs and aspirations that are most salient in the areas with which it deals, but also results in the law failing to recognise that it is not doing so. It is this that gives equity its importance as a way of dealing with structural power. Confining or ameliorating the effects of structural power requires an *alternate* set of schema and supporting narratives of justification, which have power not only at the discursive level but also at the institutional level, by being embedded in the everyday functioning of governing institutions in much the same way as the schema that are the source of structural power. The historical conceptualisation of equity's role as being concerned with 'correcting' the common law is particularly suggestive against this background, as is the concern of 19th century equity for groups within society who were particularly prone to being subject to structural power, such as widows and orphans.

Modern equity is, of course, a thing radically different from 19th century equity, and has other preoccupations.[28] The rise of commerce,

---

27. Philippe Nonet and Philip Selznick, *Law and Society in Transition: Towards Responsive Law* (New York: Harper and Row, 1978), 14–15.
28. For a particularly clear account of the shift, see Gregory S. Alexander, 'The Transformation of Trusts as a Legal Category, 1800–1914,' *Law and History Review* 5 (1987).

in particular, has resulted in a very different range of demands being made of equity, resulting—as Cotterrell has shown—in an increased focus on technical competence rather than moral trust, on the proprietary rather than the relational character of the underlying relationship, and on the systemic, transactional link between the parties (in a manner akin to contract) rather than on the social and personal link between the parties.[29] This is closely tied to the broader shift in private law that one of us has elsewhere called the 'managerial turn.' As we demonstrate in the next section through the example of the pension trust, its consequence is that modern equity no longer seeks to identify or redress the effects of structural power, even though the need for the role has not gone away.

Structural Power in Context: The Case of the Pension Trust

The pension fund, which is typically constituted as a trust, is a complex and risky beast, and the experience of the past three decades has shown that the ordinary law of trusts cannot by itself deal with the issues it creates. This was evidenced very clearly in 2001–2002 when a significant number of pensions were decimated in the Enron collapse. The Pensions Act 2004 created The Pensions Regulator (a replacement for the Occupational Pensions Regulatory Authority that had been created by the Pensions Act 1995) as a response to criticism of OPRA, and to increase public confidence in the regulatory oversight of all pension funds.[30]

The fact that the law of trusts is not a *sufficient* mechanism for dealing with the issues created by pensions funds does not mean, however, that it is no longer *necessary*. The challenge for the law is to find a regulatory framework that protects both the stability of pension funds and the interests of beneficiaries. Our argument in this section is that the current legal framework, largely as a consequence of structural power, favours the interests of fund managers and the fund itself over the expectations and needs of beneficiaries by failing to provide any legal mechanisms by which beneficiaries can seek to hold fund managers to account. The Universities Superannuation Scheme and particularly the crisis in 2017 and 2018 are a good vehicle to explore the limits of the current approach to the pensions trust

---

29. Roger Cotterrell, 'Trusting in Law: Legal and Moral Concepts of Trust,' *Current Legal Problems* 46 (1993).
30. Department of Work and Pensions, *Simplicity, Security and Choice: Working and Saving for Retirement* (Cm 5677, 2002) [3]–[7].

and its connection with structural power. USS is a unique pension fund with a significant defined benefit component complemented by a minor defined contribution scheme once the contributor earns over the current threshold of £57,216.50 (increasing annually in line with inflation).[31] It is one of largest pension schemes in the UK, with 418,964 members. USS is a multi-employer scheme which binds all the member institutions together with its 'last man standing' principle. The 'last man standing' principle means that as members go bankrupt, the remaining member institutions take on their liability, and in the event of total collapse of the sector, the last solvent institution carries the liability for the whole of the scheme's commitments. The effect of this is that the burden of risk associated with failure of the scheme falls disproportionately on some institutions.

In theory, the interests of the different persons involved in USS—the fund managers, the institutions contributing to the fund, and the members of the scheme—are balanced in a range of ways. The first is a mixture of 'soft' and 'hard' regulation. The 'soft' regulation arises from the structure of the scheme, which includes an express role for negotiations between representatives of employers and employees. The 'hard' regulation comes from the role of the Pensions Regulator (tPR). In addition, the law of trusts continues to exist as a backstop to hold trustees to their legal duties. Despite this, contributing members in 2017 began growing increasingly concerned about protecting their rights. This caused the USS pensions crisis of 2017-2018, which included the biggest industrial action in the UK higher education sector to date. The resort to industrial action raises the question of why the legal mechanisms to balance the interests of different groups failed to provide effective relief to the contributing members of the USS. As we demonstrate in the remainder of this section, the answer lies in the deference of equity to contract and regulation, whose cumulative effect is to insulate fund managers from virtually every one of the mechanisms that trust law in theory provides beneficiaries. This is a product of the third dimension of structural power discussed above—namely, a thought-style that prioritises the commercial motivations of modern pension fund trustees and their key personnel (leading to a deference to contract), and the systemic interests of the financial and retirement systems (leading to a deference to regulation) over addressing the consequences of the peculiarly vulnerable and powerless situation in which beneficiaries find themselves.

---

31. As of April 2019.

The Failure of Regulation

The Pensions Act 1995 requires defined benefit pension funds to be maintained at a level at which the fund can meet all its obligations.[32] This is calculated on the basis of an actuarial valuation of the exposure of the fund against its assets and investment performance.[33] This is also to be weighed against the 'employer covenant,' which is the employers' capacity to make additional contributions to the fund in order to ensure its ability to meet its liabilities. The USS valuation is carried out on a triennial basis. The delay in the 2017 valuation raises some significant concerns about the integrity of the regulatory framework in this area. The Pensions Regulator states that trustees should 'start their valuation process in good time and follow a project plan that leaves sufficient time for advice and analysis, as well as negotiation with the employer.'[34] Trustees that have not completed their valuation within the 15-month period may be subject to enforcement proceedings by the Pensions Regulator with a view to ensuring that an appropriate recovery plan is in place going forward.

The success of this relatively short time period seems predicated on employers and employees speaking with one voice, and negotiation being a straightforward and quick process. USS, however, is the exclusive pension scheme for 68 institutions. Although negotiation is to be carried out by the umbrella organisations Universities UK, for the employers, and the Universities and Colleges Union, for the employees, each individual employer has its own position on the risk it is willing to carry, and its relations with its employees are affected by distinct local and national issues. As a result, when it became clear in late 2017 that there was no real chance of agreement between UUK and UCU on how best to take forward the valuation, this assumption broke down. Fighting industrial action at a local level and within the context of other local employment relationship disputes led to public challenges from individual vice-chancellors to the hardline approach taken by UUK. Newcastle University's vice-chancellor broke ranks with UUK on the first strike day.[35] Much the same phenomenon also occurred on the side

---

32. The Pensions Act 1995 ss 56–59
33. Alastair Hudson, *Equity and Trusts* (Abingdon: Routledge, 2016).
34. The Pensions Regulator, *Annual Funding Statement* (April 2018), 14.
35. UCU, 'Newcastle Vice-Chancellor Backs Striking Lecturers and Calls for Talks in Pension Row,' (22 February 2018), accessed 29 February 2024, https://www.ucu.org.uk/article/9350/Newcastle-vice-chancellor-backs-striking-lecturers-and-calls-for-talks-in-pension-row.

of the employees. There were calls for the UCU general secretary to step down to change the union's approach, which escalated into a full-blown fracture between the national UCU executive and the ordinary members when branches rejected the offer from Universities UK in defiance of guidance from the national UCU team.

The question this raises is the ability of the Pensions Regulator to enforce its standards. If the USS trustees can demonstrate that they are actively trying to facilitate the necessary negotiations, and are taking account of the complex industrial relations issues that are relevant, then the Pensions Regulator is likely to simply allow them to get on with it.[36] Even if they were to seek to take enforcement action against USS, it is far from clear that any result would be forthcoming. Equally, action imposing additional contributions on the basis of the disputed 2017 valuation would simply exacerbate the dispute, especially in the wake of the Joint Expert Panel report,[37] which was intended to break the gridlock between the negotiating parties, but concluded that there were significant problems with the way that the 2017 valuation had been conducted. If law's function is to provide an arena in which conflict can be limited through a process in which different interests can compete on an equal footing, then the regulatory framework is clearly unable to discharge this function; and systemic power plays a central role in that inability.

The Failure of Trusts Law

What, then, of the ability of beneficiaries to control their trustees through the remedies in the ordinary law of trusts highlighted by Cotterrell? Collective action, in the way envisaged and approved of in *Saunders v Vautier,* is impossible because the practical issues involved in getting the circa 400,000 members to agree to the collective legal action are a complete barrier to any possibility of using *Saunders*. It is also practically impossible for the beneficiaries (including contributing members, deferred members, existing pensioners) to join together to bring the fund to an end, and resettle it on different terms. A further practical barrier arises from the complexity of pensions law, which must be navigated to initiate and continue legal action against the trustees. The legal advisors to USS are part of a magic circle law firm—

---

36. The Pensions Regulator, 'Annual Funding Statement' (2018).
37. The Joint Expert Panel on the Universities Superannuation Scheme, *Report of the Joint Expert Panel* (techspace rep, 2018).

CMS Cameron McKenna Nabarro Olswang—with a pensions law team charging a hourly rate of around £1000+VAT. Initiating and bringing legal proceedings against the trustees in relation to any of the duties the law puts them under is likely to be so prohibitively expensive as to be wholly outwith the capacity of any beneficiaries, whether acting individually or collectively.

This state of affairs is the antithesis of what we mean when we talk about equity. The point of equity is conventionally taken to be that beneficiaries of trusts have power to claim what they are entitled to, to hold the trustees to account, and to direct the trustees who work for them to act in their interests. The failure to rework the principles underlying the law of trusts, so as to make this power a practical possibility for the significantly altered entity represented by the modern pensions trust, is therefore particularly striking. The significance of the failure becomes clear when we consider the differences between these trusts and family trusts—the paradigm example of a trust in the ordinary law. Beneficiaries are entitled to their pensions, their benefits, because they are contributors to the pension fund. In the ordinary law of trusts, this means that they hold a dual role as both settlor and beneficiary. We need only make fleeting reference to the *Vandervell* litigation to illustrate the challenges that this dual role presents.[38] Further, employers–who are also settlors–are unlike settlors of family trusts paying in money in fulfilment of a contractual obligation for which the beneficiaries have given good consideration.

The position of trustees is similar. The paradigm of the trustee envisaged by much of equity is the trustee acting voluntarily in the interests of the beneficiaries—for example, the family friend who manages a testamentary trust for the children of his longstanding friend–who has no interest or ability to make a profit from this enterprise and does it as voluntary service. The reality of pension fund management is the antithesis of this. The management of a pension scheme is a professional—and typically very well remunerated—service that is established under the trust deeds. In the case of USS, the entity that carries out the management is a private limited company.[39] A corporate trustee is not acting out of beneficence. Rather, it acts because its commercial interests are served by providing a professional service for the beneficiaries.

On its face, these factors would militate in favour of a *higher*, rather than lower, level of practical power in the hands of beneficiaries.

---

38. *Vandervell v IRC* [1967] 2 AC 291. Also see Adam Gearey in this collection.
39. Company number 01167127.

Yet, in actual fact, the law does the opposite. A fundamental structural difference between the paradigm private family trustee and the corporate trustee service is the presence of an exclusion clause, which the modern law of trusts not only recognises but also facilitates. In the theory of trusts law, the exclusion clause is a way of recognising the high burden on the trustees of the fiduciary duties, by permitting them to control their potential liability. In practice, they go well beyond this. The exclusion clause that applies to USS, found in clause 72 of the USS trust deed, excludes all liability for breach of trust except for 'fraud or deliberate or culpable disregard of the interests of those actually, prospectively or contingently entitled to any relevant benefit under the scheme.'[40] If the only scope for finding the pension trustees liable is for breaches which amount to fraud, or culpable disregard for the interests of the beneficiaries, the effect is that access to justice for beneficiaries, and access to the mechanism for controlling the actions of trustees is eroded to the point of virtual non-existence.

Why, then, does the law take this stance, creating such a significant gap between the reality of the legal framework of pensions trusts and the underpinning equitable concepts? The discussion of structural power above provides us with an important part of the answer to this question. The heart of the modern legal approach to the pensions trust lies in the systemic function it plays, as a key component of social welfare provision in the UK—every person who is adequately provided for by their occupational pension fund is a person who is not dependent on the state pension or any other aspect of the welfare state for their livelihood—and as a key source of investment in the financial and capital markets. The result is that when faced with a choice of schema favouring either the beneficiaries' interests of control and accountability, or the broader systemic interests fostered by making the resilience of the fund the primary source of restraints upon the trustees' discretion, it is to the latter that governing institutions are likely to be predisposed. The law, in such a situation, will take a position that gives significant structural power to the trustees and the fund managers at the expense of the beneficiaries.

The current shape of the law of pensions trusts is consistent with this picture. The law does in fact prioritise the resilience of the trust fund, permitting the trust to resile very significantly from promises made

---

40.   Universities Superannuation Scheme, *Consolidated Rules of Universities Superannuation Scheme Incorporating all Deeds of Amendment up to and including the Fifteenth Deed of Amendment dated 9 December 2014* (April 2009). Liability is also preserved for certain duties of care and skill under Pensions Act 1995, s 33.

to beneficiaries if that is necessary to secure resilience. It permits trustees and fund managers to protect themselves against actions by framing broad exclusion clauses. And, as discussed above, this *epistemic* closure is reinforced by *institutional* closure, under which the law sets hurdles to ordinary actions in the law of trusts whose practical effect is to make those actions impossible. Beneficiaries, in consequence, have to rely on the Pensions Regulator to protect their interests, even though the standards of protection in the Pensions Act are considerably inferior to those under the ordinary law of trusts, and even though tPR acts primarily to protect the resilience of the trust fund, rather than to vindicate the beneficiaries' putative claim to hold trustees to account. As with all forms of structural power, the accompanying justification narrative, and the schema it generates, provides a powerful and attractive normative validation for this state of things being the natural, and desirable, order of things. The result is to close the doors of law to beneficiaries, leaving them with little choice but to rely on extra-legal means such as industrial action. Academia is relatively unique in involving beneficiaries with high amounts of social capital (and, hence, access to structural power in non-legal circles). Outside this specific context, it is hard to avoid the conclusion that the law of trusts has failed to discharge what ought to be a core social function.

Equity and Structural Power: Towards a New Research Agenda

Structural power is not an easy phenomenon for legal systems to deal with. Unlike instrumental power, which arises out of features of a specific jural or social relationship, structural power has more multifarious roots making it resistant to the ordinary forms of legal control. The law can set limits to relational or instrumental power in relatively straightforward way, because the ability of an agent to exercise dominion can be restrained through a range of techniques. It can be restrained by setting bounds to the power directly as, for example, the exceptions to *Saunders v Vautier* do. Alternately, it can be restrained by setting pre-conditions that seek to channel the ends to which the power can be exercised and, hence, the impact it can have on those subject to it as, for example, rules around the public benefit test for charitable trusts do. Finally, it can be restrained by setting procedural safeguards that seek to reduce the likelihood that the power will be exercised to induce someone to act against their interests as, for example, the law of undue influence does.[41] But it is hard to see how these techniques can assist in controlling structural power. As the previous section has shown, structural power arises out of 'multiple, interacting, large-scale social processes,'[42] which are deeply embedded in the institutional structure of the legal system, including not just fundamental aspects of its doctrines and processes, but also the assumptions it makes about the way the world functions. It is self-evidently unlikely that legal schemas which have a high likelihood of reflecting the same underlying predispositions can play a strong role in restraining these processes.

Our aim in this chapter has been to show that equity is no exception. Notwithstanding equity's roots in very different ways of thinking about society, the deference to regulation and to common law concepts that characterises the modern law of trusts makes it prone to the very same problems of structural power that trouble other areas of law. Many of the problems that are conventionally analysed as being connected with property, or with commerciality, are on our analysis a result of the role structural power plays within the doctrines of equity. Two cases decided within the past two decades, *Re Farepak*,[43] and *Scott v Southern Pacific*,[44] provide particularly clear illustrations. Both *Re Farepak* and *Scott* related to situations where the interests of disempowered groups came head-to-head with the interests of the financial sector, a group that enjoys an unusually high degree of structural power in modern Britain. Both cases involved situations where public regulatory frameworks failed to protect the interests of the group in question—in *Re Farepak*, because the Financial Services Compensation Scheme did not apply to the specific type of saving at issue, and in *Scott* because 'sale and lease back' schemes were not at the time a regulated activity under section 19 of the Financial Services and Markets Act 2000 (a situation that has since changed).

Given the discussion of structural power in the second section of this chapter, it is hard to avoid the conclusion that the regulatory gaps in both cases were a result of the groups in question lacking structural power and, hence, the ability to have their interests, and their vulnerability, brought onto the regulatory agenda. Structural power—or, rather, the failure to consider the relevance of structural power for the workings of equitable doctrine—also lay at the heart of the final outcomes

---

41. *Royal Bank of Scotland plc v Etridge* [2001] UKHL 44, [2002] 2 AC 773.
42. Hayward, 'On Structural Power,' 56.
43. *Re Farepak* [2008] EWHC 3272 (Ch), [2008] BCC 22.
44. *Scott v Southern Pacific Mortgages Ltd* [2014] UKSC 52, [2015] 1 AC 385.

in both sets of cases, with equity too failing to protect the groups in question. The reasoning in both cases demonstrates that the courts were overtly influenced by the now-established trend of according higher priority to contractual rights over equitable rights save where precedent clearly establishes otherwise and, less overtly but no less clearly, by the systemic importance to the economy of providing an environment in which lenders feel able to lend with security.[45] In both cases, the result was, paradoxically, that the law protected precisely those persons who were in a position to take steps to protect themselves but failed to do so, while refusing to protect precisely those persons who had little practical ability to protect themselves and, hence, were in actual need of legal protection.

The discussion of the pensions trust in this chapter shows a similar pattern. The law's task in relation to pensions trusts can be conceptualised in a number of ways. As we have shown, the expectations of beneficiaries are of no more than peripheral importance to the present framing which focuses, instead, on protecting the fund and on creating an environment within which fund managers can make investment decisions in a manner that insulates them from any broader responsibility or accountability to the beneficiaries. This stands in stark contrast to the position in the types of trusts studied by Cotterrell, and reflects the dominant influence of structural power. The systemic importance of pensions trusts as sources of funds in the financial system, and the consequent imperative of freeing fund managers to make investment decisions, means that it is their interests that will dominate policy-making agendas, and that it is towards their protection that the regulatory policy will be predisposed. Here, too, the tendency of modern equity to defer to contract and to regulation means that it has little additional relief to offer affected beneficiaries.

Our purpose in this chapter, however, is not just critique. An implicit point in our argument is that equity can in principle play a constructive role in dealing with the problem of structural power. Notwithstanding the actual outcome in the cases discussed above, the fact remains that only equitable concepts and doctrines, and not the common law or regulation, provided the claimants in those cases a language—and, more fundamentally for our purposes, a conceptual framework—in which they could seek to protect their interests. Equally, it remains the case that as things stand equitable concepts and ideas come far closer to giving legal form to the needs and expectations of the beneficiaries

---

45. Lina Mattsson, 'Harsh but Fair?' *New Law Journal* 165 (2015), 14.

of pensions trusts than do either the regulatory approach taken by tPR, or the contractual language that characterises the actual constitutive documents of the typical pensions trust. Equity, in other words, has far more potential than any other part of the legal system to form a counterweight to the structural power whose effects so profoundly influence the practical everyday working of the law, and statutory regulation, too, would be more effective if it drew on the resources provided by equitable concepts. Working to develop equity so that it does in fact realise this potential, and begin play a role in ameliorating the effects of structural power, should for that reason be an important part of the agenda of socio-legal scholarship.

10

Charity and Ideology

*Henry Jones**

'Charity [is] cold, loveless and manipulative; if a rich man wants to help the poor, he should pay his taxes gladly, not dole out money at a whim.'

Francis Beckett describing Clement Attlee's view of charity.[1]

Introduction

At the end of his 1987 article Roger Cotterrell raises the 'profound and far reaching ideological dimensions' of the law of charities.[2] Specifically, this is the construction of society as a property owner. This question is beautifully conceived in the original paper, but remains largely unanswered in trusts scholarship since then. This chapter takes forward the question of charity and ideology, to elaborate the initial observation, to develop the critique, and discover the shortcomings simply of critiquing charity as ideology.

Why charity and ideology today? The current crisis of reproduction of the capitalist mode of production, which began in 2008, has seen the greatest ever move of wealth and ownership into the hands of fewer people. Global society is more unequal than ever. Capital has been amassed in private hands like never before.[3] One of the ways this wealth is held and used is in charities, such as the Gates Foundation. Meanwhile, states have withdrawn evermore from society, removing

---

* Durham Law School, UK.
1. Francis Beckett, *Clem Attlee* (London: Richard Cohen Books, 1997).
2. Roger Cotterrell, 'Power, Property, and the Law of Trusts: A Partial Agenda for Critical Legal Scholarship,' *Journal of Law and Society* 14 (1987), 89.
3. A leading recent study of this, with a UK focus, is Danny Dorling, *Peak Inequality: Britain's Ticking Time Bomb* (Chicago: Policy Press, 2018).

public funding for everything from homelessness, healthcare and disability support to museums, libraries and the arts. Again, this gap is to be filled by private funding, often in the form of charity. Thus, the work that charity as an idea is doing in the twenty-first century is ripe for interrogation.

Charity has multiple meanings, ranging from love (often of a Christian religious sort), to specifically giving to those in need. Raymond Williams finds the dominant root of charity to be the Christian context, meaning 'Christian love, between man and God, and between men and their neighbours.'[4] The dominant meaning of giving help to the needy is established by the sixteenth century, 'and used with a new sense of abstraction from late seventeenth and early eighteenth centuries.'[5] The meaning of charity as an institution is established in the late seventeenth century. Phrases such as 'Charity begins at home' have been in common usage since the early seventeenth century. But the phrase 'Cold as Charity' which has its contemporary meaning since late eighteenth century, shows an interesting flip side to the word's meaning. Williams connects this feeling of charity as cold to resentment of accepting charity and associated feelings of wounded self-respect and loss of dignity and independence, particularly bound up with class relationships. Clement Atlee understood this when he wrote, 'Charity without loss of dignity is only possible between equals. A right established by law, such as that to an old age pension, is less galling than an allowance made by the rich man to the poor one, dependent on his view of the recipient's character, and terminable at his caprice.'[6]

Williams, surprisingly, finds the only place where charity retains its wide meaning of love and care in the specialist legal use. Otherwise he focuses on state welfare, and the clear ideology tied up in concepts such as deserving poor, welfare as being connected to returning to wage labour, and even social democratic defences of welfare as not charity but a right. Williams was a brilliant literary, cultural and political Marxist theorist, but he was not a lawyer. Examining the legal concept of charity will reveal a word just as burdened with ideological baggage, perhaps just better hidden.

The complexities of definition sharpen when the legal definition of charity is considered. In law the word charity can refer to particular forms: charitable trusts, charitable companies limited by guarantee, unincorporated associations or charitable incorporated organisations.

4.   Raymond Williams, *Keywords* (New York: Fontana Press, 1983), 54.
5.   Williams, *Keywords*, 54.
6.   Clement Atlee, *The Social Worker* (London: George Bell & Sons, 1920), 75.

It can also be defined by governance: charities are subject to supervision and reporting requirements of the Charity Commission for England and Wales. It is also useful to define charities by their legal and fiscal advantages. These include rules on certainty and perpetuity not applying to charitable trusts, benevolent construction of terms, and exemption from income, corporation and inheritance tax. The historic development of charities law is another way of defining the area, and that is where the first section will begin. It is traditional to begin with the 1601 Statute of Charitable Uses, trace the developments through eighteenth and nineteenth century case law such as *Morice v Bishop of Durham*[7] and *Special Commissioners of Income Tax v Pemsel*[8] and then to the twentieth and twenty-first century Charities Acts. The law itself throughout this history provides a definition that a charity is for charitable purposes *only*, and is for the public benefit. The meaning of the terms charitable purpose and public benefit, are broad and non-specific, and remain in Jonathan Garton's phrase 'encrusted with a luxuriant growth of case law.'[9] At the heart of all of this the actual function of charity is lost. A focus on ideology is one way to rediscover it.

In this chapter ideology and ideology critique will be explained, analysed, and critiqued. This will then be applied to the law of charities. First, attention will be given to historical development, then to specific charitable purposes. The central argument is that the law of charity performs a variety of ideological functions, but fundamentally it does more than constructing society as a property owner. It makes the problems of society a question of individual guilt and individual generosity. It allows for the celebration of generosity in the voluntary providing of food to those going hungry, or shelter to those sleeping rough, rather than exposing the injustice of any society allowing this to happen. Furthermore, it constructs these problems as misfortune, or even deserved, rather than the product of political and economic choice.

Introducing Ideology

> '[ideas] organise human masses, and create the terrain on which men move, acquire consciousness of their position, struggle, etc.'

Antonio Gramsci, *Selections from the Prison Notebooks*, 1971[10]

---

7.   (1805) 10 Ves Jun 522, 32 ER 947.
8.   [1891] AC 531.
9.   Jonathan Garton, *Moffat's Trusts Law*, 6th ed. (Cambridge University Press, 2015), 934 (hereafter cited in text as *Moffat*).
10.   Antonio Gramsci, *Selections from the Prison Notebooks* (New York: International

If charity is a hard term to define, ideology is an even more complex term. The OED defines ideology as 'a systematic scheme of ideas, usually relating to politics, economics, or society and forming the basis of action or policy; a set of beliefs governing conduct. Also: the forming or holding of such a scheme of ideas.'[11] Historically, the word originates in an academic distinction of new philosophy of mind from ancient metaphysics at the end of the eighteenth century.[12] It quickly developed its pejorative force, initially as a criticism by conservative thinkers of idealistic thought, but also as used by Marx and Engels in *The German Ideology* where ideology is thought abstracted away from the real processes of history. Ideas are 'nothing more than the ideal expression of the dominant material relationships, the dominant material relationships grasped as ideas.'[13] Ideology is that thought which doesn't grasp this, which sees the relationship between material reality and abstract thought upside down: 'in all ideology men and their circumstances appear upside down as in a *camera obscura*.'[14] This gives us a first meaning of ideology as illusion, false consciousness, a set of ideas which either are unconnected to, or fundamentally misunderstand, material reality.

The word is also used in a more neutral sense. It is not necessarily derogatory to speak of a socialist ideology, or a working class ideology, as the set of ideas capturing the material reality of one social class in its relations with another. Radical movements of the twenty-first century can be seen to reclaim socialist ideology from a neoliberal consensus that portrayed the market as post-ideological. Here what is important is the relationship between ideas and the means of production, or more generally power, whether it be political, economic, cultural or any other kind. These two elements of ideology are crucial to the meaning of the term: falsity and power. These two features are not always present, and can be understood as Williams does as two different meanings of the word, often used confusingly. This confusion is the linguistic root of the difficulty of using ideology as a critical concept. They need separating and clarifying before returning to charity's ideological function.

Publishers, 1971), 459.
11.   *Oxford English Dictionary*, s.v. 'ideology (n.), sense 4,' (July 2023): accessed 1 March 2024, doi.org/10.1093/OED/3067572701.
12.   Williams, *Keywords*, 154
13.   Karl Marx and Friedrich Engels, *The German Ideology* (Amherst (New York): Prometheus Books, 1998), 67.
14.   Marx and Engels, *The German Ideology*, 37.

First, falsity. Ideology is usually used to denote an idea informing an action where the idea is false in some way. Terry Eagleton gives the example of a racist ideology holding that some races are superior to others.[15] This is clearly false. But it is built on something true, or nobody would believe it. It is true to observe that some people are inferior to others at some things. The feelings of disempowerment and resentment which come with poverty and suffering are also true. It is ideology which misdirects these feelings. Louis Althusser sees this operating at a less conscious level, with ideology primarily about 'lived relations' with society. It is about affective, unconscious and emotional response to the world. Ideology 'expresses a will, a hope or nostalgia, rather than describing a reality.'[16] Ideology is both cognitive and affective, a matter of both rationality and emotion. Exactly where the falsity is located is also worth analysing. A statement may be ideological without being false. That unemployment is a problem and should be reduced is not a false idea. An increase in the hostility of the immigration system and a reduction in job security as a response is also not necessarily false if it achieves increased employment. What is false is the conception of social justice, the idea that this is the way to do things, which takes us back to an understanding of ideology as about ideas and their relation to material circumstances.

A second key issue is power. Ideology usually relates to the ideas of the dominant in society, a ruling ideology. But oppositional politics too have their ideology. Ideology is a useful, and not always pejorative, word to describe oppositional politics on both the left and right. A European socialist in the twenty-first century might hark back to a far bigger role for the state in daily life, and this is equally ideological as the dominant market ideology of a small state. These are also both ideological positions regardless of their falsity or falsifiability. It might be more useful to focus on ideology as about power. Michel Foucault's most general lesson about power is that it proliferates in all human relations.[17] However, there is a distinction to be drawn between every-day power relationships and those which relate to social ordering. In Eagleton's example, a breakfast table argument over burnt toast might be a power struggle, but it is ideological only when it engages questions of sexual power or beliefs about gender roles.[18] These two meanings

---

15. Terry Eagleton, *Ideology: An Introduction* (London: Verso, 1991), 12–13.
16. Louis Althusser, *For Marx* (London: Penguin, 1969), 234.
17. Michel Foucault, *Discipline and Punish* (London: Penguin, 1991).
18. Eagleton, *Ideology*, 8.

need to be disaggregated, but can be productively reconnected. After all, one's opponents' political ideas are always false in that they are derived from a different view of social and material reality, and of how to organise social and material relations.

It is also worth considering ideology's relationship with action. To what extent do people act according to their ideology? To what extent is ideology important in material relations of dominance and oppression? It is probably fair to say that ideology is important, but not determinative. It is still true today in twenty-first century Britain that most people believe in and want the public ownership of utilities, and yet voted for a long series of governments intent on privatisation.[19] To credit this to ideology is to give too much away to the governments and too little to those who are governed. Post financial crisis austerity programs have needed ideology to some extent, visible in the language of scroungers and the undeserving poor, or in the metaphors of household budgets and overspent credit cards, but this hasn't prevented opposition. People might believe in the need for austerity, but they also staff and stock food banks, give money to the homeless, and campaign to keep their local library open. The reverse of this is also true, in that the ideology might be true, and the action false. Eagleton gives the example of believing in apartheid as wrong while sitting on a bench labelled 'whites only.' This is derived from Marx's idea that the commodity supplies its own ideology, that ideology is built in to everyday material existence.[20] Thus we can be aware (conscious) of the ideology at play, but act that way anyway.

To understand ideology's relationship with action, Eagleton gives four different mechanisms by which ideology can affect action: rationalising; legitimation; universalising; naturalisation.[21] Rationalisation is a psychoanalytic category, in which it means an attempt to offer a logically consistent or ethically acceptable explanation for an idea whose true motivations are not perceived. To re-use an example, arguing that migration puts pressure on welfare and wages could be a rationalisation of a racist belief. Similarly, the oppressed might also rationalise, believing that hard work offers a route to prosperity. This self-deception

19. Eagleton, *Ideology*, 33–34. For a more recent evidence of this continued attitude, see Independent/BMG Polling poll June 2018, accessed 1 March 2024, https://www.bmgresearch.co.uk/the-independent-bmg-poll-widespread-support-for-renationalisation-of-railways-amidst-continued-disruption-to-services/.
20. Karl Marx, *Capital Volume 1* (London: Penguin, 1990), 'Chapter 1: Fetishism of Commodities'.
21. Eagleton, *Ideology*, 51–61.

might even be useful, making life more tolerable. Rationalisation is again ideology as false, but not all ideology is false as already highlighted. So ideology isn't just about rationalising. Legitimation is close to rationalisation, but is more specifically about how the ruling power secures consent. Legitimation is not always false either; it is about securing acceptance of a dominant set of ideas. Examples here might be that welfare is not a right, or that insecure working conditions are better for the worker. The unemployed person who believes these things to be true has accepted the ruling ideology, and the ruling power has been legitimised.

Universalising takes us in a different direction. This is the presentation of ideas as universal, as some how fundamentally true. Again, this is not always a false belief—the belief that the emancipation of the working class is good for all humanity, for example, may well be a universal benefit. However, it is more commonly seen in something like the belief that there have always been and always will be homeless people, an argument which is both historically and economically false. Charity has this effect by presenting individual gifts as the only option, the only way to mitigate suffering. Naturalisation is a similar effect, but does not need to be universal. Naturalising ideology closes the gap between the idea and social reality, making material facts also intellectual necessity, denying that things could ever be any other way. This is captured through John Steinbeck's aphorism that 'socialism never took root in America because the poor see themselves not as an exploited proletariat, but as temporarily embarrassed millionaires.'[22] It becomes common sense that everyone has the opportunity to be wealthy, but some have not taken it. There is no space left to question why are people poor.

Stuart Hall highlights a shortcoming in theorising around ideology which is not answered by Eagleton.[23] This is the presentation of ideas as belonging to particular classes. This is most clearly seen in Althusser's essay 'Ideological State Apparatus,' where he argues that ideologies are imposed top down through key state institutions such as schools and churches.[24] There is plenty of use in this analysis, but it misses, as Hall argues, the fluidity of ideas. Hall, drawing on Gramsci, defines common

---

22. As quoted in Ronald Wright, *A Short History of Progress* (Toronto: Anansi Press, 2004), 124.
23. Stuart Hall, 'The Problem of Ideology–Marxism without Guarantees,' *Journal of Communication Inquiry* 10 (1986).
24. Louis Althusser, 'Ideological State Apparatus,' in *Lenin and Philosophy* (London: Monthly Review Press, 1971).

sense as 'a historical, not a natural or universal or spontaneous form of popular thinking' which is 'composed of very contradictory ideological formations.'[25] Common sense is the terrain on which ideological struggle most often takes place. No class can have absolute ownership over ideas, and nobody can decisively control what ideas mean. Hall also emphasises that with ideas we are dealing with language, and language's relationship to the material world is indeterminate and changeable; an idea can change its meaning and for whom it operates. The economic remains determinate in the first instance, but after that the field is open to struggle, to making use of whatever is available.

Ideology is about the relation between ideas and the material conditions of society. These ideas are often but not always false or falsifiable. They are about political power, and often but not always about the dominant political power in society. Ideas can both inspire and prevent action, and ideas act in the world, but not always in predictable or fixed ways. What to do with ideology is another question, one that is now elaborated with the focus on the law of charity. The next section outlines the most obvious ideological functions of charity, putting some meat on the bones outlined by Cotterrell.

The Ideological Function of Charity

Illan Kapoor uses Slavoj Žižek's understanding of ideology in his critique of celebrity humanitarianism.[26] The explanation is useful here, bearing in mind everything said about ideology in the first part. Žižek explains the meaning of ideology critique by reference to a joke in the Ernst Lubitsch film Ninotchka, in which the central character visits a café and orders a coffee without cream. The waiter apologises, saying they have no cream, only milk, will the customer instead take his coffee without milk? This is how ideology functions, it is just as important what is not said as what is said, what is absent as well as what is present. The function of ideology critique is to unveil what is not said or done. In this section the ideology in the history of charities will first be revealed, before focusing on charitable purposes specifically.

25. Hall, 'Marxism without Guarantees,' 42.
26. Illan Kapoor, *Celebrity Humanitarianism: The Ideology of Global Charity* (Oxford: Routledge, 2013).

History as Ideology

Pre-modern law of charities is mostly of the religious sort, found in Ecclesiastical courts and the Church being the part of the State responsible for welfare. In England and Wales, the origins of capitalism and the historic change in the mode of production saw the Church lose power, the peasantry lose their land, and a new wealthy merchant class establish itself, whose wealth was not necessarily connected to the welfare of a local area. In *Capital Volume 1* Marx refers to the 'bloody legislation against the expropriated,' laws brought in as a response to the social destruction wrought by enclosure.[27] What he doesn't include is charity.[28] The first poor laws were enacted in 1572, drawing a distinction between deserving and undeserving poor. Here we see a profoundly ideological statement written into the law of charity from the first.

The concept of deserving poor is ideological.[29] This is not giving out of neighbourly love, but as a reward for approved social conduct. This distinction is ideological both because it falsifies—if one is needy how can one be undeserving of help?—and is in support of the dominant power, the state, which did not want to accept responsibility for the poor now disconnected from the traditional means of support. As Marx makes clear in his discussion of the poor law, the very *existence* of paupers, that is poverty as a person or social class rather than something which effects the whole of society, originates in this time. Marx quotes Frederic Eden's *The State of the Poor* (1797): 'The decrease of villeinage seems necessarily to have been the era of the origin of the poor. Manufacture and commerce are the two parents of our national poor.'[30] As Marx rightly argues, what Eden mistakes is the cause, it is not the end of villeinage, but the loss 'of the property of the agricultural labourer in the soil' which made a person a proletarian, and then a pauper.[31] Marx reveals the ideology at work even in the sympathetic history Eden tells: he has accepted that some people, when 'freed' from servitude as villeins or serfs, are unable to look after themselves. Actually, the only thing they were freed in to was wage labour.

---

27. Marx, *Capital*, 896.
28. Marx had condemned charity and philanthropy more generally in various places, as a bourgeoise attempt to convince the proletariat to rely on help from elsewhere, rather than to emancipate themselves through revolution. See Hal Draper, *Marx's Theory of Revolution Vol. 2* (London: Monthly Review Press, 1978), 150–53.
29. Williams, *Keywords*, 55.
30. Marx, *Capital*, 883.
31. Marx, *Capital*, 883.

Similarly, the idea of charity, and more specifically today state welfare, as being a last resort and something which should not offer a disincentive to work, reveals the function of charity not to relieve need but to maintain the incentive to wage labour. The function of this distinction is again to define some people as worthy of help and others as not. Poor relief remained a matter of local tariff collection within parishes, dispensed through almshouses, houses of industry, and houses of correction, depending on how deserving somebody was. The undeserving were faced with prison if they did not work, and if there was no work. Here the roots of modern charity law are found in the birth of capitalism, in the massive displacement of people from land and the social upheaval of their disconnection from traditional forms of support. The 1597 and 1601 poor law codes included a Statute of Charitable Uses, the preamble to the 1601 version went on to form the basis of the modern law of charities. The key element of the Elizabethan Acts was to make poor relief a burden for charity, and not the state.

The next major development in charity law was again connected to economic development. If the first cause is the agricultural revolution and the dislocation of people by enclosure, the second is the industrial revolution. The idea of deserving and undeserving poor continues, as Garton emphasises, with an ideology attended by Malthusian concerns about population growth and that idleness caused poverty, and hard work relieved it (*Moffat*, 890–4).[32] The 1834 Poor Law Amendment Act brought in a harsh deterrent system of poor law, with institutions such as work houses central. Voluntary giving proliferated, driven by a new bourgeois morality, with factory owners taking up the mantel of feudal landlords and setting up charities, including the YMCA, Barnardo's, and the NSPCC. Victorian philanthropists such as Joseph Rowntree provided housing and welfare for workers in their communities, but with an attendant moralising, such as housing developments without pubs. Ideologically, what is seen here is on the one hand a public disavowal that the source of the wealth of these philanthropists is the suffering of their workers, and on the other that the reason for their poverty is found in their moral failings.

Victorian philanthropy failed to alleviate poverty in any significant way. Charles Booth's study of the poverty line in London and Seebohm Rowntree's studies of the condition of the working class in York,

---

32. The historical account presented in Moffatt is drawn from Michael Chesterman, *Charitable Trusts and Social Welfare* (London: Weidenfield & Nicholson, 1979), which offers an excellent, explicitly materialist, history of the development of the law of charity.

for example, demonstrated this, and more importantly placed the blame on low wages rather than moral failing. The nineteenth century saw much contestation over the definition and scope of charity. *Morice v Bishop of Durham* (1804) saw a restriction of charitable purposes largely on the basis of allowing the testator's family their rightful due.[33] In Parliament, there were several attempts to remove the exemption from income tax from charities, or at least limit it to certain purposes. In the middle of the century, the Charity Commission was established to oversee the administration of charities.

The end of the century saw the decision in *Special Commissioners of Income Tax v Pemsel* (1891). This case is best known for Lord Macnaghten's four heads of charity: poverty, education, religion and other purposes beneficial to the public. What Macnaghten also emphasised was that charities may well benefit the rich as well as the poor, and that charities should remain exempt from taxation. As Garton emphasises, this decision, which laid the foundations for twentieth century charities law, yoked together the concepts of charitable status and tax relief (*Moffat*, 893). Lord Bramwell's dissent urged a more restrictive definition of charitable purpose, focused on 'assistance to be given to the bringing up, feeding, clothing, lodging, and education of those who from poverty, or comparative poverty, stand in need of such assistance' (*Moffat*, 895–6). He also found that several trusts upheld as within the statute of Elizabeth were without the ordinary meaning of charitable purposes.

Interestingly, here is a different ideological function of charity developed—the emphasis on benefitting rich and poor, of being a technical, specialist legal idea, and of being directly connected with tax and other privileges. It might seem that this contradicts the earlier developments, the focus on poor and of deserving and undeserving. However, the maintaining of such contradictions is another key function of ideology. By the end of the nineteenth century *poverty* is even more concerned with deserving and undeserving, with causes found in moral failure, while *charity* is concerned with technical legal decisions, with benefitting society as a whole, and with tax privileges. This echoes a general division in trusts law identified by Cotterrell as emerging in that century, between trusts as a personal relationship and trusts

---

33. Cotterrell has an excellent paper on *Morice* and purpose trusts more generally, see Roger Cotterrell, 'Some Sociological Aspects of the Controversy around the Legal Validity of Private Purpose Trusts,' in *Equity and Contemporary Legal Problems*, ed. Stephen Goldstein (Jerusalem: Hebrew University Press, 1992).

as a property receptacle.[34] Poverty is of course a foundational charitable purpose, and ideologically charity is about helping the poor, and yet the function of charity has travelled a good way away from a focus on poverty. The decision in *Pemsel* gives us that starting point for much of the jurisprudence that continues to inform the meaning of charity. In the next section the ideology at work in the definition of charitable purposes will be analysed, as well as the slippery idea of public benefit.

Ideology of Purpose

The twentieth century saw the state taking some of the burden of poverty relief in a context where private society, either through wages or philanthropy, continued to leave about 25% of the population of England in absolute poverty.[35] From 1914 until the mid-1970s the welfare state grew and developed, taking the lead in welfare provision in areas such as income maintenance, education, housing and medical care (*Moffat*, 899). In this period, the consensus changed to one of the state providing welfare, and the voluntary sector merely acting as an assistant or critical friend. This all changed In the late 1970s, in a period of economic crisis, there was an accompanying change in the dominant ideology. Garton identifies the seeds of this change in charities specifically in the 1978 Wolfenden Report, *The Future of Voluntary Organisations* (*Moffat*, 898). Here, underlying the central argument for the state to make more space for the voluntary sector, is an ideological commitment to the withdrawal of the state from welfare provision. Garton describes the ideology of the new conservative government: 'what appeared to be envisaged under this approach was a shift away from a modern social democratic welfare state towards a residual welfare state, that is, the provision of a safety net only' (*Moffat*, 900). It is here that charity developed a distinctive modern ideological role. It is not just that welfare provision is left to the voluntary sector, but that it *ought* to be delivered by the voluntary sector. In the development of charitable purposes we see a naturalising of what the state should and should not be responsible for.

---

34. Cotterrell, 'Private Purpose Trusts.' See also Roger Cotterrell 'Trusting in Law: Legal and Moral Concepts of Trust,' *Current Legal Problems* 46 (1993).
35. Booth found 31% of people in London to be in poverty, Rowntree 28% in York. For an introduction to the history of these surveys, see Howard Glennerster, 'The Context of Rowntree's Contribution' in *One Hundred Years of Poverty and Policy*, ed. Howard Glennerster, John Hills, David Piachaud and Jo Webb (Joseph Rowntree Foundation, 2004).

The Charities Act 2006 set out a new definition of a charity as 'an institution established for charitable purposes only,' and then listed these charitable purposes.[36] A charitable purpose is one which falls within the list, and is for the public benefit.[37] The Act then lists thirteen potentially charitable purposes.[38] Garton gives an excellent summary of the legislative process and political developments behind the Act (*Moffat*, 934–43). Most significant is that the Act is largely a codifying of existing common law, the stated purpose being to clarify and make more accessible the law of charities. This can be understood as another assertion of a commitment to moving the burden of welfare provision away from the state. By making the question of what is a charity a technical one, it is easier for the sector to be administered bureaucratically, by the Charity Commission, with less need for state oversight. There is not the space here to consider every purpose. Instead, the three longest established purposes of prevention and relief of poverty, advancement of education and advancement of religion will be considered.

Public benefit, separated out as a requirement in the 2006 Act but always a consideration, returns us directly to Cotterrell's original article. Charity law explicitly constructs the public as a whole as a property owner. Public benefit requires the public as a whole, or a sufficiently wide section, to be able to derive benefit from any property defined as charity. The application of this principle varies. With poverty, the test is applied very leniently. It is not particularly relevant to religious charities, as anyone could potentially join that faith. It is most significant in the case of education.

Prevention and Relief of Poverty

Prevention of poverty as a distinct purpose was new in the 2006 Act. The Charity Commission gives the example of financial advice as charitable prevention of poverty. Relief of poverty is a far wider and older concept. Poverty is often defined as meaning relative poverty, and not an absolute measure. A well-known dicta from Evershed MR in *Re Coulthurst* [1951] that 'poverty does not mean destitution ... it may not unfairly be paraphrased for present purposes as meaning persons who have to 'go short' in the ordinary acceptation of that term,

---

36. Charities Act 2006, s 1.
37. Charities Act 2006, s 2.
38. Charities Act 2006, s 3.

due regard being had to their status in life, and so forth.'[39] This individualistic and relativist approach to poverty is seen at it most extreme in a case like *Re Segelman* [1996] in which 'poor and needy' relatives who were 'comfortably off ... but not affluent' were found to be within the meaning of poverty as a charitable purpose.[40] The meaning has been found to include 'needy' (*Re Payne's Estate* [1954]) or 'of limited means' (*Re Gardom* [1914]) but not 'working class' (*Re Sanders* [1954]).[41]

Here we see the idea of poverty relief, so obviously socially necessary, being applied to a situation in *Re Segelman* [1996] where an estate worth £8m was held on trust for poor relations, with 26 potential beneficiaries at the time of death. This money could have been divided among 26 named beneficiaries in a will, but this would have given rise to taxation. Charity here is used as a tax efficient way to distribute inheritance. With poverty being relative, the ideology of charity conceals the material effect.

This is in part the product of a welfare state which should provide for anybody facing absolute poverty. However, as of the end of 2018, the Joseph Rowntree Foundation estimates that more than 14 million people in the UK live in poverty.[42] This takes us back to a more general ideological function of charity in the twenty-first century, to continue to move the burden of welfare away from the state and into private provision. Homeless shelters and foodbanks provided by charity are increasingly normalised through the ideology of charity. It is perfectly possible in one of the world's largest economies to provide for a basic standard of living and to provide shelter for everybody who needs it. To not do so is a political choice, rendered neutral through ideology. Giving, care, generosity, these virtues are made private, between oneself and one's conscience. A donation to a foodbank is sold as an opportunity to affirm ones own moral virtue, rather than an outrage at a wealthy society not being able to provide the most basic of needs.

As for the requirement of public benefit, poverty trusts are treated exceptionally leniently. For example, situations where there is a personal nexus which qualifies a beneficiary are generally regarded as not counting as a section of the public. However, there are several authorities which have established an exception for poverty, particularly

---

39. *Re Coulthurst* [1951] Ch 661, 666.
40. *Re Segelman* [1996] Ch 171, 190.
41. *Re Payne's Estate* [1954] 11 WWRNS 424; *Re Gardom* [1914] 1 Ch 662; *Re Sanders* [1954] Ch 265.
42. UK Poverty 2018 (Report, Joseph Rowntree Foundation, 2018).

poor relations or poor employees.[43] This type of trusts can confer on a small number of people, only going short in regard to their status in life, the full fiscal benefits of charitable status. Why relatives who are (relatively) poor should be entitled to receive an inheritance free of tax in this way, which could have come to them anyway through the normal operation of a will, is, as Garton says, 'difficult to defend on any policy ground' (Moffat, 983). That is putting it mildly.

Something as narrow as Re Segelman is uncommon, but the shrinking of public good to private interests seen there is most effective in poverty trusts. Charity is providing ideological cover for a legal tool which keeps capital in the hands of a small few. Beyond the extreme inheritance example, allowing poverty trusts to define the beneficiaries so specifically allows a huge amount of power to accrue to such a charity in choosing who and how to apply its money. This isn't just deception, it is the use of charity to continue a characterisation of deserving and undeserving poor, and giving the power to help over to wealthy individuals rather than systemic solutions to a systemic problem.

Advancement of Education

Formal education is one of Althusser's ideological state apparatuses, a mechanism for the imposition of official thinking. But as a charitable purpose it is more subtle than that, allowing for rulings on what knowledge is worthwhile. Educational purposes developed from the preamble into a very wide ranging category, extended to include culture and sport, both of which now have their own category. This historic use of the category as being one which other purposes could be squeezed in to is well noted, and it is a category which is particularly associated both with incidental benefits problems and with the question of fee charging (Moffat, 950).[44] It also includes some interesting precedent related to public benefit.

To start with, consider the contrast between Re Shaw [1957], where George Bernard Shaw's testamentary gift for research into a new alphabet was refused charitable status, and Re Hopkin's [1965], where research into demonstrating that Francis Bacon was the true

---

43. Dingle v Turner [1972] AC 601.
44. Independent Schools Council vs Charity Commission for England and Wales [2011] UKUT 421 (TCC), [2012] Ch 214.

author of some of the plays of William Shakespeare was approved.[45] These might both seem like trifling matters, but they reveal the class interests of the judiciary. The continuation of the research of socialist playwright and critic Shaw into a new phonetic alphabet for English pronunciation was deemed 'merely the increase of knowledge.'[46] The promotion of the idea that plays regarded as the some of the greatest writing in the English language must be the product of nobility rather than a commoner was considered a benefit 'to improve the sum of communicable knowledge.'[47]

Education highlights another aspect of public benefit. In principle, formal education is a public service provided by the state. Schools, colleges and universities are publicly funded. Alongside the publicly funded system there is a fee paying system of private schools, allowing for the wealthy to opt out of the system. This is a key part in forging class identity and reinforcing class privilege. There are vastly disproportionate number of privately educated people studying in top universities and working in powerful or well paid jobs, including politics and the law. The system also provides an ideological justification of class difference as based on ability rather than exploitation. There are a variety of ideological justifications for this, including freedom of choice or an insistence on the need for a free market in education. One particularly important element is that schools are charities, that even fee paying schools benefit the public, by relieving the system for example, or providing bursaries or access to facilities. This function can be seen in the law itself.

In *Independent Schools Council vs Charity Commission for England and Wales*,[48] this is expressed plainly in the judgment. The case concerned the guidance published by the Charity Commission that where benefit is restricted, it must not be unreasonably restricted by the ability to pay any fees, and that people in poverty must not be excluded from the opportunity to benefit. The Charity Commission presented evidence that fee-paying schools actively dis-benefit society, by reducing diversity and social mobility. This was dismissed by the Tribunal, as deciding if fee-paying schools benefit society is 'an essentially political exercise.'[49] However, the Tribunal went on to endorse the wider benefit of private education later, mentioning specifically the reduction of the burden

---

45. *Re Shaw* [1957] 1 WLR 729; *Re Hopkin's Will Trusts* [1965] Ch 669.
46. *Re Shaw*, 737 (Harman J).
47. *Re Hopkins' Will Trusts*, 680 (Wilberforce J).
48. [2011] UKUT 421 (TCC), [2012] Ch 214.
49. In *Independent Schools Council*, 96.

on local authorities. To highlight the absurdity, imagine claiming that Michelin starred restaurants ease the burden on foodbanks, or mansions the burden on homeless shelters. In this move, from criticism of private schools being political, to endorsing the benefits of private schools being relevant to the decision and not political, we see the ideology of charity at work.

Advancement of Religion

Advancement of religion is the third charitable purpose which goes back to the statute of 1601. It is again a very wide category, covering potentially any form of religion. One historical exception, which is revealing about of the general motivation, is the exclusion of Catholicism. Garton generously glosses this as 'an interpretation of the public benefit requirement' which regards Catholicism as focused on 'purely spiritual activity rather than "good works"' (*Moffat*, 953). The exclusion of Catholicism from being a religion which benefits the public is clearly tied to the origins of charity in general as being in Christianity, and during a period of struggle between protestants and Catholics in England and throughout Europe. Behind this application of charity law is a portrayal of Catholicism as a selfish and inward looking practice, not really a religion, and certainly not one which helps others.

This struggle is now historic, with religion having liberalised as a charitable purpose considerably. The refusal of scientology and paganism demonstrate that limits are still in place, but in general the beneficial role of a wide range of religious practices is now accepted. What becomes a more interesting question is why religion should keep this position in a twenty-first century England and Wales where over 50% of the population define themselves as having no faith.[50] One response is that charity is itself a defining aspect of most religions. Another though would focus on the ideology.

Making religion charitable makes it public rather than private, and establishes that all religions have some relationship with the state, not just the state religion. This bringing in of religions, gathering them all together, can be seen as one element of effectively blunting the radical history and potential of religion. The history of religion is deeply political, centuries of warfare were fought in the propagation or defence of specific religions. A third element is that there is something useful

---

50. NatCen Social Research, 'British Social Attitudes Survey 33' (2016), accessed 1 March 2024, https://natcen.ac.uk/publications/british-social-attitudes-33.

in keeping the idea of religion as central to society even when it is so diminished. This picture of social cohesion around religious groups, which while different all work together to benefit society, is false but useful. Problems of social cohesion—whether they be attributed to race, religion, or ethnic tensions, are ultimately often explicable by a lack of investment, a lack of opportunity, a dissatisfaction with the material conditions of daily life. Making this the work of charity, particularly religious charities, allows the state to wash its hands. The problem of social cohesion is portrayed as a question of faith, rather than a question of finance.

Conclusion: The Function of Charity Revealed?

It is worth re-iterating what the ideology of charity is. It is the securing of consent for an economic and political system which produces massive inequality, nationally and globally. Charity offers the only solution to this as individual generosity alleviating some of the otherwise inevitable suffering in the world. It offers charity as a horizon; more homeless shelters, rather than fewer homeless people. That there are homeless people becomes a fact, when actually it is a product of political and economic choice. This is the work that ideology does, not always by falsifying, not always in the same way or at the same scale, and not always consistently, but throughout charity law it can be found in the gaps between what is said and what is done.

This chapter has elaborated upon a specific observation of Cotterrell's, that charity law performed an ideological function by constructing the general public as a property owner. Charity does far more than that. It is not the law of charity which is responsible for maintaining consent for the current mode of production. But charity does play a significant role in manufacturing consent for otherwise unacceptable situations created by political and economic choice.

Poverty in the UK, described by UN Special Rapporteur Philip Alston as 'not just a disgrace, but a social calamity and an economic disaster,' is entirely a political and economic choice in the world's fifth largest economy.[51] As Alston also says 'many of the problems could readily be solved.' Instead, they are handed over to charity, to food banks and homeless shelters. In 2008, the year of the global financial crisis, the UK

---

51. Statement on Visit to the United Kingdom, by Professor Philip Alston, United Nations Special Rapporteur on extreme poverty and human rights (London, 16 November 2018).

had about 100 foodbanks. As of September 2018, estimates are around 1000. The Trussell Trust, the UK's biggest provider of food banks, went from providing tens of thousands of emergency food parcels a year to well over a million in that period.[52] And the cause of this is a choice.

The individual charities are generally not at fault. People, often many volunteers, are trying honestly and seriously to help others. It is the idea that this is the only thing to be done that needs to be challenged. As highlighted at the end of the section introducing ideology, ideas are not the property of just one class or set of interests. Maybe, where charity has been used to contain and direct the forces of social change found in mass movements, there is a bottled genie. This is the genie of human generosity, compassion, and solidarity. Charity is not a bad idea, ideas themselves cannot be morally culpable. It is the way the idea is used, the material effects it has in the world, which has been the subject of this critique.

---

52. Trussell Trust end of year stats, available at https://www.trusselltrust.org/news-and-blog/latest-stats/end-year-stats.

11

The Gendered Trust

Lisa Sarmas[*]

Introduction

In his article 'Power, Property and the Law of Trusts,' Roger Cotterrell argued that the trust creates a distancing effect that reinforces and conceals the property-power of the beneficiary, thereby obscuring 'private power' and perpetuating the 'legal ideology that human beings appear as equal subjects before the law.'[1] In this chapter I draw on and further develop Cotterrell's claim about the distancing effect of the trust by suggesting that when analysed as a *gendered* private power device, the trust may be observed as effecting a more complex dialectic of both distance and intimacy as it metaphorically takes on the gendered characteristics of 'male' and 'female' *form* respectively. This chapter explores, in a preliminary and provisional way, this dialectic at work in a number of doctrines and conceptual debates within trusts law. The chapter's focus is on these metaphorical manifestations of gender, rather than on its material effects, which have been explored elsewhere.[2] Nevertheless it is tentatively suggested that the trust's gendered dance of intimacy and distance works to reproduce (rather than to challenge) the gender binary and thereby to reinforce gender-power, as well as (as identified by Cotterrell) to reproduce and reinforce class power—including new

[*] Melbourne Law School, Australia.
1. Roger Cotterrell, 'Power, Property and the Law of Trusts: A Partial Agenda for Critical Legal Scholarship,' *Journal of Law and Society* 14 (1987), 82–86.
2. See Lisa Sarmas, 'The Gendered Nature of Trusts Law,' *Precedent* 144 (2018). There is also a significant and increasing volume of work about the gendered effects of specific trusts doctrines, particularly as they relate to acquisition of interests in the family home: see, e.g. Simone Wong, 'Sharing Homes by Unmarried Cohabiting Couples in England and Wales: Rebutting Presumptions and Exceptional Conduct,' *FamPra.ch* (2016).

forms of class power that have evolved since Cotterrell published his article in 1987. The conclusion drawn is that the trust is a particularly malleable and resilient legal form that is well-adapted to (and complicit in maintaining) the current gendered neo-liberal order.

Form, Gender and the Trust

In his epic 1924 work on 'The General Theory of Law and Marxism,' Evgeny Pashukanis identified the form of law that emerged in capitalist societies as the 'commodity form,' a legal form that parallels the process of 'commodity fetishism' in capitalist exchange by invoking notions of formal equality, abstract subjects, free will and free exchange, on people with unequal power and material resources.[3] Cotterrell's 1987 analysis of the trust as serving the ideology that 'human beings appear as equal subjects before the law' by in effect hiding the property power of the beneficiary, is consistent with Pashukanis's theory of the commodity form of law and suggests that the trust is an important English common law addition to reinforcing that particular form.[4]

Just as Pashukanis, and others,[5] have argued that the form of law may be 'homologous to deep structures within capitalist exchange,' that there is a 'capital logic' to it, so too feminists and others have argued that language and other social phenomena (including the form of law) are structured in ways that are homologous to the gender binary. Drawing on the work of Claude Lévi-Strauss and Monique Wittig, Margaret Davies, for example, has analysed the concept of property through the lens of the gender binary.[6] She suggests that

> property takes on stereotypically masculine characteristics; but at the same time, the object of property is sometimes said to be structurally female, because the owner/owned, subject/object distinctions all correlate socially and epistemologically to the male/female distinction.[7]

The idea developed in this chapter is that the *form* of trusts law is influenced both by 'capital logic' *and* the gender binary, the latter being

---

3. Dragan Milovanovic, introduction to *The General Theory of Law and Marxism*, by Evgeny Pashukanis (New Brunswick (USA) and London (UK): Transaction, 2003), vii–xxiv.
4. Cotterrell, 'Power, Property and the Law of Trusts,' 82–83.
5. See, e.g. Isaac Balbus, 'Commodity Form and Legal Form: An essay on the "Relative Autonomy" of the Law,' *Law and Society Review* 11 (1977).
6. Margaret Davies, 'Queer Property, Queer Persons: Self-Ownership and Beyond, *Social & Legal Studies* 8 (1999).
7. Davies, 'Queer Property, Queer Persons,' 329.

the focus of the present chapter.[8] Drawing on Judith Butler's phrase,[9] I suggest that the trust 'performs' gender by variously taking on 'masculine' and 'feminine' characteristics in specific contexts. As I discuss below, while the trust in its 'masculine' form has the distancing effect identified by Cotterrell, in other contexts the trust takes on a 'feminine' form that produces instead what I call an 'intimacy effect' whereby the trust is subject to close scrutiny and potential regulation or 'penetration' by courts and the legislature, and the beneficiary's interest, in particular, is subject to the exercise of discretion/power by both trustees and the courts. The idea that modern, 'big money' trusts appear to combine elements of both 'masculine' and 'feminine' form is also explored. Ultimately, it is suggested that the trust's ability to flip from male to female (from distance to intimacy) and, at times, to combine elements of both, exposes it as a particularly flexible, chameleon-like device that likely serves to reiterate, rather than to challenge, the gender binary, while at the same time providing a fit-for-purpose vehicle for the facilitation of current modes of capital investment and exchange.

The Feminine Trust

In this section I explore a number of doctrines and conceptual debates within trusts law in which I suggest the trust takes on a 'feminine' form that evokes the 'intimacy effect' identified above. In these contexts, I argue, the trust takes on the 'feminine' characteristics of passivity, malleability, penetrability and powerlessness, as it is subjected to penetration by the state and the power and discretion of the trustee.

The Discretionary Trust and the Intimate Power of the Trustee

It is a basic principle of trusts law that beneficiaries of discretionary trusts have no proprietary interest in the trust assets. They have what is sometimes called a 'mere expectancy' (not an enforceable right) that the trustee may (or may not) exercise its discretion/power to distribute assets in their favour. The very question of whether a beneficiary will get a distribution of capital or income from such a trust is at the discretion or power of the trustee, who must exercise this power in accordance with so-called 'fiduciary' principles. In the words of Lord Wilberforce

---

8. Of course other forms of power, such as race, are also at play and are of equal importance.
9. Judith Butler, *Gender Trouble: Feminism and the Subversion of Identity* (New York: Routledge, 2007), 175-193.

in *McPhail v Doulton*, in order to properly exercise their power of appointment, the trustee of a discretionary trust:

> would examine the field, by class and category; might indeed make diligent and careful inquiries, depending on how much money he had to give away and the means at his disposal, as to the composition and needs of particular categories and of individuals within them; decide upon certain priorities or proportions, and then select individuals according to their needs or qualifications. If he acts in this manner, can it really be said that he is not carrying out the trust?[10]

Lord Wilberforce's statement is suggestive of the intimate nature of the obligation involved in the trustee's exercise of power to distribute in the context of a discretionary trust. Assessing needs, qualifications, being diligent, careful and deciding on priorities and proportions between potential beneficiaries requires a proximity to, and knowledge of, as well as power over, potential recipients of the trust funds. In this context the trust is a penetrable, flexible and passive creature, subject as it is to the power, scrutiny and attention of the trustee. This renders the beneficiary, too, as relatively powerless, without *rights* to property and dependent on the trustee's close scrutiny and assessment of their needs and qualifications. While the power possessed by the trustee to intimately examine and choose beneficiaries marks them here as distinctly 'male,' the trust itself is represented as distinctly *feminine* in form, characterised as it is by the feminine traits of passivity, penetrability, flexibility and powerlessness. Moreover, far from creating a distancing effect that obscures the property power of the beneficiaries of the trust, the beneficiaries are here brought into *focus* and made distinctly visible as they are subject to the trustee's close examination and scrutiny.

The Trust as a 'Personal Obligation'?

The beneficiary's lack of property rights under a discretionary trust (and the concomitant power of the trustee over the beneficiary's interests) is often contrasted to the obligations and rights inherent in fixed trusts in which the beneficiary is said to have a proprietary right to the trust assets which is not subject to the discretion of the trustee.[11] The question of the precise nature of the beneficiary's rights under a trust features

---

10. *McPhail v Doulton* [1971] AC 424 (HL) 449.
11. The beneficiary of a fixed trust may, of course, be subject to the exercise of other discretions by the trustee, for example discretions related to the investment of trust assets.

centrally in ongoing debates about whether the trust is best conceived of as a 'personal obligation' or as conferring 'proprietary rights.'[12]

Anne Bottomley has explored the interplay of the metaphors of 'proprietary right' and 'personal obligation' as they apply to the operation of the 'beneficiary principle' in the context of fixed and discretionary trusts.[13] The 'beneficiary principle' states that to be valid, a trust must be for the benefit of individuals, rather than for a stated purpose, unless that purpose falls within the legal definition of 'charity.'[14] Bottomley cites the rule in *Saunders v Vautier* (where beneficiaries under a fixed trust who are all ascertained and of full age and capacity can bring an end to the trust and force a distribution of property despite the settlor's stated intention to the contrary)[15] as an example of the trust in its 'proprietary manifestation' (ie the beneficiaries have the power to do this because they are the 'owners' of the trust property), while *McPhail v Doulton* (where the test of certainty of objects for discretionary trusts was watered-down)[16] and *Re Denley* (where a non-charitable purpose trust was held to be valid)[17] are viewed as instances of a 'loosening up of the proprietary aspect' of the trust.[18] Bottomley convincingly suggests that the operation of the beneficiary principle in the discretionary trust context 'weakens the narrative of beneficial ownership of the fund,'[19] as it is difficult to conceive of the beneficiaries as 'owners' of the trust property if trusts law does not require that all beneficiaries of the trust be known, or indeed if it does not require there to be beneficiaries at all, as in *Re Denley*.

This 'weakening of the narrative of beneficial ownership of the fund' in the operation of the beneficiary principle in discretionary trusts feeds into the conception of the trust as a personal obligation rather than

---

12. See, e.g. Peter Jaffey, 'Explaining the Trust,' *Law Quarterly Review* 131 (2015).
13. Anne Bottomley, 'Our Property in Trust: Things to Make and Do,' in *Feminist Perspectives on Equity and Trusts*, ed. Susan Scott-Hunt and Hilary Lim (London: Cavendish Publishing, 2001).
14. See, e.g. *Re Astor's Settlement Trusts* [1952] Ch 534.
15. (1841) 49 ER 282.
16. *McPhail v Doulton* [1971] AC 424 (HL). In this case the test for certainty of objects for discretionary trusts was watered-down from a requirement that all potential beneficiaries be identified (the requirement of 'list certainty') to a looser requirement of 'criterion certainty,' which does not require the identification of all beneficiaries.
17. [1969] 1 Ch 373. In this case a non-charitable purpose trust -which is generally invalid as a trust- for the construction and maintenance of a sports field for employees of a company was held to be valid on the basis that the employees were 'indirect beneficiaries.'
18. Bottomley, 'Our Property in Trust,' 260.
19. Bottomley, 'Our Property in Trust,' 267–273.

as conferring proprietary rights, and, I would suggest, lends support to the notion that the discretionary trust may be characterised as distinctly 'feminine' in form. As a 'personal obligation,' the trust is weaker, more passive, less secure, the trustee having the ultimate power to closely, intimately examine and scrutinise it. The beneficiary is rendered relatively powerless, without property rights, while at the same time being the focus of close attention, examination and scrutiny.

Violence, Penetration and the Family Trust

The family trust is another instantiation of the trust in its 'feminine' form. The typical family trust in Australia is based on a discretionary trust model where the founder or real (as opposed to nominal) settlor (the main breadwinner) appoints a trustee (usually a company which they control) to receive and, at its discretion, to distribute capital and income among a class of beneficiaries which include the family of the real settlor. Such trusts are usually used to minimise tax by splitting income among a range of family members (the beneficiaries) and thereby taking advantage of a progressive taxation system (including, in Australia individual tax-free thresholds of $18,200). They can also potentially protect the income and capital 'earned' by the main breadwinner from being available to their creditors, including an ex-spouse. In 2014–15 there were 823,448 trusts in Australia with assets of $3.1 trillion and revenue of $349.2 billion, with 642,416 of those trusts being discretionary trusts used to minimise tax.[20]

So far legislators have only really tinkered at the edges (largely ineffectually) at stopping the worst excesses of the use of such trusts in tax minimisation. However in 2017, the Australian Labor Party, one of the two major political parties in Australia, released a well-publicised policy which stood in marked contrast to the usual 'hands off' approach of the major parties. The headlines were dramatic:[21]

Trust buster: Bill Shorten promises $17.2 billion tax crackdown

Bill Shorten will slam the door shut on tax loopholes that let high income earners legally use trusts to slash their tax bills, in a move designed to raise $17.2 billion over 10 years. …

---

20. James Massola, 'Trust Buster: Bill Shorten Promises $17.2 Billion Tax Crackdown,' *The Sydney Morning Herald*, 30 July 2017, accessed 1 March 2024, http://www.smh. com.au/federal-politics/political-news/trust-buster-bill-shorten-promises-172-billion-tax-crackdown-20170729-gxlf3s.html.
21. Massola, 'Trust Buster.'

> If he wins the next election, he will introduce an across-the-board minimum 30 per cent tax rate on discretionary trust distributions to people over the age of 18. ...
>
> The bold plan to change the rules for discretionary trusts—put in the too-hard basket by previous governments—will be framed as a tough but necessary decision to tackle Australia's ballooning debt. ...
>
> 'We need to make the tough decisions to build a fairer tax system, a stronger budget, a stronger nation. This must include cracking down on artificial income splitting to avoid tax' Shorten said.

The substance of the reforms suggested in the Labor Party's policy are radically interventionist in that they demonstrate a never-before seen willingness to significantly intervene in and penetrate the family trust at a legislative level. The introduction of a minimum 30 percent tax rate on trust distributions would have a considerable (and welcome) impact on the existing tax-minimisation potential of such trusts. Moreover, the language used in the report is particularly graphic, invoking a distinctly violent image of the trust having things done to it; having the door slammed on it, being cracked-down on, being busted.

This willingness to intervene in and penetrate such trusts and the use of distinctly masculinist metaphors conjures up a distinctly passive and objectified 'feminine' image of the trust in this instance.

Courts too, in Australia, have shown a greater willingness to penetrate the family trust and to look beneath it. An interesting instance of this is demonstrated in the decision of the High Court in the case of *Kennon v Spry*.[22] Dr Spry, a prominent Australian equity academic and QC, lost his bid to 'protect' substantial assets which were held in a discretionary family trust from being included as 'property of the parties to the marriage' for the purposes of a claim by Ms Spry (his former wife) for a property order under section 79 of the Family Law Act 1975 (Cth). Dr Spry was settlor and trustee of the trust and Ms Spry was one of several discretionary beneficiaries, which included the children of the parties. French CJ held that the relevant 'property' of the parties was 'the trust assets, coupled with the trustee's power...to appoint them and her [Ms Spry's] equitable right to due administration.'[23] Gummow and Hayne JJ held that it was Ms Spry's 'right to be considered under

---

22. (2008) 238 CLR 366.
23. (2008) 238 CLR 366 [62]–[64]

the husband's power of distribution that formed part of the relevant property.'[24]

These findings came as somewhat of a surprise to trusts lawyers (and they were indeed surprising and disappointing to Dr Spry).[25] Given that Dr Spry (as trustee) was not, under the trust instrument, compelled to distribute to Ms Spry, and that Ms Spry was only one of several potential genuine 'objects' of the trust, each of whom had a right to be considered for a distribution of trust property, it is difficult to see, from a traditional trusts law perspective, how the trust assets could be viewed as the 'property of the parties to the marriage' (i.e. the property of Dr and Ms Spry). The Court's decision in this respect is clearly not in line with ordinary discretionary trust principles, which state that beneficiaries of such trusts have no proprietary interest in the trust assets unless and until the trustee exercises their discretion to distribute in their favour.[26]

Yet the Court in *Kennon v Spry* was willing to look beyond and beneath the formal categories and well-worn trusts concepts of discretion and beneficial ownership (or rather, *no* beneficial ownership) in order to reach its decision. In the court's judgment, we can observe an interesting tension at play as the Court takes an interventionist approach to penetrate the trust so as to confer rights of a proprietary nature on a discretionary beneficiary while at the same time emphasising the power of the trustee and the closeness of their relationship to the beneficiary: it is Ms Spry's *right to be considered* by the trustee (Dr Spry) and the trustee's *power of distribution* that forms the basis for finding that she has property rights.

The family trust in *Kennon v Spry* can therefore be characterised as 'feminine' in a number of ways: it is both penetrated by the Court and strangely reliant on the exercise of the trustee's power and discretion—it is doubly passive, so to speak. Moreover, it displays a remarkable degree of malleability in that the mere expectancies it confers on a range of discretionary beneficiaries are ostensibly transformed into 'property of the parties to the marriage.'

---

24. (2008) 238 CLR 366 [125]–[126]

25. Dr Spry somewhat unconventionally circulated letters criticising the judges in the case: see 'I Spry,' posted on *Justinian*, accessed 1 March 2024, https://justinian.com.au/archive/i-spry.html.

26. The Court's decision is, of course, to be applauded from a gender justice perspective, as it limits the ability of men to use the trust as a means of shielding assets from potential distribution to their former spouse.

The Remedial, Discretionary, Soft and Unentitled Australian Constructive Trust

Another doctrine that brings to the fore the more 'feminine' aspects of the trust is the Australian remedial constructive trust. Australia has parted ways with the jurisprudence of England and Wales on the nature of constructive trusts. In England and Wales such trusts are said to be institutional; they are awarded as of right, and they endow the beneficiary with proprietary rights.

The approach in England and Wales is illustrated clearly by Lord Browne-Wilkinson in *Foskett v McKeown*:

> The rules establishing equitable proprietary interests and their enforceability against certain parties have been developed over the centuries and are an integral part of the property law of England. It is a fundamental error to think that, because certain property rights are equitable rather than legal, such rights are in some way discretionary. This case does not depend on whether it is fair, just and reasonable to give the purchasers an interest as a result of which the court in its discretion provides a remedy. It is a case of hard-nosed property rights.[27]

This institutional non-discretionary approach to the constructive trust in England and Wales appears to extend to the 'common intention' constructive trust that continues to be the main basis upon which beneficial interests over the family home are determined in that jurisdiction. Anne Bottomley has made the interesting point that the proprietary basis of this approach to family home disputes is to be preferred to a remedial approach which marginalises the claims of women and makes them dependants rather than rights holders. The common intention constructive trust, she says, treats women as citizens with property rights.[28]

In Australia, constructive trusts in most (but not all)[29] contexts are said to be remedial, flexible and awarded at the courts' discretion.

---

27. *Foskett v McKeown* [2000] 3 All ER 97 (HL) 102.
28. Bottomley, 'Our Property in Trust,' 283. See also, Claire de Than, 'Equitable Remedies: Cypher Wives, Weak Women and "Equity's Special Tenderness",' in *Feminist Perspectives on Equity and Trusts*, ed. Susan Scott-Hunt and Hilary Lim (London: Cavendish Publishing, 2001). De Than argues that as 'the grant of any equitable remedy is discretionary, courts are able to cloak policy decisions and unjustified assumptions behind what appears to be no more than a series of decisions made only on relevant facts': De Than, 'Equitable Remedies', 197.
29. Cf the common intention constructive trust, which still exists in Australia alongside the remedial unconscionability constructive trust e.g. *Parsons v McBain* (2001) 109 FCR 120.

The Australian approach is typified by the following statement of the High Court in the equitable estoppel case of *Giumelli v Giumelli*:

> Before a constructive trust is imposed, the court should first decide whether, having regard to the issues in the litigation, there is an appropriate equitable remedy which falls short of the imposition of a trust ... the various factors to be taken into account, ... [include] the impact upon relevant third parties, in determining the nature and quantum of the equitable relief to be granted.[30]

This Australian approach is also well-illustrated in the following extract from the judgment of Deane J in *Muschinski v Dodds*, whose formulation of the constructive trust in that case is viewed as heralding a new 'progressive' era in which courts could now impose an 'unconscionability based' constructive trust in the family home context. Deane J described the relevant trust as follow:

> [I]n this country at least, the constructive trust has not outgrown its formative stages as an equitable remedy and should still be seen as constituting an in personam remedy attaching to property which may be moulded and adjusted to give effect to the application and inter-play of equitable principles in the circumstances of the particular case ... [A] declaration of constructive trust by way of remedy can properly be so framed that the consequences of its imposition are operative only from the date of judgment or formal court order or from some other specified date ... Lest the legitimate claims of third parties be adversely affected, the constructive trust should be imposed only from the date of publication of reasons for judgment of this Court.[31]

In *Grimaldi v Chameleon Mining NL (No 2)*,[32] the Full Court of the Federal Court accepted that contrary to the old authority of *Lister & Co v Stubbs* (which said that a fiduciary who received a bribe could only be personally liable to the principal as a debtor),[33] a bribe taken by a fiduciary can be held on constructive trust for the principal. In doing so the Court was in basic agreement with the approach now taken by the Privy Council in *Attorney General for Hong Kong v Reid*,[34]

---

30. [1999] HCA 10, (1999) 196 CLR 101 [10]. See also Fiona Burns, '*Giumelli v Giumelli* Revisited: Equitable Estoppel, the Constructive Trust and Discretionary Remedialism,' *Adelaide Law Review* 22 (2001), 123.
31. *Muschinski v Dodds* (1985) 160 CLR 583 [8] and [20].
32. (2012) 200 FCR 296.
33. (1890) LR 45 Ch D 1 (CA).
34. [1994] 1 AC 324 (PC) (on appeal from New Zealand).

and by the UK Supreme Court in *FHR European Ventures LLP v Cedar Capital Partners LLC.* [35] But in contrast to those authorities, which indicated that a constructive trust would be granted in such cases, the Court in *Grimaldi* emphasised that in Australia such relief would not be granted as of right and that the interests of third parties would be considered first:

> In Australia, the constructive trust in this setting is a discretionary remedy ... [T]o accept that money bribes can be captured by a constructive trust does not mean that they necessarily will be in all circumstances. As is well accepted, a constructive trust ought not to be imposed if there are other orders capable of doing full justice. ... Such could be the case, for example, where a bribed fiduciary, having profitably invested the bribe, is then bankrupted and, apart from the investment, is hopelessly insolvent.[36]

Clearly, apart from a few exceptions,[37] the Australian approach to the constructive trust is that it is a remedy at the discretion of the court, conferring primarily personal rather than proprietary rights. Moreover, it is a discretionary remedy of last resort and any perceived claim of the putative beneficiary will give way to the superior rights of third parties. This conception of the constructive trust stands in marked contrast to Lord Browne-Wilkinson's conception of 'hard-nosed property rights' that are awarded as of right.[38]

The Australian remedial constructive trust fits (perhaps too neatly) into the trope of the 'feminine' form of the trust. The putative beneficiary of this trust is not the real holder of 'property-power' as conceptualised by Cotterrell. Rather, any rights that the putative beneficiary might acquire are subject to the court's discretion, which will first consider whether there might be an appropriate remedy that falls short of the imposition of a trust and that will always put the rights of third parties before those of the putative beneficiary.

The remedial constructive trust can therefore be characterised as soft, malleable, flexible; always coming in second to third parties and frequently giving way to 'more appropriate' (read non-proprietary) remedies. The remedial constructive trust is 'kept close' by the court,

---

35. *FHR European Ventures LLP v Cedar Capital Partners LLC* [1994] 1 AC 324 (SC).
36. *Grimaldi v Chameleon Mining NL (No 2)* (2012) 200 FCR 296 [582]–[583].
37. Cf common intention constructive trust e.g. *Parsons v McBain* (2001) 109 FCR 120.
38. *Foskett v McKeown* [2000] 3 All ER 97 (HL) 102.

its possibility closely scrutinised lest it overreach its appropriate role. The notion of the property-power of the beneficiary is displaced here by the discretionary power of the court to limit, if not completely deny, proprietary relief. This stands in contrast to what might be considered the more 'masculine' form of the constructive trust in England and Wales, which confers solid proprietary rights that are not subject to the court's discretion.

The remedial constructive trust, together with the family trust and the discretionary trust, each manifest the trust as marked by the 'feminine' metaphors of penetrability, malleability, lack of entitlement, powerlessness and passivity. The 'beneficiaries' of discretionary trusts and remedial constructive trusts have no property *rights* as such and are subject to the *close* scrutiny, discretion and power of trustees and courts. The family trust too is increasingly subject to *close* scrutiny and penetration by courts and the state. Rather than producing the 'distancing effect' that hides the beneficiary's power as identified by Cotterrell, the 'feminine' trust brings the beneficiary into focus, granting them little or no 'property power' as such (unless the trustee, or the court, grants it).

These feminised iterations of the trust, where the trust itself is marked as distinctly female, evidence another side to the trust that is not captured by Cotterrell's 1987 conceptualisation. This 'other side' to the trust suggests a homologous relationship to the gender binary, reinforcing it at a metaphorical level through the well-worn feminine stereotypes of weakness, penetrability, passivity and so forth.

The Masculine Trust

'Feminine' manifestations of the trust may be compared to those manifestations in which the trust takes on an arguably more 'masculine' form. In this section I outline a number of contexts in which the trust takes on an institutional and proprietary flavour, impenetrable by courts and the state and less vulnerable to the discretions of trustees. It is these more 'masculine' manifestations of the trust that more closely resemble the elements identified by Cotterrell in his 1987 article.

Reference has already been made to the institutional constructive trust of England and Wales as evocative of the 'masculine' form of the trust, standing strong, protecting the 'hard-nosed property rights' of the beneficiary and impenetrable by courts. However perhaps the most obvious and more basic example of the trust in its 'masculine' form is the fixed trust. In a fixed trust trustees must distribute the trust funds to the specified beneficiaries and they must do so in the proportions or amounts specified in the trust.[39] This gives beneficiaries an equitable proprietary interest, and this interest is *fully* proprietary in the sense that it can be bought and sold and devised by will. Fixed trusts confer 'hard-nosed property rights' on beneficiaries which are not subject to the discretions of trustees or courts.

Quistclose and Yet So Far...

Another instance of the trust operating in a 'masculine' form is the so-called 'Quistclose' trust, at least as it currently operates in Australia.[40] In a 'Quistclose' trust the trust acts as an informally created, largely unregulated and unregistered security device for the repayment of money loaned for a specific purpose. Interestingly, while the legislature in Australia has intervened to require that other security interests over personal property are registered,[41] those created under 'Quistclose' and other trusts are specifically excluded from such registration requirements.[42] The 'Quistclose' trust remains immune to regulation mandated for other forms of personal security interest in Australia.

The registration and regulation of personal security interests was aimed at bringing a degree of certainty into this particular commercial context by providing a central register that would record such interests.[43] The effect of excluding 'Quistclose' trusts from these requirements is to allow the continued creation and operation of invisible security interests which transform the lender into a secured creditor or, to put it

---

39.   John D. Heydon and Mark J. Leeming, *Jacob's Law of Trusts in Australia* (Australia: LexisNexis Butterworths, 2006) [524].

40.   The 'Quistclose' trust is named after the case of *Barclays Bank Ltd v Quistclose Investments* [1970] AC 567. The case involved a loan made to a company for the specific purpose of enabling it to pay dividends to its shareholders. The company went into liquidation before it was able to pay the dividends. The lender was, however, able to recover all the money 'lent' by successfully claiming that, the specified purpose having failed, a trust over the money had been created in its favour, thereby conferring on it rights that prevailed over those of other creditors. It is to be noted that there is considerable academic debate about the nature of the 'Quistclose' trust (see e.g. William Swadling, ed., *The Quistclose Trust: Critical Essays* (Hart Publishing, 2004), but it is fairly settled that in Australia the 'Quistclose' trust is conceived as a species of express trust: see *Legal Services Board v Gillespie-Jones* (2013) 249 CLR 493. It should also be noted that 'Quistclose' trusts may operate outside of the loan context: see *Twinsectra v Yardley* [2002] 2 AC 164 (HL).

41.   See Personal Property Securities Act 2009 (Cth).

42.   See Personal Property Securities Act 2009 (Cth), s 8(1)(h).

43.   Robert McClelland (Attorney General), Second Reading Speech, Parliament of Australia, *Hansard* (24 June 2009) 6960.

in trust terms, into a beneficiary with 'hard-nosed property rights.' These rights are invisible to, and thus obscured from, the outside world quite literally. This conferral of property rights and the immunity to state intervention or penetration makes the 'Quistclose' trust a particularly apt candidate for inclusion as a 'masculine' manifestation of the trust. Here, the very real property-power of the 'Quistclose' beneficiary is both reinforced and concealed, thereby creating the 'distancing effect' noted by Cotterrell.

Investment of the Trust Fund and the Financial Maximisation Principle

Another area of trusts law that arguably evokes the metaphor of the 'masculine' is the operation of trustees' duties relating to the investment of the trust fund, and particularly the duty to seek financial maximisation for the trust and to ignore social investing. The principle is stated most clearly by Megarry VC in *Cowan v Scargill*:

> [T]he power must be exercised so as to yield the best financial return for the beneficiaries ... Trustees may have strongly held social or political views. They may be firmly opposed to any investment in South Africa or other countries, or they may object to any form of investment in companies concerned with alcohol, tobacco, armaments ... [I]f investments of this type would be more beneficial to the beneficiaries than other investments, the trustees must not refrain from making the investments by reason of the views that they hold ... Trustees may even have to act dishonourably (though not illegally) if the interests of their beneficiaries require it.[44]

This oft-cited passage conveys an arguably 'masculine' image of the trust. It is a vehicle for financial maximisation that leaves no room for feelings (or ethics or social conscience) and requires trustees to be impartially focussed on profit-making and objective capital management. Impartiality and rationality are of course stereotypically marked as male traits.

It could be argued, however, that the financial maximisation rule instantiates a more complex and ambiguous gendering of the trust. While the rule may mark the trustee as gender-male (the impartial, amoral profit-maximiser), the absolution of trustees from any social or moral responsibility for their investment choices points towards a more ambiguous gendering of the trust device as a whole. The notion

---

44. [1985] Ch 270, 287–288.

that ethical and moral issues should not get in the way of trustees' pursuit of profit reinforces the narrative that trustees should be as free and as unfettered as possible in the pursuit of this end. Arguably, this shifts the locus of power within the trust towards the trustee, diluting the beneficiary's property-power. It also serves to instil an ideal image of the trust itself as a flexible, malleable and therefore perhaps less 'masculine' capital maximisation device.[45]

Softening of the Masculine Trust?: Systems Trusts and Exculpation Clauses

Where commercial and 'big money' applications of the trust are concerned, for example unit trusts, superannuation trusts—'systems trusts' as Cotterrell called them—one might, at first blush, consider that these too are examples of the trust in a 'masculine' manifestation. These commercial applications appear to sit comfortably with the 'masculine' metaphors of 'hard-nose property rights,' objective capital management, financial maximisation, and a hands-off approach when it comes to state intervention in their underlying basic private law trust structure. However, as I have suggested in relation to the financial maximisation principle above, there may also be elements of 'gender ambiguity' in this context, particularly when it comes to the possible dilution of the beneficiary's property-power in the name of greater flexibility and power conferred on trustees to maximise returns as capital managers.

Others in this collection have noted the shift in power towards trustees.[46] This 'ambiguous' tendency is also present in the increasing use—also flagged by Cotterrell—of wide-ranging exculpation or exemption clauses which exculpate trustees from potential liability for a wide range of breaches of trust (barring those that are dishonest).[47] Such clauses give trustees significant power without the concomitant

---

45. Another oft-cited authority on the principle of financial maximisation is *Harries v Church Commissioners for* England [1993] 2 ALL ER 300, which involved the investment choices of a religious charity. There the court held that even in the charitable trust context, trustees should generally choose investments based on financial maximisation for the trust rather than considerations of morality or social policy. It is interesting to note that the rule for charities was recently changed by statute in England and Wales, and charities now have power to make socially motivated investments: see Charities (Protection and Social Investment) Act 2016. This softening to the call of social conscience and the willingness of the state to legislatively intervene (penetrate) in this area may be indicative of further 'gender ambiguity' in relation to this particular trust principle.
46. See Michael Bryan and Arvind and Stirton in this collection.
47. *Armitage v Nurse* [1998] Ch 241 (CA).

responsibility and lend further support to the notion of a shift in power away from the beneficiary and towards the trustee.[48] In terms of gender metaphors, systems or big money trusts evince a more fluid blending of both 'male' and 'female' elements.

This fluidity or blending is also suggested in research conducted by Gino Dal Pont, which analysed the Australian High Court's trusts jurisprudence over the last three decades. Referring to High Court case law that suggests that *discretionary* beneficiaries' interests may, in some contexts, be viewed as 'property,' Dal Pont notes that:

> the elapsing of 30 years has witnessed a breaking down of the assumption that the unit trust and the discretionary trust are polar opposites so far as beneficiaries' 'interests' are concerned. The historical dichotomy has .... yielded to a more contextual inquiry, where fixed rules have less to play.[49]

This blending of elements of 'male' and 'female' is indicative of the emergence of a more ambiguous trust form that variously combines the beneficiary's property-power and 'hard-nosed property rights,' with flexibility, discretion, state intervention, personal obligation, and increasing trustee power, to effect a complex dialectic of *both* distance and intimacy.

The Contemporary Trust: Non-Binary and Queer?

The interplay of this dialectic raises the question as to whether we might be witnessing the emergence of a trust form that is non-binary; a queer, transgressive trust that challenges existing systems of power. Margaret Davies pondered a similar question in her analysis of the concept of property through the lens of the gender binary, and concluded that property is 'basically straight':

> To speak of queer property, then, is itself a rather ambiguous and in many respects politically sensitive project which must be undertaken as a contingent, even tentative, exploration. Property—at least in the popular and traditional conceptions I have alluded to—is basically straight, and I mean that it reflects and enforces a conventional heterosexual symbolism which is hierarchical.[50]

---

48. While the freeing up of the trustee from their usual obligations of prudence and against self-dealing can be injurious to the interests of beneficiaries, it can also maximise their property power within a neo-liberal profit driven 'unregulated' framework.

49. Gino Dal Pont, '1984–2014: The Life of the (Non-constructive) Trust in the High Court,' *Adelaide Law Review* 36 (2015), 186.

50. Margaret Davies, 'Queer Property, Queer Persons: Self-Ownership and Beyond,'

I suggest that it is also likely that the trust is 'basically straight.' While it is clear that the form of the trust in contemporary trusts law is more nuanced than the 'distancing' device (essentially the masculine trust) identified by Cotterrell in 1987, the fact that in some contexts the trust takes on a feminine, or even an ambiguous, gender form, is not necessarily indicative of its transgressive potential. Rather, the trust's ability to flip from male to female and its more recent tendency towards gender ambiguity may simply work to reinforce the gender binary (as suggested earlier) while at the same time ensuring that the modern trust is particularly well-equipped to facilitate current modes of capital investment and exchange.

While a more definitive assessment of the trust's transgressive potential must await further critical engagement with the trust, I tentatively suggest that the metaphor that best befits the modern trust is that of the 'metrosexual.' The Merriam Webster dictionary defines the 'metrosexual' as:

> a usually urban heterosexual male given to enhancing his personal appearance by fastidious grooming, beauty treatments, and fashionable clothes ...

> A metrosexual [...] is happy getting a pedicure and a manicure. He's hip, urban, sophisticated and, above all, stylish.[51]

Whilst on the surface, the trust may at times appear to transgress gender boundaries, much like the modern metrosexual, the modern trust is a malleable, savvy, slippery and elusive figure, difficult to pin down and control. It likely does little to challenge the gender binary and is actually a very nice fit for the neo-liberal capitalist economy.[52]

This chapter has, in a preliminary way, attempted to further develop Cotterrell's essentially masculinised conceptualisation of the trust by demonstrating that the contemporary trust takes on a *range* of gendered forms. I have suggested that these forms bear a homologous relationship to the gender binary, and as such they work at a metaphorical level to reproduce and reinforce gender power. A fertile area of enquiry for future critical trusts scholarship will be to explore the specific ways in which these gendered expressions of the trust interact with its material effects.

Social & Legal Studies 8 (1999), 332.

51. Meriam Webster entry for 'metrosexual,' accessed 1 March 2024, https://www.merriam-webster.com/dictionary/metrosexual.

52. See Adam Gearey, 'Equity and the Social Reproduction of Capital,' *Pólemos* 11 (2017).

12

The Bank of England's Directors as Trustees in Walter Bagehot's *Lombard Street*

*Iain Frame**

This chapter draws inspiration from Roger Cotterrell's 'Power, Property and the Law of Trusts' to offer an interpretation of Walter Bagehot's famous defence of central banking.[1] In *Lombard Street*, Bagehot argues that in a crisis the Bank of England (BoE) should use its reserve of banknotes to act as a Lender of Last Resort (LOLR): in other words, it should lend freely at a high rate of interest to solvent but temporarily illiquid banks.[2] Bagehot justifies his argument by asserting that the BoE held its reserve on trust for the benefit of 'the public.' In Bagehot's own words, 'The directors of the [BoE] are in fact, if not in name, trustees for the public, to keep a banking reserve on their behalf' (LS, 36–37); and, 'At present the Board of Directors are a sort of semi-trustees for the nation. I would have them real trustees, and with a good trust deed' (LS, 75).

This chapter's first task is to explain why Bagehot refers to the trust in relation to the BoE's role as a LOLR. Providing this explanation takes us to the Bank Charter Act 1844. According to contemporaries who adhered to the so-called 'currency principle,' that legislation 'rendered [the BoE] an ordinary bank of deposit and discount,'[3] and barred it

* Kent Law School, UK.
1.   Roger Cotterrell, 'Power, Property and the Law of Trusts: A Partial Agenda for Critical Legal Scholarship,' *Journal of Law and Society* 14 (1987).
2.   Walter Bagehot, *Lombard Street: A Description of the Money Market*, 10th ed. (London: Kegan Paul, 1892), 198–200 (hereafter cited in text as LS). The first edition was published in 1873.
3.   Robert Torrens, *The Operation of the Bank Charter Act of 1844* (London: James Ridgway, 1847), 35.

from 'affording assistance to the mercantile world.'[4] Instead of relying on the BoE's reserve of banknotes, the banks of *Lombard Street* ought to embrace the values of self-reliance and self-discipline and secure reserves of their own.

Bagehot considered such an arrangement counter-productive, and to bolster his argument he employed the concept of the trust. Cotterrell's 'Power, Property and the Law of Trusts' helps us to understand why he did so. As Cotterrell counsels,

> A useful strategy in developing a critical analysis of any area of doctrine is to start from its most central and fundamental ideas and to ask what social (as contrasted with professional legal) significance they may have, and what resonance such ideas may have beyond the world of profes- sional legal practice in the consciousness of ordinary citizens.[5]

Bagehot's use of the trust in *Lombard Street* had the potential to res- onate beyond the world of legal professionals because the idea of the trust suggests both a formal, technical legal device and a communal, collective social vision. Bagehot employs the latter idea of the trust, one that blends the trust with fiduciary duties and by so doing 'enshrines an important notion of sacrificing one's own interests to those of others, or treating others' interests as one's own.'[6] Whether the BoE's directors were 'trustees for the public' in the opinion of a lawyer or a court was less important to Bagehot than persuading the BoE's directors to see their position as 'in some respects trustlike,'[7] as calling for sacrifice for the benefit of the public.

If this reading of Bagehot is right, it takes us to this chapter's second task. Here the chapter again draws inspiration from Cotterrell, this time to suggest that Bagehot's reference to the BoE's directors as trustees served to present the country's banks, these holders and distributors of 'the many Millions in Lombard Street' (LS, 17), as vulnerable members of the public 'meriting protection' rather than as 'possessors of property-power.'[8] Bagehot accepts as self-evident that these 'possessors

---

4. Robert Peel, *Speeches of the Right Honourable Sir Robert Peel in the House of Commons, May 6th and 20th, 1844, on the Renewal of the Bank Charter Act* (London: John Murray, 1844), 75.

5. Cotterrell, 'Power, Property and the Law of Trusts,' 81.

6. Roger Cotterrell, 'Trusting in Law: Legal and Moral Concepts of Trust,' *Current Legal Problems* 46 (1993), 77. See also Gregory S. Alexander, 'The Transformation of Trusts as a Legal Category, 1800-1914,' *Law & History Review* 5 (1987).

7. Leonard Sedgwick Sealy, 'Fiduciary Relationships,' *Cambridge Law Journal* 20 (1962), 72

8. Cotterrell, 'Power, Property and the Law of Trusts,' 88.

of property-power' merit this protection. But perhaps that which Bagehot considered self-evident presents us with an opportunity: what do banks owe in return for the public support they receive?

Walter Bagehot

Walter Bagehot's 'vigorous pen'[9] covered a broad range of subjects, from literature to biography, politics to economics. Today he is known to political scientists as the author of *The English Constitution* (1867), 'the inevitable starting-point for any account of how British government has come to be what it is now,'[10] and to monetary economists as the author of the 'bible of central banking,' the much-cited *Lombard Street* (1873).[11] As the editor of *The Economist* from 1861–1877, Bagehot was well placed to observe monetary affairs. His opinions proved influential: he advised William Gladstone during the banking crisis of 1866 and his general influence was such that Woodrow Wilson, a great admirer of Bagehot, later saw him as a 'sort of supplementary Chancellor of the Exchequer.'[12] In the mid twentieth century the Victorianist G.M. Young awarded Bagehot the title 'The Greatest Victorian.'[13]

Whether the greatest or not, Bagehot's work captures something of the equipoise of the mid-Victorian period, its uneasy compromises and unresolved conflicts.[14] Bagehot sought the support of the Liberal Party on each of his unsuccessful attempts to enter parliament and, in many ways, he was a liberal.[15] His 'positions were individualistic and evolutionary' and he 'was unwavering in his support for the … minimalist state associated with the age of laissez-faire.'[16] And yet there was a 'Janus faced' quality to Bagehot's thinking.[17] Alongside the 'liberal

9. Joseph Schumpeter, *History of Economic Analysis*, ed. E. B. Schumpeter (London: Allen & Unwin, 1954), 792.

10. Brian Harrison, *The Transformation of British Politics, 1860-1995* (Oxford: Oxford University Press, 1996), 1.

11. Peter Conti-Brown, 'Misreading Walter Bagehot: What *Lombard Street* Really Says to Modern Central Bankers,' *The New Rambler* (2014), 2.

12. Gregory C. G. Moore, 'The Practical Economics of Walter Bagehot,' *Journal of the History of Economic Thought* 18 (1996), 230.

13. George Malcolm Young, 'The Greatest Victorian,' *The Spectator*, 18 June 1937, 9.

14. William Burn, *The Age of Equipoise: A Study of the Mid-Victorian Generation* (London: George Allen & Unwin, 1964).

15. William Selinger and Greg Conti, 'Reappraising Walter Bagehot's Liberalism: Discussion, Public Opinion, and the Meaning of Parliamentary Government,' *History of European Ideas* 41/2 (2015), 264.

16. Roger Middleton, 'Walter Bagehot (1826-77): A Man for All Seasons?' 10–11, available at SSRN: https://ssrn.com/abstract=2942627 (accessed 8 March 2024).

17. Roger Middleton, 'Walter Bagehot (1826-77): A Man for All Seasons?', 9.

ideals of the individual, Smilesian self-help and the civilising effects of mercantile progress' we find a Bagehot influenced by 'a Burkean faith in the slowly-evolving English conventions, the need to preserve the social fabric, and the conviction that no political prescription can engender complete confidence.'[18] This chapter draws on this latter Bagehot, a pragmatic Bagehot sensitive to the grip of what he called 'the cake of custom.'[19]

It was this cake of custom, the entrenched weight of past practice and 'instinctive confidence generated by use and years' (LS, 71), that prompted Bagehot to describe proposals for a 'many-reserve system of banking' as 'childish' (LS, 70). A system in which each bank kept its own reserve rather than turn to the BoE was, Bagehot agreed, the 'natural system' (LS, 69) but he feared (LS, 71)

> [n]obody would understand it, or confide in it ... Those who live under a great and firm system of credit must consider that if they break up that one they will never see another, for it will take years upon years to make a successor to it.

Bagehot wrote *Lombard Street* to defend this 'great and firm system of credit' by arguing that the BoE ought to use its reserve of banknotes to serve as a LOLR. He felt compelled to make this argument because many of his contemporaries favoured the currency principle.[20] In accordance with that principle these contemporaries supported a 'many reserve system of banking,' one in which the BoE behaved as any other bank and 'should take care to provide for its own liabilities, and leave other people to provide for theirs.'[21] These supporters of the currency principle called on the Bank Charter Act 1844 to buttress their position, and it is to this legislation that we now turn.

The Bank Charter Act 1844 and the Currency Principle

Controversy hounded the BoE in the nineteenth century, chiefly owing to tensions between its various roles. The BoE's exclusive privileges

---

18. Moore, 'The Practical Economics of Walter Bagehot,' 236.
19. Kunal M. Parker, 'Repetition in History: Anglo-American Legal Debates and the Writings of Walter Bagehot,' *UC Irvine Law Review* 4 (2014) 132.
20. On the currency principle, see Arie Arnon, *Monetary Theory and Policy from Hume and Smith to Wicksell: Money, Credit, and the Economy* (Cambridge: Cambridge University Press, 2011), chapter 11. On the rival banking school, with which Bagehot is often associated, see Arnon, chapter 12.
21. Anon [Marmaduke Sampson], *The Currency Under the Act of 1844* (London: John Van Voorst, 1858), 14.

made it a 'great engine of State,'[22] yet it had private shareholders who expected generous dividends. One such privilege allowed the BoE to create paper money to any extent that it pleased, yet preserving the value of that money required that it stand ready to convert these notes into gold on demand. The strain of balancing these roles intensified during commercial crisis: other banks pressured the BoE to expand its note issue and lend to them, yet if the BoE provided such support at a time when its gold reserve was falling (as it would be during commercial pressure), many feared that the BoE would be unable to uphold its commitment to convert BoE notes into gold.[23]

To uphold convertibility, the Bank Charter Act 1844 separated the BoE into two departments, an issue department and a banking department. All of the BoE notes created by the issue department had to be backed by their equivalent in gold coin or gold bullion, with the exception of a £14 million issue backed by securities such as government debt.[24] The banking department accepted deposits, advanced loans, and discounted bills of exchange. Its reserve of notes consisted of those notes created by the issue department minus those in circulation,[25] which meant that neither it nor the issue department could create notes ex nihilo: as Bagehot summarizes '[the BoE] can no more multiply or manufacture bank notes than any other bank can multiply them' (LS, 27).

Leading advocates of the currency principle seized on the impression that the banking department now had 'no more concern with the regulation of the circulation'[26] by employing it to counter a matter

---

22. Adam Smith, *The Wealth of Nations* (New York: Modern Library, 2000), 348. From its establishment in 1694, the BoE was the only joint-stock bank in England with corporate privileges. All other banks in England were restricted by law to no more than six partners but could issue demand notes. Legislation in 1826 permitted banks outside a 65 mile radius around London to operate as joint-stock banks but corporate privileges were only extended slowly over later decades. Legislation in 1833 permitted joint-stock banks to operate in London but retained restrictions on note issuing within the 65 mile radius and made BoE notes legal tender. Legislation in 1844 placed restrictions on the capacity of banks outside of the 65 mile radius to issue notes. To summarize, by the time Bagehot published *Lombard Street* in 1873, the BoE had a near monopoly over the note issue but now shared joint-stock status and corporate privileges with banks across the country. Bagehot provides an overview of the English banking system of his day in chapters VIII–XI of *Lombard Street*. See also Michael Collins, *Money and Banking in the UK: A History* (London: Routledge, 1988).
23. See, for example, Samuel Jones Loyd, *Remarks on the Management of the Circulation* (London: Pelham Richardson, 1840), 91–92.
24. Bank Charter Act 1844, s. 11.
25. Ralph George Hawtrey, *A Century of Bank Rate* (London: Frank Cass, 1962), 19–20.
26. Torrens, *The Operation of the Bank Charter Act of 1844*, 32.

they considered 'grave and serious':[27] the practice whereby other banks 'habitually look to the Bank ... "to promote the prosperity of our commerce and to temper its occasional reverses"'[28] by demanding that the BoE do 'everything in its power to afford general assistance in times of Banking or commercial distress.'[29] Currency principle adherents considered the matter grave and serious because they feared that 'unwarrantable dependence upon the Bank of England'[30] led to a loss of 'a discipline most severe but wholesome'[31] and undermined the lesson 'that commercial stability can be insured only by individual prudence and moderation.'[32]

To restore this lost discipline and cultivate self-reliance, supporters of the currency principle argued that the note issue limitation 'rendered [the banking department] an ordinary bank of deposit and discount.'[33] As such, the banking department should conduct its affairs 'just as any private banker would do'[34] since it was now 'relieved from all charge of the public interests,' and so could with 'perfect liberty employ the funds intrusted [sic] to it to its own best advantage.'[35] Unable to rely on the BoE, other bankers would have to demonstrate self-discipline by showing 'timely precaution and restraint'[36] in their lending 'to maintain an adequate reserve for their own protection'[37] since 'their sole reliance now must be only on their own till.'[38] Even when the government

---

27. Samuel Jones Loyd, *Effects of the Administration of the Bank of England. A Second Letter to J. B. Smith, Esq. President of the Manchester Chamber of Commerce* (London: Pelham Richardson, 1840), 47.

28. Jones Loyd, *Effects of the Administration of the Bank of England*, 47.

29. Thomson Hankey, *The Principles of Banking* (London: Effingham Wilson, 1867), 26.

30. John G. Hubbard, *Report from the Select Committee on the Bank Acts* (HC 1857, 220–X), Appendix, 12.

31. John G. Hubbard, *A Letter to Sir Charles Wood on Monetary Pressure and Commercial Crisis of 1847* (London: Longman, Brown, Green, and Longmans, 1848), 49.

32. Hubbard, *A Letter to Sir Charles Wood*, 49.

33. Torrens, *The Operation of the Bank Charter Act of 1844*, 35.

34. John Fullarton, *On the Regulation of Currencies*, 2nd ed. (London: John Murray, 1845), 196. Fullarton is associated with the banking school. The quotes from *On the Regulation of Currencies* are from his summary of the consequences of the Act of 1844 for the BoE's banking department, a summary he provides to then criticize the Act of 1844 and the currency principle.

35. Fullarton, *On the Regulation of Currencies*, 196.

36. Anon. [Samuel Jones Loyd and Robert Torrens], *The Petition of the Merchants, Bankers, and Traders of London, against the Bank Charter Act; with comments on each clause* (London: Pelham Richardson, 1847), 18.

37. Hubbard, *Report from the Select Committee*, 12.

38. Sheffield Neave, *Report from the Select Committee on the Bank Acts* (HC 1857,

suspended the note issue limit, as happened during the commercial crises of 1847, 1857, and 1866, each suspension was only temporary. And with the restoration of the Act of 1844, those who adhered to the currency principle could once again insist that the BoE 'assimilate to the conduct of every other well-managed Bank in the United Kingdom.'[39]

Developing Instincts Contrary to 'The First Instinct of Everyone' Else

When interpreted in accordance with the currency principle, the Act of 1844 tried to render it both impossible and unnecessary for the BoE to provide what we today describe as LOLR support. *Lombard Street* challenged the role the currency principle assigned to the BoE. This part of the chapter sets the stage for our discussion of that challenge by emphasizing the dynamics of financial booms and busts and the collective action problems these generate.

Consider the dilemma faced by depositors whose money is held by a bank that is rumoured to be on the verge of collapse. It is individually rational for a depositor to withdraw funds because if the bank does collapse the depositor's funds are safely in their possession, and if the bank does not collapse the depositor loses nothing. It is rational to withdraw, and irrational not to do so. Yet if all depositors try to withdraw at the same time they will bring about the outcome they fear: the collapse of the bank. And should the bank collapse, the vast majority of depositors will be left with nothing. When aggregated collectively, individually rational decisions turn out to be irrational and self-defeating.[40]

Examples of collective action problems from the world of finance extend beyond bank runs. Consider both asset price bubbles and asset 'fire sales.' Concerning the former, it is individually rational for an investor to buy assets today if they expect the price will be higher tomorrow. Other investors who expect the same price increase will do likewise. But where all investors buy today rather than tomorrow, prices are pushed higher than they would have been but for these purchases. The investors create or worsen the price increases they fear. Yet for any single investor to have refrained from purchasing the asset would not necessarily have prevented the price increase: more likely it would

39. Hankey, *The Principles of Banking*, 26.
40. See Robert Hockett, 'Are Bank Fiduciaries Special?' *Alabama Law Review* 68/4 (2017), 1071, 1075–1079, 1086–1087. See also Morgan Ricks, *The Money Problem: Rethinking Financial Regulation* (Chicago: University of Chicago Press, 2016), 52–73.

have left the investor paying more for an asset that they could have bought for less.[41] Asset fire sales resemble bank runs. The holder of the asset hears a rumour about the credibility of the asset's issuer. In such circumstances it is individually rational to sell the asset before others do so to safeguard against losses. Yet when everyone tries to sell the asset the price collapses and the majority of investors end up holding an asset of little or no value.[42]

Bagehot at no point uses the language of collective action problems, but it is nonetheless instructive to read *Lombard Street* from that perspective. Bagehot wished to challenge the view that the BoE was 'only a Bank like any other bank' with 'no peculiar duties, and no public duties at all' (LS, 43). Throughout *Lombard Street* Bagehot stresses the need for the banking department to maintain a large reserve of BoE notes in ordinary times to help it respond to the demand for BoE notes during a panic. And yet he also recognized that the effective deployment of that reserve during a panic might be impaired by the banking department either depleting its reserve during normal times to compete with other banks or hoarding its reserve during a crisis rather than use it to assist others.

The banking department might use its resources to compete with others by matching the discount rate offered by bill dealers like Overend Gurney. And the banking department might be inclined to so compete, not only because the Act of 1844 seemed to encourage this, but because the profits that this extra business might generate pleased the BoE's shareholders. As Bagehot remarks, the BoE's directors desire 'to make a good dividend for their shareholders. The more money lying idle the less, caeteris paribus, is the dividend; the less money lying idle the greater is the dividend' (LS, 39). But despite the temptation to compete, it would be 'erroneous' (LS, 321) for the BoE to do so. Although Bagehot doesn't expand on the point in *Lombard Street*, many contemporary and later commentators highlight the BoE's contribution to the asset price bubble of the 1840s that ended with the crisis of 1847.[43] Instead of competing with other banks by offering cheap credit as it had done in the 1840s, the BoE should, argued Bagehot, prioritize its 'first duty ... to protect the ultimate cash [reserve] of the country' (LS, 321).

---

41. Hockett, 'Are Bank Fiduciaries Special?' 1081–1084.
42. Hockett, 'Are Bank Fiduciaries Special?' 1088–1089.
43. See, for example, Thomas Tooke, *A History of Prices*, 4th ed. (London, Longman 1848), 293–302; and Wilfred Thomas Cousins King, *History of the London Discount Market* (London: Routledge, 1936), 102–112.

Protecting the reserve could be distinguished from hoarding it in all circumstances. Should the BoE try to 'keep aloof in a panic' (LS, 190) by relying on its large reserve to protect only itself it would find bankers desperate for liquidity withdrawing their deposits from the BoE. And if the BoE responded to the loss of these deposits by attempting to 'replenish its reserve' (LS, 190), it would only be able to sell its assets at low prices because 'in a panic there is no new money to be had; everyone who has it clings to it' (LS, 191). Rather than hoard its reserve the BoE should undertake to do exactly the opposite. As Bagehot explains (LS, 55),

> The ultimate banking reserve of a country ... is not kept out of show, but for certain essential purposes, and one of these purposes is the meeting a demand for cash caused by alarm within the country ... we keep that treasure for the very reason that in particular cases it should be lent.

And yet casting the banking department as 'an ordinary bank of deposit and discount'[44] would see it cling to its reserve when it should lend it and compete with other banks when it should stand aloof. By so acting the banking department contributed to rather than countered asset price bubbles and asset fire sales. But these outcomes were not inevitable. One way of countering a collective action problem, as Robert Hockett explains, is through an agent who acts on behalf of the collective 'to change the calculus of each individual, to make it no longer individually rational to pursue the collectively irrational outcome.'[45] To achieve that outcome the collective agent commits to do that which no one else will do: in a panic it buys when everyone else wishes to sell, and by so doing makes it irrational for everyone else to continue to sell.

Bagehot's task was to recast the BoE as that collective agent. He had to convince his audience that the BoE was more than the ordinary bank pictured by supporters of the currency principle; that it had special public duties to perform, duties that would see it put its own self-interest to one side and prioritize the interests of others. To fulfil these duties, the BoE had to act 'In opposition to what might be at first sight supposed' (LS, 50) as the rational option by developing instincts contrary to '[t]he first instinct of everyone' else (LS, 50). When the instincts of others told them to hoard and cover their own liabilities, Bagehot advised the BoE to cultivate a contrary instinct and advance

---

44. Torrens, *The Operation of the Bank Charter Act of 1844*, 33
45. Hockett, 'Are Bank Fiduciaries Special?' 1090.

whatever cash reserves it had 'most freely for the liabilities of others' (LS, 53).[46] It was to further this contrary and oppositional logic that Bagehot described the directors of the BoE as 'trustees for the public.'

Acknowledging 'A Principle ... Handed down ... for More than a Century'

Two logics underpinned by two sets of competing values.[47] Supporters of the currency principle wished to see the banking department act in the manner of other banks: to seize on profitable opportunities, to take responsibility for its own solvency, and to leave other banks to take care of their own affairs. Bagehot saw that logic and these values as incompatible with the role the BoE ought to perform: if the BoE imitated other banks it alongside these banks fuelled asset price inflations and precipitated periods of discredit. To avoid these outcomes, Bagehot encouraged a different logic supported by a different set of values, in accordance with which the BoE ought to forego profitable opportunities, embrace other-regarding moral obligations, and see the problems of others as its own problems.

These competing logics and their competing values left the BoE in an ambiguous position. Joseph Pease, the observant coal-mine owner from Durham, agreed by explaining that the BoE 'frequently appears to me to act as a private individual would act, and then at other times it appears to act as having certain national objects to sustain or difficulties to meet.'[48] By inviting the BoE's directors to act as 'trustees for the public,' Bagehot nudged them towards embracing values that justified and legitimized the BoE 'as having certain national objects.' Trustees must not make personal profits from their dealings with trust property; they must not allow their interests to come into conflict with their duties; they must act with disinterested devotion for the benefit of others, and so on.[49] If the banking department acted in accordance with these values the use of its reserve promoted 'certain national objects.'

---

46. See also Fred Hirsch, 'The Bagehot Problem,' in *Financial Crises, Contagion, and the Lender of Last Resort: A Reader*, eds., Charles Goodhart and Gerhard Illing (Oxford: Oxford University Press, 2003), 187–200.

47. On the theme of conflict between social visions in the context of the law of trusts in nineteenth century America, see Gregory S. Alexander, 'The Dead Hand and the Law of Trusts in the Nineteenth Century,' *Stanford Law Review* 37 (1984–1985), 1189.

48. Testimony of Joseph Pease, *First Report from the Secret Committee on Commercial Distress* (HC, 1847–48, 395–VIII) Q. 4613.

49. See Jonathan Garton, *Moffat's Trusts Law: Text and Materials* (Cambridge: Cambridge University Press, 2015), 403–405.

Why? Because it held its reserve on trust for the benefit of the public. And, as a rhetorical move, as a way of setting a different tone for the conversation about the responsibilities of the BoE's directors, Bagehot's approach has merit. The fiduciary duties traditionally associated with the role of trustees carry connotations suggestive of selflessness and gratuitousness, and in was these connotations which I think Bagehot was trying to capture.

He was joined in his efforts by contemporaries who also cast the BoE as honouring obligations beyond its own self-interest. Occasionally, the idea of the trust reappears in these representations, such as in portrayals of the BoE as 'filling a high public trust'[50] or 'fulfilling the trust confided to it by Parliament.'[51] More typically, contemporaries expected the BoE's directors to act in accordance with 'a principle which had been handed down from their predecessors for more than a century – a principle under which legitimate commercial bills ... were always discounted, and which they never dreamt of refusing.'[52] The reports of parliamentary enquires often confirmed these expectations: 'the Bank is a public institution' said one such report,

> possessed of special and exclusive privileges, standing in a peculiar relation to the Government, and exercising ... great influence over the general mercantile and monetary transactions of the country.[53]

And it was owing to these privileges and this influence that the BoE had 'the duty of a consideration of the public interest.'[54] In *Lombard Street* Bagehot too casts the BoE as duty bound (LS, 168), as obliged by custom to discount bills of exchange when no one else will do so. If the BoE's directors continued to find it difficult to acknowledge openly that custom, Bagehot invited them to embrace the figure of the trustee, of someone who resists the temptation to pursue their own self-interest by prioritizing a sense of obligation to others.

---

50. *The Times* (1834), quoted in David Kynaston, *Till Time's Last Stand: A History of the Bank of England 1694-2013* (London: Bloomsbury Publishing, 2017), 130.
51. Lord Monteagle, *Report from the Select Committee on the Bank Acts* (HC 1857–58, 381–V), Appendix, 496. On the history of the idea of the 'public fiduciary or trustee,' see Paul Finn, 'Public Trusts and Fiduciary Relations,' in *Fiduciary Duty and the Atmospheric Trust*, eds., Ken Coghill, Charles Sampford and Tim Smith (Aldershot: Ashgate, 2011), 31–41.
52. R. J. Blewitt, HC Deb, 2 December 1847, vol 95, col 590.
53. *First Report from the Secret Committee on Commercial Distress* (HC 1847–48, 395-VIII) iv.
54. *First Report from the Secret Committee on Commercial Distress* (HC 1847–48, 395-VIII) iv.

'Possessors of Property-Power'

In a recent essay on Walter Bagehot, Peter Conti-Brown argues that the BoE's 'failure to acknowledge that they kept the central reserve, that they were the lender of last resort' inspired Bagehot to write *Lombard Street*.[55] And yet if Bagehot sought to encourage 'plain speaking'[56] in 'plain words' (LS, 1) about the realities of central banking, in the spirit of Roger Cotterrell's understanding of critical legal scholarship this chapter concludes by probing *Lombard Street's* 'unexamined assumptions'[57] to reveal that which it 'tends to disguise.'[58] As Cotterrell astutely observes, 'The idea of fiduciary obligation of the trustee ... induces us to see the trust beneficiary not as the possessor of property-power but as a person meriting protection.'[59] Bagehot's use of the trust does exactly that. Although Bagehot characterizes the BoE's directors as trustees for 'the public' his discussion privileges the problems experienced during a panic by 'the money market' (LS, 1) or 'Lombard Street' or 'our credit system' (LS, 36): in short, by the country's banks. And so Bagehot induces us to see the country's banks, these holders and distributors of 'the many Millions in Lombard Street' (LS, 17), as vulnerable members of the public 'meriting protection' rather than as 'possessors of property-power.'

As in Bagehot's time, the reality today is that banks are 'possessors of property-power' precisely because the central bank protects them. That reality is sometimes obscured by descriptions of banks as intermediaries between savers and borrowers.[60] In reality, banks are dynamic creators of money, extending credit to others by creating promises to pay in the state's currency. This is a dynamic arrangement because it allows the credit system to respond to the needs of those capitalists the banks deem of sufficient creditworthiness. But it's also a fragile arrangement because the credit advanced is a bet on future productivity. The role played by the central bank is a response to this fragility: by ensuring that the liabilities created by commercial banks are convertible at par into the state's currency, the central bank acts as a guarantor; it extends

---

55. Conti-Brown, 'Misreading Walter Bagehot,' 16. Emphasis in original.
56. Conti-Brown, 'Misreading Walter Bagehot,' 13.
57. Cotterrell, 'Power, Property and the Law of Trusts,' 80.
58. Cotterrell, 'Power, Property and the Law of Trusts,' 86.
59. Cotterrell, 'Power, Property and the Law of Trusts,' 88.
60. Robert Hockett and Saule Omarova, 'The Finance Franchise,' *Cornell Law Review* 102 (2017), 1151.

the credit of the sovereign to commercial banks.[61] The property-power of banks follows from this relationship. Banks are 'privileged purveyors'[62] of the sovereign's currency.

Bagehot's objective was to normalize that privilege. The idea of the trust served as a rhetorical device in the service of that objective: it invited the BoE's directors to privilege the banks of *Lombard Street*; and it invited the banks to 'really regard public money as their own and assume for themselves the right to constant convertibility of the bills of exchange discounted by them.'[63] Once normalized, the longer-term outcome was 'the victory of the Bagehot Principle,'[64] and the appearance of central banks across the world increasingly willing to use LOLR powers to overcome the collective action problems that mark financial panics.[65] So acting secures financial stability by countering the vulnerabilities inherent in the banking system.[66] Yet Bagehot's own analysis omits any consideration of the distributional consequences that follow from this support.[67] The task of raising that issue fell to Bagehot's opponents, such as the supporter of the currency principle and former Governor of the BoE, Thomson Hankey. In a response aimed at Bagehot, Hankey emphasized that

> there are many other parties in England who are engaged in carrying on works of great public importance who might equally put in their claim to [support from the BoE] ... Why should not contractors for public works, railway companies and railway contractors, ship-builders and ship-owners, house holders and house-builders, dock companies, and

61.   Christine Desan, *Making Money: Coin, Currency, and the Coming of Capitalism* (Oxford: Oxford University Press, 2015), 428.
62.   Hockett and Omarova, 'The Finance Franchise,' 1164.
63.   Karl Marx, *Capital: A Critique of Political Economy, Vol. III* (London: Lawrence & Wishart, 1974), 534.
64.   Frank Whitson Fetter, *Development of British Monetary Orthodoxy, 1797-1875* (Cambridge (MA): Harvard University Press, 1965), 257.
65.   Perry Mehrling updates Bagehot's position to account for modern conditions in *The New Lombard Street: How the Fed Became the Dealer of Last Resort* (New Jersey: Princeton University Press, 2011).
66.   Keep in mind, however, Bagehot's advice, that a central bank should provide this support at a high rate of interest to solvent but temporarily illiquid banks. In other words, the central bank's support should be conditional, and it retains the option of withdrawing that support. These points were emphasized by the English courts following the collapse of Northern Rock. See *R (on the application of SRM Global Master Fund LP) v Treasury Commissioner* [2009] EWHC 227 (Admin), referring specifically to Bagehot at [10]; and *R (on the application of SRM Global Master Fund LP) v Treasury Commissioner* [2009] EWCA Civ 788, referring specifically to Bagehot at [8].
67.   Nadav Orian Peer, 'Negotiating the Lender-of-Last-Resort: The 1913 Fed Act as a Debate over Credit Distribution,' *NYU Journal of Law & Business* 15 (2019).

222 CRITICAL TRUSTS LAW

a host of others all carrying on business in which the country at large is deeply interested ... be equally entitled to benefit by any favours for which the public have a right to look from such an institution as the Bank of England?[68]

Hankey's cure for these distributional dilemmas followed the prescription of the currency principle: the BoE should take care of its own liabilities and refuse all requests for assistance, whether from banks or from anyone else. As Bagehot so eloquently explains, such an approach fails to address the dynamics of financial panic. And yet even if we accept the necessity of a LOLR there remains a further often unexamined question of profound distributional significance: what parts of our economy, and what sorts of assets, merit the privileged support that follows from the use of LOLR powers?

---

68. Hankey, *The Principles of Banking*, 29–30.

13

Afterword: Trust and Critique
after Three Decades

*Roger Cotterrell**

When I heard that a conference on critical studies of trust law would be held at the University of Kent in 2017 it was a pleasant surprise also to learn that an inspiration for it was an article that I had published three decades before.[1] That paper had proposed 'a partial agenda for critical legal scholarship', especially in the context of the law of trusts. It was the first of three closely interconnected essays that I wrote on trusts in the space of half a decade. They tried to map out new ways to view trusts in a socio-legal perspective at a time when trust law had received very little modern critical socio-legal scrutiny. Now, this book, arising from the Kent conference, gives an unexpected opportunity to revisit my essays, to consider the contexts that informed them and to indicate how some of their themes have been reflected in later work.

'Power, Property and the Law of Trusts', published in 1987, was explicitly linked to the project of critical legal studies. It was followed by a second essay (on private purpose trusts)[2] which tried to show how doctrinal problems in trust law might be illuminated by adopting a sociological approach; in this paper a seemingly narrow inquiry about an arcane kind of trust was used to develop wide conclusions about the historical trajectory and changing socio-economic functions of trusts in general. A third and final essay, 'Trusting in Law',[3] building directly

* Queen Mary University of London, UK.
1. Roger Cotterrell, 'Power, Property and the Law of Trusts: A Partial Agenda for Critical Legal Scholarship,' *Journal of Law and Society* 14 (1987).
2. Roger Cotterrell, 'Some Sociological Aspects of the Controversy around the Legal Validity of Private Purpose Trusts,' in *Equity and Contemporary Legal Problems*, ed. Stephen Goldstein (Jerusalem: Hebrew University, 1992); reprinted in Cotterrell, *Living Law: Studies in Legal and Social Theory* (Abingdon: Routledge, 2008).
3. Roger Cotterrell, 'Trusting in Law: Legal and Moral Concepts of Trust,' *Current*

on the second, tried to link a perspective on trust law with the then developing literature on trust in social theory—a literature that has flourished since.

After these papers I wrote no other substantial studies of trust law.[4] I had been teaching trusts for a decade and a half before the first of the essays was written but ceased to teach the subject from around 2004. Thereafter my work has been almost entirely in jurisprudence, sociology of law, and comparative law. However, ideas from the trusts essays found their way into the seemingly quite different kinds of research I did later. And the concept of trust, as a social rather than specifically legal idea, has been very important in the socio-legal theory I have tried to develop over the past two decades.

What Is Critique?

'Power, Property...' was written in the mid-1980s when the American critical legal studies (CLS) movement was flourishing. Parallel but differently oriented movements were also developing in the UK and various continental European countries.[5] In that context, the essay criticised the orientation of American CLS, arguing that critical legal scholarship should be linked closely with social scientific studies of law and not confined (as American CLS mainly was) to being a law school movement. CLS had to be more than an 'internal' lawyers' critique of legal doctrine and had to draw on empirical and theoretical social scientific research. And it needed to ask what kind of knowledge is sought by critique and for what purposes.

Today I would say that critical study cannot, if it is to be productive, *only* be critical. It has not only to point out what may be problematic, incoherent, mystifying, misguided or iniquitous in what it studies but also how, if at all, change can be brought about in what it critiques, and what principles or values should guide this constructive critique. If, for example, there is much wrong with the law of trusts and the way it is used in various social and economic contexts, how (using what intellectual tools?) might critique indicate ways to move legal development

Legal Problems 46 (1993); reprinted in Cotterrell, *Living Law*.
4. A brief, schematic paper, Cotterrell, 'Context and Critique in Law Teaching (with Reference to Property and Trusts),' is in *Examining the Law Syllabus: The Core*, ed. Peter Birks (Oxford: Oxford University Press, 1992), 28–32.
5. See e.g. Michel Miaille, *Une Introduction Critique au Droit* (Paris: Maspero, 1976); Peter Fitzpatrick and Alan Hunt, eds., *Critical Legal Studies* (Oxford: Blackwell, 1987); Roel de Lange and Koen Raes, eds., *Plural Legalities: Critical Legal Studies in Europe* (Nijmegen: Ars Aequi Libri, 1991).

and interpretation in different ways? How might it point to resources to be called on to do this? How then can critique help to construct law in more satisfactory ways? And how can we theorise practically what 'satisfactory' might mean—in other words, what might be realistically expected from law? What might be hoped for and worked towards, using the tools of academic legal and social scientific research?

American CLS did have a constructive side and this was focused on legal practice, especially in the courtroom; it focused on the possibility that sharp lawyers with progressive values (and sympathetic judges hearing these lawyers' persuasive arguments) might be able to 'flip' legal ideas in clever, persuasive interpretation, eloquently fitting out these ideas with new meaning or significance, to make them potentially liberating rather than repressive; progressive rather than reactionary, socially enlightened rather than narrowly conservative. In a way, this is what progressive lawyers always do and have done. But I thought, and still think, that both theory and empirical study are needed to ground this approach; to make the values and policies that progressive practising and academic lawyers urge on legal doctrine something more than a matter of personal, subjective preferences or convictions.

In this context, empirically-oriented social theory may have much to offer. While social science cannot itself prescribe values, it has the potential through empirical and theoretical research to illuminate the likely effects of following certain policies or trying, through law, to implement certain values. And it can clarify why some moral or political issues seem to become important in debate at certain times and unimportant or irrelevant at others. When and why, for example, does (or does not) slavery become a matter of moral contention—or abortion, or same-sex marriage, or poverty, or corruption? How, at various times and in various places, is the agenda of moral (and legal) debate set, so that some issues seem meaningful and urgent in some historical and social contexts, but not in others?

Critical study of law surely needs criteria to set its directions constructively. Social science is one important means of helping to clarify those criteria—not by purporting to prescribe the criteria themselves but by providing means of understanding the contexts in which certain criteria can seem meaningful, practical and relevant; the contexts in which these criteria are chosen, and the consequences of the choices made. In this way it can help to inform a socially aware jurisprudence.[6]

---

6. Roger Cotterrell, *Sociological Jurisprudence: Juristic Thought and Social Inquiry* (Abingdon: Routledge, 2018).

Despite its limitations, early CLS emphasised two critical concepts that are still strikingly easy to apply to the field of trust law. One is the concept of *reification*.[7] American CLS claimed, following earlier theories, that much of the ideological power of law comes from making *social relations*—such as those of contracting parties, or those centred on possession, control and use of benefits—appear as *things*.

Social relations in certain forms are *reified*—they seem to become social 'objects', solid entities, their existence and nature normally unchallenged and unchallengeable. For example, relations between parties negotiating with each other are reified (turned into a social object) in the form of a *contract*—which has a definable existence in time and, often, the quality of being an assignable asset. So, the contingency of social relations (with all their variable qualities, for example as regards power and dependence) is turned into the impersonally neutral, objective form of a contract—a legal entity.

More generally, social relations arranged around the use of resources are understood in terms of *property*. The idea of property as a thing distinct from its owner is part of the everyday furniture of social life in modern societies—and law protects rights in this thing which is property. On this basis, the right generally to amass capital without limit and use it freely is an assumption not only of law but of everyday life.

The most perfect legal example of reification may be the trust. Trusting relations pervade social life in innumerable ways. But they become reified in certain ways as *a trust*—a social object—under specific conditions. The trust is undeniably a legal 'thing', though rooted in general social relations centred on trust. But its thing-like quality is such that it has a legal life of its own circumscribed not by the moral and sometimes emotional circumstances that surround trusting in everyday life but by legal rules.

The intimate, often ambiguous and fragile social condition of trusting someone (or something) is, in a sense, drained of its social complexity and contingency. Its richness is reduced to a set of defined powers and responsibilities. If trusting has at its heart a moral relation centred on the risks and responsibilities of dependence of one person on another, in law it becomes primarily a rule-bound device for holding and managing wealth and for distributing and controlling rights in this.

---

7. Peter Gabel, 'Reification in Legal Reasoning,' *Research in Law and Sociology* 3 (1980).

Thus, legal trust becomes a shadow of what trust often is in social interaction. But the compensation, which law provides for this impoverishment, is that, as Maitland enthused long ago,[8] the trust is potentially an instrument of almost unlimited flexibility. It can legally define property relations with the precision necessary to fix the exact amount of freedom or restriction to be attached to individuals or entities entrusted with managing assets in which other people or entities have legitimate claims.

The other early CLS notion readily applicable in studying trust law is *tilt*.[9] Because the trust is so flexible, it is a classic case of a legal concept susceptible to 'tilt'—that is, it may be open to many interpretations of its nature and function but tilts towards some more powerfully than others in practice, although legal thought may underemphasise or even not recognise this tilt. The trust form can be applied for 'good' or 'bad' purposes, as judged from various perspectives.

It can tilt, for example, to surround wealth with secrecy, technicality and obfuscation, perhaps freeing it from diminution by taxation, or from claims that might otherwise attach to it. But it is also a device for distributing wealth, for pursuing public charitable purposes, for safeguarding vast funds intended to benefit large numbers of individuals (as in major pension funds), or simply for promoting a basic, essential legal value of security (in this case, security of property holding). In the form of resulting or constructive trusts, it can be a means of holding otherwise free-floating assets where, for example, transactions have failed, intentions have been misunderstood, or wrongs need to be redressed by legally shifting entitlements.

The trust is eminently 'tilt-able'. Critical trusts scholars can ask how far the trust in practice is tilted towards certain purposes and understandings more than others and with what consequences, how far it can be tilted in socially valuable ways, and what obstacles exist in legal thought and practice for doing this.

Power and Dependence

The 'Power, Property...' essay was concerned with reification more than with tilt. Its key argument is that the reification of property and trust as social entities obscures the social relations that underpin them—

8. Frederic W. Maitland, *Equity: A Course of Lectures*, revised ed. (Cambridge: Cambridge University Press, 1936), 591–2.
9. Wythe Holt, 'Tilt,' *George Washington Law Review* 52 (1984).

which are almost inevitably power relations. So the trust as a device serves to disguise relations of power, putting in the forefront of legal attention instead technical issues of managing (and allocating rights and responsibilities attaching to) an independent object—the trust fund as a fund of value—distinct from its creators, owners and managers.

The essay suggests that, in general, power in the trust concept ultimately lies with the beneficiaries because the trustees, although legal owners, must act in the interests of beneficiaries and are legally controlled for this purpose. Law seems to reverse the normal power-dependence relationship between the person trusted and the person who trusts (and who is thus dependent on and has to take the risk of trusting the other). However, I soon realised that I had stated this conclusion in too sweeping a manner because law can never take away all the risks in entrusting one's wellbeing to another. Law portrays beneficiaries as the weaker parties in the trust, requiring protection against the legal owners of the trust property, but this power-dependency situation is not always reversed by law enforcing their status as beneficial owners.

The ideological significance of the separation of equitable and legal ownership remains very important—it is certainly the key to trust law's capacity to obscure the holding of wealth, to make ultimate relations of power and dependency hard to unravel in complex cases and often utterly opaque to the non-specialist. But, as my two later essays discuss in detail, the power relations between settlors, trustees and beneficiaries can be very varied, depending on different trust structures and on socio-economic factors often not explicitly recognised in legal doctrine itself.

The 'Trusting in Law' essay emphasises that two factors—'size' and 'expertise'—immeasurably complicate the picture if we try to generalise about power-dependency relations across the whole range of private trusts. In what that essay calls 'big trusts' (those with huge capital funds and often vast numbers of beneficiaries as in major pension trusts), management tends to operate in practice almost entirely beyond the knowledge or influence of most individual beneficiaries. It typically has considerable freedom to act on available expertise to optimise investment returns, so that the well-being of the capital fund, rather than that of any specific beneficiaries as such, appears as the primary imperative. The result is that power in the big trust structure lies routinely mainly not with beneficiaries but with those controlling the trust investments.

In the two later essays the position of the settlor of the trust is also looked at in much more detail than in my first paper. So, 'Trusting in Law' argues that, in 'big trusts', the relationship between settlor and trustees or trust managers has often tended to be much closer, formally or at least informally, than in traditional kinds of trusts where the settlor is normally assumed—at least according to orthodox trusts doctrine—to relinquish control of the trust property in favour of the trustees who are to act solely in the interests of the beneficiaries.

'Power, Property...' formed part of a 1987 collection of articles[10] looking at various areas of law from CLS perspectives. But very soon after CLS had declared itself on the UK scene, the nascent movement (with which I never wholly identified) began to dissolve or transform into different orientations. As in the United States, some critical legal scholars in Britain identified themselves as legal historians and developed careers in socio-historical research on law. Some others identified themselves as postmodernist legal theorists, producing critical writings that were often thought-provoking but sometimes seemed diffuse and unfocused, at least to this reader. Feminist legal scholarship also rapidly developed,[11] as did critical scholarship informed by minority perspectives. Some researchers already saw the future of critical inquiry as being in empirical and theoretical socio-legal scholarship drawing strongly on the social sciences, and especially focused on applying insights from empirically-oriented social theory to legal inquiry. This last orientation, which I shared, was signalled in 'Power, Property...' but exhibited more fully in the two subsequent papers and by many other writings outside the field of trust law.

The 1992 paper, 'Some Sociological Aspects of the Controversy around the Legal Validity of Private Purpose Trusts', has a much wider ultimate focus than its title suggests. It notes that, in several common law jurisdictions, it has proved extremely difficult to develop, in case law and in juristic commentary, a satisfactory analysis of the nature of trusts for (abstract) non-charitable purposes—and even to decide conclusively whether these can exist as valid trusts—despite centuries of experience with them. While matters were solved practically in some jurisdictions by legislation bypassing the juristic controversies, the controversies themselves remained unsolved. It seems that they still are today.[12]

The essay argues that, for a long time in the historical development of trust law, purpose trusts were assumed to be legally permissible,

10. Fitzpatrick and Hunt, *Critical Legal Studies*.
11. As regards trusts, see the pioneering essay collection, Susan Scott-Hunt and Hilary Lim, eds., *Feminist Perspectives on Equity and Trusts* (London: Cavendish, 2001).
12. See e.g. Geraint Thomas and Alastair Hudson, *The Law of Trusts*, 2nd ed. (Oxford: Oxford University Press, 2010), 153–8.

although they might fail for a range of reasons. Even *Morice v Bishop of Durham*,[13] later interpreted as establishing the principle that all non-charitable trusts must have human beneficiaries, was not initially seen as propounding such a principle. Purpose trusts came to be seen as problematic by their very nature only as they began to be used for socially and economically ambitious purposes that raised important policy issues bearing on the very existence and functions of trusts. Cases of valid purpose trusts that once may have been treated as of no particular legal interest now had to be marginalised carefully as anomalies, or rare and exceptional concessions to human weakness or sentiment, in a new legal environment where the place of trusts in a modern economy had become clearer. A moral reverence for the settlor's intentions, perhaps reflected in old cases, now had to be clearly distinguished from a modern view of the function of trusts as receptacles of property in which well-defined economic interests could be safeguarded as beneficiaries' assets.

This analysis points far beyond a study of a tiny enclave of arcane trusts doctrine. It founds a claim that the history of trust law shows two distinct conceptions of the trust—a 'moralistic' one in which an essentially moral obligation to carry out the settlor's intentions is paramount, and a 'property-receptacle' conception in which the trust is seen as a property-holding device in which clear rights of ownership (legal and equitable) in property are defined and protected. Both conceptions survive but the latter dominates in orthodox doctrines of modern trust law.

The 'Trusting in Law' paper takes the analysis a step further—especially in the light of the proliferation of 'big trusts'. It argues that the property-receptacle conception of the trust has now split into two different variants. The first is an 'individual property' variant (i.e. the traditional form of modern trust governed by the beneficiary principle, usually requiring clear identification of beneficiaries or beneficial interests, and thus secure allocations of property entitlements). The second, a newly prominent kind of trust, is the 'capital management' variant. In this, the primary aim is not to define distinct beneficial interests as settled property entitlements but to preserve, control and enhance (often large) capital resources with maximum flexibility in changing economic conditions, and to set up typically wide powers to manage the capital, sometimes in ways that the settlor ultimately controls.

---

13.   (1804) 9 Ves 399; (1805) 10 Ves 522.

The landscape of trusts could thus be best conceptualised in socio-legal terms in terms of this three-fold schema—of *moralistic, individual property*, and *capital management* trust conceptions. I leave it to others to decide whether this schema, supposing it had validity in the early 1990s, has some purchase today. It does, at least, suggest that the relative power of settlors, trustees and beneficiaries is likely to vary greatly depending on which of these trust conceptions dominates in practice. Ultimately the moralistic, individual property and capital management orientations of trusts are mutually incompatible, even though moralistic elements can still be identified in some kinds of modern trusts and, equally, the idea of the trust as a property receptacle was probably always important in some form.

What may be new is the pattern of typical features of the capital management conception of the trust: for example, the relaxing of trustees' duties or liabilities in significant respects and very wide powers and discretions given to them in some trusts; the flourishing of discretionary trusts in which management flexibility and overall trust purposes are much more important than precisely defined beneficial interests; the validation and flourishing of purpose trusts of wide scope in several jurisdictions; and arrangements by which trustees are sometimes put in a position close to that of agents of the settlor.

Trust in Law and in Social Life

It should be stressed that no claim of historical evolution is being made here; contrasting trust orientations surely all co-exist in the contemporary landscape of trusts despite their theoretical incompatibility. But perhaps their relative significance is shifting. That would be an issue for socio-legal inquiry. My interest in them today is mainly in what they can suggest about wider social and economic change. The 'Trusting in Law' paper suggested that it would be good to ask how analysis of the legal concept of trust might aid better understanding of general social or moral notions of trust.[14] That project still remains uncompleted. However, increasingly, the phenomenon of social trust—trust as a feature of everyday life, in economic and social relations—is a topic for social science research.[15]

---

14. Cotterrell, 'Trusting in Law,' 76.
15. For a sample from a large literature see Niklas Luhmann, *Trust and Power* (Cambridge: Polity, 2017). Bernard Barber, *The Logic and Limits of Trust* (New Brunswick NJ: Rutgers University Press, 1983); Diego Gambetta, ed., *Trust: Making*

It is possible to live, at least to some extent, on a basis of *distrust*, so that precautions are taken in all social relations, suspicion reigns, reliance on others is avoided as much as possible, defences are erected and maintained, and solitary individuals (and perhaps their families) are the only significant social units recognised in an atomised society. But arrangements avoiding all social trust are widely recognised as costly in time, energy, and material and emotional resources. Community is important—not in some archaic, romantic, pre-modern sense but understood as a diversity of flexible, complex and impermanent but effective social bonds. At the heart of those bonds are relations of mutual interpersonal trust.

Since my trusts essays were written, I have tried to explore this idea of communal bonds, seeing these bonds as of several radically different types which typically combine in an infinity of ways in social life; I have argued that law must be understood as a regulatory framework of these communal bonds, a legal framework of community.[16] State law is the law of a national society politically organised as a communal network. In this perspective, for some purposes, state law can be regarded as just one kind of law among many (even if it is often the most prominent and most formalised), because all networks of community can potentially inspire their own law-like regulation. The relation between state law and numerous kinds of law-like communal self-regulation is one of the standard topics for research in sociology of law, as it has been throughout the history of this research field.[17]

From one point of view, the side-lining of moralistic understandings of trust in law in favour of a property-receptacle understanding, which eventually culminates in impersonal capital management structures, suggests a sad shrivelling of the trust's moral underpinnings. Capital funds held in 'big trusts' seem often very far removed from interpersonal trust relationships. Where does trust lie in these structures? Does it still have meaning as a moral idea?

---

and Breaking Cooperative Relations (Oxford: Blackwell, 1988); Karen S. Cook, ed., *Trust in Society* (NY: Russell Sage Foundation, 2000); Russell Hardin, *Trust and Trustworthiness* (NY: Russell Sage, 2002); Barbara A. Misztal, *Trust in Modern Societies: The Search for the Bases of Social Order* (Cambridge: Polity, 1996); Piotr Sztompka, *Trust: A Sociological Theory* (Cambridge: Cambridge University Press, 1999).

16. Cotterrell, *Law, Culture and Society: Legal Ideas in the Mirror of Social Theory* (Abingdon: Routledge, 2006).

17. See e.g. Eugen Ehrlich, *Fundamental Principles of the Sociology of Law* (New Brunswick, NJ: Transaction, 2002).

The sociologist Niklas Luhmann writes that the complexity of modern life is such that interpersonal trust relations have often become impossible and in their place confidence is attached to impersonal systems.[18] He thinks of these as systems of communication. Examples could be banking, financial or administrative systems. Often, individuals have no choice as to whether they will put their trust in these systems; they have to do so. At the same time, most individuals understand little of their workings. A profound moral distance separates the systems from the individuals who rely on them. I argued in 'Trusting in Law', however, and still argue today, that interpersonal trust remains crucially important for social and economic life.

Law can support this interpersonal trust, providing structures that encourage and protect it in social and economic relations. But trust law has long understood that trust is fragile and easily disappointed, full of risks, dangers and vulnerabilities. Perhaps this understanding now dominates the law of trusts less than in the past, as its attention moves beyond moralistic and individual property to capital management orientations. But confidence in systems is rooted, however remotely and indirectly, in interpersonal trusting relations, an argument developed in the 'Trusting in Law' essay.[19] Systems (perhaps including vast capital management systems) are not ultimately self-sustaining without there being a willingness on the part of those people who depend on them to continue to trust those (often unknown) other people who manage such systems. Studies of trust law should examine, as part of their agenda, how and under what conditions law can assist and encourage trusting relations—understanding these relations not merely as legal forms but also as building blocks of stable social life.

---

18. Niklas Luhmann, 'Communications Media and System Trust,' in Luhmann, *Trust and Power*.
19. See further, Cotterrell, *Law's Community: Legal Theory in Sociological Perspective* (Oxford: Clarendon Press, 1995), 329–32; and Cotterrell, *Law, Culture and Society*, 73–6.

www.ingramcontent.com/pod-product-compliance
Lightning Source LLC
Chambersburg PA
CBHW071554210326
41597CB00019B/3235